MW00807113

Numanities - Arts and Humanities in Progress

Volume 20

Series Editor

Dario Martinelli, Kaunas University of Technology, Kaunas, Lithuania

The series originates from the need to create a more proactive platform in the form of monographs and edited volumes in thematic collections, to contribute to the new emerging fields within art and humanistic research, and also to discuss the ongoing crisis of the humanities and its possible solutions, in a spirit that should be both critical and self-critical.

"Numanities" (New Humanities) aim at unifying the various approaches and potentials of arts and humanities in the context, dynamics and problems of current societies.

The series, indexed in Scopus, is intended to target an academic audience interested in the following areas:

– Traditional fields of humanities whose research paths are focused on issues of current concern;
– New fields of humanities emerged to meet the demands of societal changes;
– Multi/Inter/Cross/Transdisciplinary dialogues between humanities and social and/or natural sciences;
– Humanities "in disguise", that is, those fields (currently belonging to other spheres), that remain rooted in a humanistic vision of the world;
– Forms of investigations and reflections, in which the humanities monitor and critically assess their scientific status and social condition;
– Forms of research animated by creative and innovative humanities-based approaches;
– Applied humanities.

More information about this series at http://www.springer.com/series/14105

Natalya V. Sukhova · Tatiana Dubrovskaya ·
Yulia A. Lobina

Editors

Multimodality, Digitalization and Cognitivity in Communication and Pedagogy

 Springer

Editors
Natalya V. Sukhova
Department of Modern Languages
and Communication
National University of Science
and Technology 'MISiS'
Moscow, Russia

Tatiana Dubrovskaya
English Language Department
Penza State University
Penza, Russia

Yulia A. Lobina
English Language Department
Ulyanovsk State University of Education
Ulyanovsk, Russia

ISSN 2510-442X ISSN 2510-4438 (electronic)
Numanities - Arts and Humanities in Progress
ISBN 978-3-030-84070-9 ISBN 978-3-030-84071-6 (eBook)
https://doi.org/10.1007/978-3-030-84071-6

This Springer imprint is published by the registered company Springer Nature Switzerland AG
The registered company address is: Gewerbestrasse 11, 6330 Cham, Switzerland

Contents

Editors and Contributors

About the Editors

Natalya V. Sukhova is Associate Professor at National University of Science and Technology 'MISiS' (Moscow, Russia). She got her Ph.D. in Philology from the Moscow Linguistic University (2004). She taught ESP courses at Lomonosov Moscow State University (School of Public Administration) and was affiliated with the Institute of Linguistics of Russian Academy of Sciences where she took part in the project on multichannel linguistics and gesture studies. She has published over 50 articles on pedagogy, gesture studies and English Phonetics and 5 textbooks on teaching English for Specific Purposes. She is an editorial board member in *Numanities* series (Springer) and a member of Association of Public Relations Educators (Russia). The main interests are non-verbal semiotics and gesture studies, English Phonetics and foreign language teaching.

Tatiana Dubrovskaya is Habilitated Doctor, Professor and Head of the English Language Department at Penza State University, Russia. She is also affiliated with Belgorod National Research University, Russia, as a Professor at the Department of Communication Studies, Advertising and Public Relations. She has published extensively in the areas of linguistic pragmatics, political, legal and media discourse, cross-cultural communication in internationally acknowledged journals, such as *Discourse and Communication, Critical Discourse Studies* and *Discourse Studies.* She co-edited a few volumes, including *Young Scholars' Developments in Linguistics: Tradition and Change* (Cambridge Scholars Publishing, 2015). She is a member of the Russian Communication Association and the International Society for the Study of Argumentation.

Yulia A. Lobina is Professor at the English Language Department at Ulyanovsk State University of Education (Ulyanovsk, Russia). She got her Ph.D. in Language Theory from Ulyanovsk State University (Russia, 2002). She teaches courses in introductory linguistics, cross-cultural studies and English for Academic Purposes. She has published over 60 articles on genre studies, cross-cultural communication and pedagogy and edited/co-edited 5 volumes of young scholars' research papers. The main interests are academic discourse, genre studies and language teaching.

Contributors

Lilia V. Bondareva National University of Science and Technology 'MISiS', Moscow, Russia

Irene Clark California State University, Northridge, CA, USA

Jasmin B. Cowin Touro College and University System, New York, USA

Tatiana Dubrovskaya Penza State University, Penza, Russia; Belgorod National Research University, Belgorod, Russia

Natalya Koshkarova South Ural State University, Chelyabinsk, Russia

Grzegorz Kowalski University of Warsaw, Warsaw, Poland

Evgeniy Kozhemyakin Belgorod National Research University, Belgorod, Russia

Andrei N. Kuznetsov Center of Education Systems Management, Institute of Education Management of Russian Academy of Education, Moscow, Russia

Yulia A. Lobina Ulyanovsk State University of Education, Ulyanovsk, Russia

Tatiana V. Potemkina National University of Science and Technology 'MISiS', Moscow, Russia

Irina V. Privalova Saratov State Medical University, Saratov, Russia; Leading Research Fellow of the Research Laboratory, "Intellectual Technologies of Text Management", Institute of Philology and Intercultural Communication, Kazan (Volga region) Federal University, Kazan, Russia

Yulia V. Pushkina National University of Science and Technology 'MISiS', Moscow, Russia

Dana S. Saulembekova National University of Science and Technology 'MISiS', Moscow, Russia

Ekaterina N. Shchaveleva National University of Science and Technology 'MISiS', Moscow, Russia

Raluca Sinu Transilvania University of Brașov, Brașov, Romania

Natalya V. Sukhova National University of Science and Technology 'MISiS', Moscow, Russia

Igor Ž. Žagar Educational Research Institute & University of Primorska, Ljubljana, Slovenia

Chapter 1
Communication Challenges in Modern Social Practices

Tatiana Dubrovskaya, Natalya V. Sukhova, and Yulia A. Lobina

Abstract Communication challenges to the twenty-first century humankind are as serious as materialistic ones. Search for meaning, the ever-present focus of human praxis, has gained new urgency in the current age of diversity and rapid transformations in all social spheres. This chapter is an overview of research on meaning-loaded forms in social interactions presented in the current volume. Modern communicative practices are characterized by a profound change in their shapes and formats: both everyday and institutional communication is becoming increasingly multimodal and digital. These new formats of communication require new approaches that would reveal underlying processes happening in the participants' cognition.. In their contributions, the authors explore the connection between new communication patterns, technological innovations and underlying cognitive processes in an array of communicative situations in both physical and virtual environments. Recent decades have seen a singularly close integration of verbal and visual semiotic systems, which has become essential for social meaning construction and interpretation. Technological advances bring to the fore the role of digital competency in educational environments, generating intense discussions on the impact of video games, corpus technologies, online projects and other digital pedagogy techniques of effective classroom communication. In their observations on and theoretical implications of the diverse communicative patterns the authors draw on recent advances in neuroscience, genre theory, psychology and psycholinguistics. The volume may provide a point of reference for further discussions of multimodality, digitalization and cognitivity as the phenomena pertaining to the present day communicative and educational contexts.

T. Dubrovskaya (✉)
Penza State University, Penza, Russia

Belgorod National Research University, Belgorod, Russia

N. V. Sukhova
National University of Science and Technology 'MISiS', Moscow, Russia

Y. A. Lobina
Ulyanovsk State University of Education, Ulyanovsk, Russia

1

Keywords Postmodernity · Communication · Education · Multimodality · Digital environments · Teaching methodologies · Cognition

The challenges that the twenty-first century humanity is facing are described in predominantly materialistic terms. The humanity is threatened with population growth, poverty, resource depletion, environmental crisis, wars, terrorism, and pandemics, while non-materialistic complications of postmodernity hardly receive as much attention. Yet, now that the humankind is re-considering multiple aspects of its existence, the humanities should step forward in defining axiological dimensions for the future. The postmodern state of the world is endowed with diversity and rapid transformations in all social spheres, including communication, cognition and culture. Bauman characterised the postmodernity as "the era of unstoppable and accelerated dynamism of forms and patterns" (Bauman 1999: xx). The diversification of cultural forms and patterns has resulted in blurred boundaries between numerous phenomena that once were conceived as paradigmatically opposed: individual vs social, private vs public, national vs cross-cultural, humanities vs science, theoretical vs practical, verbal vs non-verbal, real vs virtual, games vs learning, functional vs aesthetic, the list can go on and on. Confronting the eclectic mixtures in life, the humans need to give structure and meanings to them, since

> human praxis, viewed in its most universal and general features, consists in turning chaos into order [...] – order being synonymous with the intelligible and meaningful. (Bauman 1999: 96)

Although the debate is open as to whether postmodernity is "dead and buried" (Kirby 2006), it seems that the humans still seek to discover order, dispose of vagueness and make sense of the world irrespective of the label attached to it.

This volume is the result of contemplations and research on some aspects of contemporary social life, where the humanities come to the fore and offer pluralistic analyses of social phenomena, highly pertinent to the realities of the future. The title of the volume *Multimodality, Digitalization and Cognitivity in Communication and Pedagogy* implies that we tackle issues related primarily to communication and education. However, the concept of communication is construed most widely, in an interdisciplinary spirit, and pertains to both physical (specifically, phonetic) and cognitive processes, verbal and non-verbal (visual and multimodal) interactions, between heterogeneous actors and in a variety of situations across cultures. Communication also provides an essential basis for educating activities; therefore, pedagogy design appears to be inextricably intertwined with the ways ideas and meanings are conveyed.

Modern communicative practices are characterized by a profound change in their shapes and formats: both everyday and institutional communication is becoming increasingly multimodal and digital. Multimodal patterns gain popularity in various social practices, which include making promotional videos on the Internet, organising public interactions through public signs, as well as teaching languages through corpus technologies, video games or virtual worlds, to name but a few. New formats of communication definitely require new approaches that would reveal under-lying cognitive processes happening in the participants' brains. Without turning to the biology of brain, which is beyond their competence, the authors of the volume address cognition through the study of meaning-making in communication. Whether we consider interpretation of multimodal texts, pedagogical evaluation, imitation processes in language learning, or emotion transmission in teaching, these phenomena involve a cognitive constituent. Thus, attempts have been made to connect new communication patterns, technological innovations and cognitive processes in an array of communicative situations in both physical and virtual environments.

The authors from around the world, including Russia, Poland, Romania, the USA and Slovenia, focus on meaning-loaded forms and instruments in communication. The eclectic forms under study require eclectic approaches and methodologies, and the authors cross disciplinary boundaries drawing on philosophy, linguistics, semi-otics, computational linguistics, mathematics, cognitive studies, and neuroaesthetics. Such a combination emphasizes both internal links within the humanities and their external nexuses.

Part I *Studies in multimodality* includes three chapters. All of them take a semiotic approach and are interrelated through the object of study, which is multi-modal communication in its different displays, covering promotional video in crowd-funding project presentations, multimodal public signs of prohibition, and visuals as arguments.

In his paper on promotional videos, **G. Kowalski** claims that discourse anal-ysis has recently become open to non-verbal material, and aspires to grasp logico-semantic progression in multimodal texts, specifically in crowdfunding project presentations. He is specifically interested to discover the degree to which patterns of written discourse organization are realized in non-textual modes. In his study, Kowalski identifies three types of interaction between verbal and non-verbal discourse patterns, thus contributing to the debate on resemiotization, i.e. recon-strual of meaning from one semiotic system into another. Methodology wise, the scholar argues that a relevant framework should be devised in order to represent multimodal communication in its dynamism and complexity.

Interaction between verbal and non-verbal modes of communication is also central to the two other papers in the part. **E. Kozhemyakin** and **T. Dubrovskaya** explore how different semiotic resources, such as words, fonts, frames, colors and images co-operate to produce the pragmatic effect of prohibition in public signs. The authors construct a multi-dimensional model of a public sign, since they associate different types of semiotic resources with two opposing aspects of social behavior regulation—legal and naïve. They show that the legal aspect is rendered through words mostly, while the naïve aspect draws predominantly on multimodal resources, which offer a ready-made version of a social norm. Considering the results in a wider perspective, the implication can be drawn that the signs (verbal or multimodal) are connected not only to a signified object, but also they constitute a meaningful system through entering relations between themselves.

In the last chapter in the multimodality part **I. Ž. Žagar** refers to the field of argumentation, which, as the author claims, is becoming more open to non-traditional approaches that are not based on either logic or language. Specifically, Žagar tackles visuals as arguments and advances an express claim on the impossibility of reasoning without turning to the verbal context when reconstructing the meaning of visuals. The methodology applied to visuals involves experimenting with respondents as well as the enchronic analysis, and the concluding part of the paper offers a step-by-step dynamic procedure of meaning-making moves. The scholar also poses a conceptual question on the necessity to reconsider traditional argumentation through encompassing enchrony.

Part II *Language teaching methodology for digital environments* contains four chapters, which present a balanced picture of varied teaching methodologies that have emerged as a result of and response to modern technological changes and new societal challenges as well. This part of the volume approaches the pedagogical context in a higher education system as a whole considering the faculty, the future language teachers and the teaching methodology in the digital environments.

Hence, the chapter by **J. Cowin and D. Saulembekova** addresses the specific competency requirements for future language teachers and a higher education faculty in the epoch of the *Fourth Industrial Revolution*. The authors carry out a comparative analysis of the educational systems of Russia and the United States. More precisely, they try to uncover the program design, education degrees and certifications of future language teachers and current faculty in both countries. The scholars suggest a perspective where language study programs and teacher preparation programs would adapt to the ever-changing world with the technologies enabling more holistic teaching and learning experiences.

One way to obtain such an experience is the use of video games in the teaching process. Undoubtedly, the modern pedagogical context as noted by **L. Bondareva and T. Potemkina** demonstrates the possibility of using video games to develop cognitive skills when learning a foreign language. The authors present a systematic review and analysis of current research in the field. They delve into vocabulary development, communicative responses, word choice, speech strategies as well as reading and writing skills. Interestingly, Bondareva and Potemkina show the diverse and often opposing results regarding the impact of video games on the skills development: it can be either positive or negative, but mostly it is rather limited.

In her study, **N. Koshkarova** examines possible ways of using corpus technologies in teaching English to the speakers of other languages. Along with some theoretical claims on the essence of corpus linguistics, this practice oriented paper demonstrates how to develop teaching materials based on the real language use. It seems that apart from its practical value, the chapter bears very important societal implications: first, employing real-life native linguistic resources overcomes geographical borders and builds a bridge between cultures; second, corpus technologies, their designers, teachers and students can all be viewed as actors in a network (in the spirit of the Actor-network theory by Latour), that are mutually shaping one another's needs, opportunities and capacities.

The pedagogical potential of another example of advanced technology—the online dictionary—is shown by **R. Sinu** in her chapter. Two online lexicographic projects were used in a master program to perfect the students' grasp on both theory of lexicography and practice of dictionary making and dictionary use. The theoretical input the students received in class enabled them to go successfully through each stage of the lexicographic process as part of their obligatory research activity. The author argues that involvement in dictionary compiling can help improve students' dictionary consultation skills, turning them into more competent dictionary users. The online medium they used contributed greatly to merging theory with practice in their dual role as dictionary makers and dictionary users.

Part III *Cognitive approaches to language and pedagogical design* comprises five chapters, focusing on problems of personality development and search for identity, which have been brought to the fore by the diversification of cultural forms and patterns. The contributors concentrate on the sphere of pedagogy as the principal realm where cognitive skills vital for taking on the challenges of postmodernity are acquired. Different factors influencing the achieved level of skill and the rate of personal development are discussed, including approaches to instructing, teaching objectives, the teacher's personality and assessment strategies. Also, an overview of the most popular psycholinguistic methods lending validity to research in the sphere of cognition is offered.

I. Clark suggests reconsidering imitation as a valid approach to teaching writing. Crossing disciplinary boundaries and drawing on recent advances in neuroscience, the author argues that imitating either experienced writers' behaviour in the creative process or the result of such process can enable students to develop a *writerly identity*. Clark and her colleagues carried out a project using imitation in first year writing classes. Several possibilities for utilizing imitation in the classroom are described in the chapter. As a result, student anxiety about their writing ability decreased and their self-rating as writers increased. Given the salience of written forms in the present-day discourse, a view of oneself as a good writer is essential in coming to terms with rapid transformations in postmodern social life.

Mastering spoken genres, nevertheless, can also result in broadening cognitive and communicative skills, as shown in the chapter by **Yu. Lobina**. The author maintains that defining the objective of learning a spoken genre precisely, with Vygotskian zones of proximal development clearly designated in the educational model of the target genre, can enhance a foreign language student's cognitive development. Careful scaffolding of skill acquisition within those zones gives the students access to new ways of conveying ideas and meanings to diverse audiences. The main method of identifying the zones of proximal development is comparing genres within and between cultures, as well as investigating the students' prior genre knowledge.

Another crucial factor in developing students' cognitive skills is the teacher's personality. **E. Shchaveleva, A. Kuznetsov and Yu. Pushkina** in a well-designed investigation including surveys, interviews, comparative analysis, and computational method reveal the influence of the teacher's personal qualities on students' personalities and their academic and professional development. A four-phased analysis produced a list of the most relevant qualities and established their correlation with various parts of a teacher's performance. The chapter makes it evident that shaping a teacher's personality during both teachers' pre-service and in-service periods is a way of helping graduates face the complexities of postmodernity, forge their axiological standpoint and make sense of the world.

One of the key elements of language teaching –assessment—is tackled by **N. Sukhova** in her paper on L2 pronunciation assessment. The author claims that the teachers (raters) frequently evaluate the students' speech as the viewers evaluate the paintings in the art gallery. The methodological underpinnings come from the neuroaesthetic model (The Vienna Integrated Model of Art Perception) where the rater's personality, background experiences and personal differences in processing information play a great role. The phoneticians and non-phoneticians assessed the student's speech sample in the survey, and their answers were collected and compared to the stages of the model. Sukhova suggests that there is a high degree of congruency between the way raters (teachers) assess the speech sample and the way viewers assess an art object. The methodological novelty prompts unexpected results and highlights the difficulty in phonetic and phonological competency assessment.

The methodological consistency of the psycholinguistic research is addressed by **I. Privalova**. The author argues that the most popular psycholinguistic experimental approaches (the method of speech activity observation, semantic analysis, the method of semantic differential, free and directed associative experiments) are effective and valid. Privalova supports this claim with the results of her experiments. Invaluably, the advantages of these methods are discussed as well as the prospects of their employment to language and pedagogical design are shown.

It is hoped that by signalling some questions and suggesting ideas on multi-modality, digitalization and cognitivity, the phenomena pertaining to the contemporary life, we have managed to outline the communicative and educational contexts that we live and work in. We believe that the book will find its readers among linguists, semioticians, language teachers and scholars in the humanities, as well as providing a point of reference for further discussions in the field.

References

Bauman, Zygmunt. 1999. *Culture as Praxis*, 2nd ed. London: SAGE.
Kirby, Alan. 2006. The Death of Postmodernism and Beyond. *Philosophy Now. A magazine of ideas, 58.* https://philosophynow.org/issues/58/The_Death_of_Postmodernism_And_Beyond Accessed 27 June 2020.

Part I
Studies in Multimodality

Chapter 2
Patterns of Discourse Organization in Multimodal Discourse of Crowdfunding Project Presentations

Grzegorz Kowalski

Abstract Rapid development of multimodal communication stimulates scholarly interest in elaborating methods and tools capable of investigating this phenomenon in its structural and functional complexity. One such approach is multimodal discourse analysis (MDA). Of relevance to the origins of MDA are social semiotics and systemic-functional linguistics, providing rationale to approach different modes as meaning-making systems on the one hand, and to investigate multimodal texts as communicative acts in context on the other. Having said that, there still seem to be unchartered areas in the vast universe of multimodal communication, all the more so as research can hardly keep pace with the constantly emerging and promptly popularized Web 2.0 technologies of communication. One important aspect that is still to receive a thorough scientific account is logico-semantic progression in multimodal texts, in particular the extent to which patterns of discourse organization, originally identified in written texts, are realized in non-textual modes. The study discusses how patterns of discourse organization are realized in simultaneously received modes in the multimodal genre of promotional video in crowdfunding project presentations. Three types of interaction between the patterns, their moves and the modes of expression are identified: (1) transfer of moves across modes; (2) move-and-pattern overlap; and (3) rupture of intermodal cohesion. The insights presented in this paper may be relevant not only to related studies of multimodal discourse but also for more effective content management in crowdfunding project presentations.

Keywords Multimodality · Discourse organization pattern · Discourse analysis · Crowdfunding · Kickstarter

G. Kowalski (✉)
University of Warsaw, Warsaw, Poland
e-mail: g.kowalski@uw.edu.pl

© The Author(s), under exclusive license to Springer Nature Switzerland AG 2021
N. V. Sukhova et al. (eds.), *Multimodality, Digitalization and Cognitivity in Communication and Pedagogy*, Numanities - Arts and Humanities in Progress 20, https://doi.org/10.1007/978-3-030-84071-6_2

9

2.1   Introduction

It is generally agreed that contemporary interpersonal communication is more often than not multimodal (Kress 2010). At the same time, interactants more readily exploit non-verbal semiotic systems, e.g. visual (Iedema 2003: 39), and when language resources are applied, they are often used as complementary to non-verbal ones. In general, multimodal content is neither produced in nor received from alternately used modes; instead "most of the communication we come across happens in different modes simultaneously" (Machin 2014: 6).

To guarantee that modes are well orchestrated (Kress 2010: 161) in this simultaneous use, and do not lead to a semiotic cacophony, interactants need to refer to some generally recognized principles of discourse organization. Such principles in turn ensure that the resources applied in the co-occurring modes do not disrupt semiosis. This role is fulfilled, among other things, by conventional patterns of discourse organization (Hoey 1983, 2001).

Patterns of discourse organization are particularly vital in the case of Internet genres, not only due to their multimodal complexity but also in terms of the multidimensional context in which they are produced and received. The latter is pertinent to crowdfunding project presentations, which are addressed to two distinctive groups: future customers and potential investors. As a result, a crowdfunding project presentation will be, respectively, an advertisement for a product and a company business portfolio. As a result, customer-targeted content and investor-targeted content need to be separated, a task all the more challenging in the case of multimodal texts realized simultaneously in two or more channels (e.g. video with voice-over commentary). Here patterns of discourse organization serve a regulatory function, managing the flow of information destined for the different target groups of crowdfunding project presentations.

However, as the present paper aims to show, patterns of discourse organization, while present in multimodal genres, do not unfold in the same way as in monomodal ones. The former involve variations to the prototypical patterns (as originally discussed in Hoey 1983, 2001), including: (1) transfer of moves across modes; (2) move-and-pattern overlap; and (3) rupture of intermodal cohesion. Empirical grounds for distinguishing these three types of interaction between the Problem-Solution pattern, its moves and modes of expression are provided in my earlier case studies of English and Polish crowdfunding project presentations, notably in the Technology category (Kowalski 2017, 2018, 2019). By contrast, in this paper I develop a more general theoretical framework for grasping the complex interaction between patterns of discourse organization, not limited to Problem–Solution, and simultaneously received modes in the multimodal genre. The phenomena discussed are illustrated with examples excerpted from a Kickstarter project presentation.

The paper begins with an overview of MDA as the theoretical background for my research (Sect. 2.2), followed by a general presentation of patterns of discourse organization and their application in multimodal discourse (Sect. 2.3 and 2.4). Section 2.5 describes a crowdfunding platform and crowdfunding project presentation as a genre, with Kickstarter used as reference, while Sect. 2.6 outlines the aims, methods and materials. The three types of interaction between patterns of discourse organization, their moves and modes of expression are defined and discussed in Sect. 2.7. The final part of the paper provides concluding remarks and proposes directions for future research.

2.2 Multimodal Discourse Analysis

Interpersonal communicationislargely multimodal nowadays; some scholars even go as far as to venture claims that monomodal communication has ceased to exist at all, or that it has never existed (Kress 2010; Machin 2007; O'Halloran and Smith 2011). While this view may be too radical to be accepted, one cannot deny that multimodality has become fundamental to contemporary interaction. This status is a corollary of the technological revolution, which, among other things, provides diverse digital media, whose users can communicate by means of multiple semiotic systems.

More and more affordable and easy to use, digital media have been changing interpersonal communication practices, which in turn has drawn considerable scholarly interest in social studies and linguistics. The ever-increasing popularity of research topics related to multimodality may in fact denote a "visual turn" (Machin 2014) in said disciplines. In this respect, the digital revolution has not only contributed to the emergence of new genres of interpersonal communication treated as the source of research data, but also enabled their analysis by developing advanced tools capable of grasping the semiotic operation of these genres in all its multimodal complexity (Jones 2013). Such tools include, among others, dedicated software for corpus analysis of multimodal discourse, which has been recently developed (Bednarek 2015; O'Halloran et al. 2010; Rohlfing et al. 2006).

The "visual turn" has been observed in particular in social semiotics and discourse analysis, leading to the emergence of "social semiotic multimodality" approaches and "multimodal discourse analysis", respectively (Jewitt 2009). Drawing a dividing line between them may, however, seem irrelevant in the end as they in fact share not only the subject of study but also origins in Halliday's (1978) systemic functional model of language as social semiotic. However, soon after the publication of Halliday's work social semioticians became more interested in semiotic systems other than language (Hodge and Kress 1988; Kress and van Leeuwen 1996; O'Toole 1994). The latter has often been analysed as complementary to non-verbal modes, or treated instrumentally when models of language grammars were adapted to represent other semiotic systems, e.g. visual (e.g. Kress and van Leeuwen 1996).

It is the recent interest in multimodality that has brought language back into the focus of social semiotic inquiry, recognizing its vital role in multimodal communication in interaction with other semiotic systems. And just as social semiotics has now restored its interest in language when used in multimodal communication, so discourse analysis has now become open to non-verbal material. All in all, then, the difference between social semiotic multimodality research and multimodal discourse analysis may no longer be significant, and perhaps refers to disciplinary affiliation claimed by particular authors.

In line with my field of study, I consider MDA to be of greater relevance for the research perspective adopted in this paper than the social semiotic multimodality approach.[1] MDA is defined as

> an emerging paradigm in discourse studies which extends the study of language per se to the study of language in combination with other resources, such as images, scientific symbolism, gesture, action, music and sound. (O'Halloran 2011: 120)

In addition to this line of development of MDA, i.e. extending the scope of semiotic modes for research, the origins of the approach can also be traced back to *mediated discourse analysis* (Jones 2013; Norris and Jones 2005), which in turn emerged from interactional sociolinguistics and intercultural communication studies. The resultant multimodal interactional analysis is represented in the works by Rodney and Sigrid Norris (2004, 2011), Norris and Jones 2005, Scollon 2001, Scollon and Wong Scollon 2004).

Three major areas of theoretical modelling and empirical analysis are identified in MDA:

> (a) Modelling semiotic resources that are fundamentally different to language.
>
> (b) Modelling and analysing intersemiotic expansions of meaning as semiotic choices integrate in multimodal phenomena.
>
> (c) Modelling and analysing the resemioticization of multimodal phenomena as social practices unfold.
>
> (O'Halloran 2011: 124)

Specifically, area (a) refers to the above-mentioned problem of the applicability of grammatical models to semiotic systems other than language. While some scholars (e.g. Machin 2009) reject such a possibility, mainly due to differences in the structural organization of semiotic systems, others have developed comprehensive grammars of non-verbal semiotic systems (e.g. Kress and van Leeuwen 1996 for visuals and O'Toole 1994, O'Toole 2010 for mathematical and scientific images, urban architecture or museum exhibitions). Area (a) is also of relevance to my research on how patterns of discourse organization, originally identified in the written medium, are realized in the visual-verbal material of promotional videos in crowdfunding project presentations.

My previous and current research also refers to area (b), by examining the ways in which the content presented in two modes, namely film and voice-over commentary, contributes to the semiosis in the promotional video in crowdfunding project

---

[1] As regards social semiotic multimodality, an interested reader may find comprehensive theoretical models and analytical frameworks, e.g. in Kress and van Leeuwen (2001), Kress (2010) and Bateman (2014). In addition, specific areas of social semiotic approach to multimodality, along with reviews of relevant literature, are presented in related papers in the *Encyclopedia of Applied Linguistics* (Chapelle 2013), for instance Djonov (2013) on multimodality and hypermedia or Knox (2013) on multimodality and systemic functional analysis. Finally, a number of case studies are discussed in Machin (2014).

presentations. It should be noted here that intersemiotic (Jones 2013) relations in multimodal genres remain a major methodological challenge in MDA, especially in the case of dynamic and/or digital media, such as Web content (Lemke 2002) or film (Wildfeuer 2014; Bednarek 2015), though to a lesser extent in the case of static content (e.g. text and image; see, for example, Martinec and Salway 2005; Bateman 2008).

Finally, area (c) focuses on *resemioticization* (or *resemiotization*, as Iedema 2003 puts it), i.e. reconstrual of meaning from one semiotic system into another, either diachronically or cross-culturally. The phenomenon is critically addressed in terms of transferability of meaning across semiotic systems, each of which has its own resources, not necessarily compatible with those available in others (Lemke 1998). This issue, however, is not central to my research.

While these three major areas of MDA set the scene for empirical research, there is still much work to be done in terms of defining the field's basic concepts, describing its methodology and analytical frameworks (Jewitt 2009; O'Halloran and Smith 2011). The call for this meta-scientific work has been addressed since the mid-2000s, as shown in contributions by Bateman (2008), Bateman et al. (2017), Bednarek and Martin (2010), Norris and Maier (2014), O'Halloran (2005), O'Toole (2010), and Seizov and Wildfeuer (2017). The aim of this paper is to contribute to this meta-scientific work on MDA by identifying and defining three types of interaction between patterns of discourse organization, their moves and modes of expression in a multimodal genre.

Simultaneously, this paper also contributes to the burgeoning critical thread in MDA, an approach that "does not as yet have a clear academic identity of its own" (van Leeuwen 2013), and which has not yet proposed a comprehensive methodology or research framework. In fact, for the time being, MDA has not fully developed a critical perspective, and critical discourse analysis has not offered a model suitable for analysing multimodal texts. One possible solution is to adapt frameworks and methodologies originating in social semiotics, where a critical approach has a history dating back to the 1960s works of French semioticians, e.g. Barthes' ([1964] 1977) analysis of press photographs and visuals in advertising. More recently, Hodge and Kress (1988) applied a critical stance to show how resources of language and other semiotic systems are used to express specific ideologies. It is, however, only in the last decade or so that there has appeared a significant interest in a critical approach to multimodality, as exemplified in case studies collected in Djonov and Zhao (2016), Stocchetti and Kukkonen (2011) and Zhao et al. (2017).

2.3 Patterns of Discourse Organization

Patterns of discourse organization are defined by Hoey (2001: 119) as "culturally popular" ways of arranging verbal content in different genres. The list compiled by Hoey (2001) includes such patterns as General-Particular, Goal-Achievement, Opportunity-Taking, Knowledge-Filling, Question–Answer and Problem–Solution, the latter considered "the most common pattern of all (or at least the most thoroughly described)" (Hoey 2001: 123). Indeed, most literature in the field discusses Problem–Solution in different written and spoken genres (e.g. Dudley-Evans 1994; Flowerdew 2003, 2008; Grimes 1975; McCarthy 1991; Paltridge 1996). It has also received a comprehensive description by Hoey (1983) himself, with supplementary material being provided in his more recent works (e.g. Hoey 1994, 2001; Hoey and Winter 1986).

Each pattern provides a structural frame for discourse to unfold in a predictable way, which facilitates the process of text production and interpretation. For instance, the Problem-Solution pattern consists of four basic steps: Situation, Problem, Solution and Result/Evaluation. Specifically, Situation portrays a broad context in which a particular Problem is identified. In response to the latter a Solution is proposed, the outcome of which is simply acknowledged (Result), or commented upon with reference to some axiological system (Evaluation). By contrast, the Goal-Achievement pattern opens with the Situation, in whose context a particular Goal is identified. This is followed by Method of Achievement, leading to Evaluation and/or Result.

Methodologically, specific moves of a pattern of discourse organization are signalled by lexical and grammatical triggers (Hoey 2001: 128). The former include certain keywords, e.g. *problem/issue/challenge* for Problem, or *solution/answer* for Solution in Problem–Solution text. Lexical triggers are further classified into *inscribed signals* (explicitly referring to a given move, e.g. *problem* and *challenge* as signals of Problem in Problem–Solution, or *want to, would like to, aim* and *objective* as signals of Goal in Goal-Achievement), *inscribed evaluations* (merely alluding to the move, e.g. *unfortunately* as a signal of Problem in Problem–Solution), and *evoking signals* (presuppositions requiring more general common-sense knowledge to be properly understood as signalling a particular move, e.g. *had no money* recognized as Problem in Problem–Solution).

By contrast, grammatical triggers include signals of sentence subordination and discourse markers, for instance Cause and Consequence markers, which are identified with the Problem–Solution transition, or Instrument and Achievement markers, which correspond with the Solution-Result transition (Hoey 1983). Also, questions can act as grammatical triggers: direct questions can represent the Situation and/or the Problem as a shared experience familiar to both author and reader, while *How to* … questions would act as triggers to Goal in Goal-Achievement (Hoey 2001).

Identifying the triggers and associating them with a particular discourse pattern are basic steps in the analytical framework described by Hoey (2001). Recently, it has been postulated (e.g. Flowerdew 2008) that empirical material for establishing lists of recurrent lexical and grammatical triggers may be provided by corpus analysis. This approach was adopted by Flowerdew (2008), who used Martin and White's (2005) Appraisal system to classify triggers in the moves of the Problem-Solution pattern in technical reports.

It should, however, be remembered that while triggers are explicit markers, easily retrieved in corpus analysis, specific moves in discourse patterns and transitions between them can remain implicit. As Hoey (2001: 128) notes,

[t]he greater the knowledge that the reader shares with the writer, the less need there is for the writer to make explicit linguistic reference to the pattern being followed.

Another challenge to analysis of the patterns is that the boundaries between specific moves do not necessarily correlate with the boundaries of grammatical units, be they clauses, sentences or paragraphs. And, finally, to complicate the task even more, the components can appear in a non-linear order, and/or may be used repetitively (see, for example, Flowerdew 2008: 2; McCarthy 1991: 28).

2.4   Patterns of Discourse Organization in Multimodal Discourse

Central to this study, the question of transferability of discourse organization patterns from text to multimodal discourse has been addressed in discourse analysis only recently. For instance, the structure of narrative has been discussed in *multimodal narrative analysis* (De Fina and Johnstone 2015) in terms of its presence in genres as different as Internet fiction and Web-based personal stories (cf. the variety of genres discussed as multimodal narratives in the volumes edited by Page 2011 and Schiffrin et al. 2010).

Another line of related research focuses on logical organization of multimodal content. For instance, in her study of public reports, Harvey (1995) discusses how text and diagrams co-construct meaning, noting that the latter may resemiotize the textual content in a simplified form (Explanation pattern), or provide evidence to the claim formulated verbally (Claim-Evidence pattern). Logico-semantic relations between image and text are also analysed by Martinec and Salway (2005) in a comparative analysis of several multimodal genres ("electronic encyclopaedias, print advertisements, news websites, online gallery sites, anatomy and marketing textbooks", Martinec and Salway 2005: 341). Martinec and Salway (2005: 349) define three basic relations between image and text: general–specific / general–example (*elaboration*), adding new information (*extension*) and elaborating on the context, including temporal, spatial and/or causal relations (*enhancement*). In general, then, the patterns of multimodal discourse organization, as distinguished in the models by Harvey (1995) and Martinec and Salway (2005), do not differ significantly from the patterns prevalent in monomodal discourse.

Surprisingly, little research has been devoted to the Problem-Solution pattern in multimodal discourse, a topic of direct relevance to my study, despite the fact that it is recognized as "one of the most common rhetorical patterns in our society" (Ferreira and Heberle 2013: 112; see also Jordan 1984; Hoey 2001; Fairclough 2003). At the same time, it is considered to be a major pattern of content organization in advertising discourse (Flowerdew 2008; Hoey 2001), under which type can also be subsumed crowdfunding project presentations. Traditionally, however, the scope of research has only involved the verbal dimension, "leaving aside any visual semiotic resource that may have been deployed" (Ferreira and Heberle 2013: 112) in advertising discourse.

Among the few papers that discuss intersemiotic realization of the Problem-Solution pattern in multimodal advertisements are Machin and van Leeuwen (2007) and Ferreira and Heberle (2013). In their brief analysis of a wellness clinic advertised in the Dutch edition of *Cosmopolitan* 2001, Machin and van Leeuwen (2007) show that the Situation move does not appear in the advertisement analysed, whereas all other moves of the Problem-Solution pattern, i.e. Problem–Solution-Result-Elaboration of Solution and Result, are expressed verbally. By contrast, the visual medium in general represents only one move at a time: Problem, e.g. "expressed by a picture of a blemished skin", Solution, e.g. "picture of the product", or Result "a picture of an unblemished skin" (Machin and van Leeuwen 2007: 108). The authors do not, however, offer a more detailed study of this example, and conclude with a vague statement that "some stages may be realised visually and others verbally" (Machin and van Leeuwen 2007: 108).

A more comprehensive study is presented in Ferreira and Heberle (2013), discussing the *Diners Club International* advertisement originally published in *Newsweek*—Latin America Edition on 23rd December 2002. The paper combines a variety of research perspectives, including Mitchell's (1995) semiotic model of *textimage* that accounts for interaction of verbal and visual systems in multimodal discourses, Kress and van Leeuwen's (1996) concept of *reading path* that accounts for different patterns of navigation across multimodal content, and the critical approach to discourse as social practice (Fairclough 2003), which also focuses on the advertisement as a representation of *consumer culture* (Bauman 2007). Ferreira and Heberle (2013) show that visual and verbal elements concurrently realize the key moves in the Problem-Solution pattern, depicting the Problem metaphorically as a locked door, to which the Solution is claimed—and shown—to be the payment card in question.

In contrast to Machin and van Leeuwen (2007) and Ferreira and Heberle (2013), who analyse printed advertisements in magazines, I focus on the multimodal genre of promotional video, combining film with simultaneous voice-over commentary. Also, my research is not limited to Problem–Solution but also includes other patterns of discourse organization, for instance General-Particular and General-Example.

Empirical material referred to in this paper was sampled from promotional videos of project presentations showcased on Internet crowdfunding platforms, a genre that I discuss in the following section.

2.5 Crowdfunding Platform and Project Presentation: Kickstarter

Internet crowdfunding platforms hold an important position in the contemporary marketing landscape. They have also popularized a new advertising genre, project presentation, which exploits the affordances of digital multimodality, as shown in my previous studies (Kowalski 2017, 2018, 2019).

While the number of crowdfunding platforms is ever increasing, and each of them may make use of a specific interface, they will in general structurally and functionally resemble Kickstarter, the oldest and largest crowdfunding platform. The latter has also established the template for the genre of crowdfunding project presentation, now widespread on other platforms, e.g. the Polish *PolakPotrafi* and *Beesfund*. For this reason I take Kickstarter and its presentation template as my reference for defining a crowdfunding platform and the genre of project presentation.

Kickstarter (www.kickstarter.com) is a leading global crowdfunding platform. Launched in 2009, it promotes reward-based projects (i.e. supporters of a project receive some related merchandise, its value being dependent on the amount of donation) on an all-or-nothing basis; that is, the sum raised is transferred to the project's developer only if it reaches the preset threshold, or otherwise the donations are returned to the backers. Kickstarter thus offers a virtual showcasing platform for new business ventures, falling into one of the 15 thematic categories: Art, Comics, Crafts, Dance, Design, Fashion, Film & Video, Food, Games, Journalism, Music, Photography, Publishing, Technology and Theater. The sheer number of projects and financial turnover prove Kickstarter's leadership in the crowdfunding market: as of 26th November 2019, the platform has promoted 468,483 projects, with 4.68 billion USD worth of donations. As for the Technology group, which has been the focus of my analysis, the respective figures are 40,775 projects and 883.85 million USD backing.

The ever-increasing popularity of Kickstarter among project developers would have probably led to randomness of form and/or content in project presentations but for administrators' strict regulatory mechanisms. These include: (1) explicit content-related policy; (2) explicit form-related policy; and (3) the reviewing process. To this set one may also add (4) the interface, a regulatory mechanism whereby users can narrow down the enormous database into a manageable subset of their choice.

Explicit content-related policy refers to Kickstarter's approval of reward-based, all-or-nothing projects only. In addition, specific regulations stipulate that: (a) projects must create something to share with others; (b) projects must be honest and clearly presented; (c) projects can't fundraise for charity; (d) projects can't offer equity (i.e. the investors can only receive some reward for their payments, but not shares in the company); and (e) projects can't involve prohibited items.[2]

Explicit form-related policy, on the other hand, determines that project presentations fit into a preset template. In general, the project is announced in a headline part, which also contains hyperlinks to Campaign, FAQs, Updates, Comments and Community. The Campaign web page is the project presentation proper, providing both informational content (general information about the project, the developer's details, the product's specification) and promotional content (links to media materials on the project, experts'/testers' opinions, results of tests against similar, already available solutions). An ever-present element on the right side of the website is the Back This Project button, followed by a list of rewards in return for donations at successive thresholds. In each case the donation option is provided with the data on

---

[2] See here: https://www.kickstarter.com/rules?ref=faq-basics_whatfor; DOA: 11th October 2019.

the time and mode of shipment of the goods offered as reward, and the number of backers who have already chosen the given option.

The reviewing process is an executive procedure whereby administrators control the project presentation's compliance with both form- and content-related policies. The rejection rate is claimed to be maintained at the moderate level of 20%.[3]

Finally, Kickstarter's interface is a regulatory mechanism that allows the user to reduce the pool of the project presentations displayed to those meeting the pre-specified browsing criteria.

In addition to the above-listed explicit regulatory instruments (explicit content-related policy; explicit form-related policy; the reviewing process; interface), there can be distinguished one important implicit regulatory mechanism in Kickstarter project presentations: patterns of discourse organization, especially Problem–Solution, as discussed in this paper. They act as a logico-semantic scaffolding for the promotional content of the presentation, whereby it unfolds along generally recognized lines (e.g. Problem–Solution, General-Particular, General-Example). As a result, relations between the discursive moves are easily retrieved, which in turn warrants the clarity of the argument.

2.6   Aims, Methods and Materials

The present paper concludes my series of earlier case studies (Kowalski 2017, 2018, 2019), in which I analysed a number of crowdfunding project presentations in the Technology category, showcased on Kickstarter versus PolakPotrafi reward-based crowdfunding platforms and CrowdCube versus Beesfund equity-based crowd-funding platforms. The results obtained in contrastive research (global versus local platforms, reward-based versus equity-based platforms) show certain regularities in the way the patterns of discourse organization are realized in simultaneously received modes in the multimodal genre of promotional video in crowdfunding project presentation. This paper develops a general theoretical framework for grasping the complex interaction between patterns of discourse organization, their moves and the content simultaneously received in visual and verbal modes in the said genre. Specifically, three types of such interaction are identified and discussed: (1) transfer of moves across modes; (2) move-and-pattern overlap; and (3) rupture of intermodal cohesion.

The phenomena discussed are illustrated with examples excerpted from the promotional video of *Knocki*, a "wireless device that instantly transforms ordinary surfaces [...] into powerful yet easy to access [touch] remotes".[4] Further examples

---

[3] See here: www.kickstarter.com; https://com/blog/everything-you-need-to-know-about-the-pro ject-review-process; DOA: 17th October 2019.

[4] See here: https://www.kickstarter.com/projects/knocki/knocki-make-any-surface-smart, DOA: 16th October 2019; video: https://ksr-video.imgix.net/projects/2424950/video-668848-h264_high. mp4.

of the phenomena in question as found in other project presentations are discussed in Kowalski (2017, 2018, 2019).

2.7 Patterns of Multimodal Discourse Organization in Promotional Videos of Crowdfunding Project Presentation

The results of my earlier case studies show that the advertising content of crowdfunding project presentations is partly realized monomodally, and hence received linearly (e.g. written text), and partly realized multimodally, which in turn requires simultaneous reception from two or more channels. The latter is the case for promotional videos, which combine the film medium, including feature and/or animation, with voice-over commentary and/or actors speaking. Such multimodal presentation of the advertising content in two or more simultaneously unfolding channels entails variations in the patterns of discourse organization, compared with their primarily linear realization in monomodal discourses, as originally discussed in Hoey (1983, 2001).

2.7.1 Transfer of Moves Across Modes

The first variation in the patterns of discourse organization found in promotional videos of crowdfunding project presentations is *transfer of moves* of the same pattern *across modes*. In the case of the projects showcased in the Technology category, the video promoting a device can discuss general features of the product in the voice-over commentary (General move of the General-Particular pattern), while the simultaneous film scenes show its operation (Particular move of the General-Particular pattern). For instance, the off-camera commentary at the beginning of the Knocki promotional video (00:27–00:34) makes a general presentation of the device, *"Knocki is a small wireless device that instantly transforms ordinary surfaces in your environment into remote controls"*, whereas the simultaneously running video represents examples of "ordinary surfaces in your environment": inner wall, underside of the tabletop and door. Martinec and Salway (2005) identify a similar relation for General-Example, which they classify as *Exemplification*.

Transfer of moves across modes can also concern other patterns of discourse organization apart from General-Example and General-Particular, for instance Problem–Solution or Goal-Achievement. The latter can be illustrated with the opening scenes in the promotional video of Knocki. The voice-over commentary represents the Goal (*"I find myself thinking there has to be a more natural and accessible way to control the devices around us"*, 00:08–00:14), while the video running in parallel already depicts the Method of achievement move, with the images of the company's R-and-D laboratory and employees working on the CAD design of the device.

2.7.2   Move-And-Pattern Overlap

The second variation in the patterns of discourse organization identified in promotional videos of crowdfunding project presentations is *move-and-pattern overlap*, which is actually embedded in the transfer of moves across modes (see Sect. 2.7.1). Specifically, it refers to a move of the pattern that extends across modes (i.e. *transfer of moves across modes*), and which simultaneously constitutes another complete discourse pattern. This is the case for *micro-narratives* (Kowalski 2017, 2019) realized in the film medium, depicting the operation of the product promoted (Particular move of the General-Particular pattern), with the simultaneous voice-over commentary discussing its general features (General move of the General-Particular pattern). The micro-narrative itself is, however, not only a move in the General-Particular pattern, but constitutes a complex pattern of its own, namely Problem–Solution.

The move-and-pattern overlap is frequently used in Knocki's promotional video, which contains 11 micro-narratives, taking in sum a significant 1 min 26 s of the 3'44"-long video. Eight of these micro-narratives feature the move-and-pattern overlap. A case in point may be the first narrative (00:46–00:58), which realizes simultaneously the Particular move (triggered by the General move in the preceding voice-over commentary) and the entire Problem-Solution pattern. Specifically, the film presents the backyard of a house, with a man playing football casually (Particular/Situation overlap), unaware of a delivery man approaching the front door (Particular/Problem overlap). The delivery man knocks, which instantly activates the Knocki smartphone application, displaying the message "Someone at front door" (Particular/Solution overlap). The man opens the door and is given a package (Particular/Positive Result overlap). The accompanying voice-over commentary, however, takes a general perspective on Knocki's diverse applications: "*Knocki can control a wide variety of devices around us. But the true beauty of our technology is that what it can do is only limited by your imagination*" (General), with no direct reference to the micro-narrative simultaneously displayed.

2.7.3   Rupture of Intermodal Cohesion

Finally, the third variation in the patterns of discourse organization in promotional videos of crowdfunding project presentations is simultaneous realization of different, unrelated patterns in video and voice-over commentary, with no interweaving moves across the two modes. As a result, the content unfolds in two separate lines, a phenomenon that can be termed *rupture of intermodal cohesion*. Illogical as it may seem from the point of view of the flow of communication, the phenomenon can in fact be motivated by at least two reasons.

Firstly, rupture of intermodal cohesion may be due to the general conciseness of advertising genres, to which belong not only the crowdfunding project presentation but also the project's promotional video embedded therein. The latter may thus exploit the advantages of multimodality and represent the marketing content in a twin-track manner, thus—hypothetically—presenting the message in up to half the time that would otherwise be necessary in a monomodal genre. Having said that, it should be noted that the two narrative lines are not totally unrelated, inasmuch as they share the same topic (the product marketed), and hence their overall semantic integrity, or coherence, is not affected. What follows is that their simultaneous reception should not pose a problem for the audience. An empirical study is here recommended to verify this hypothesis.

Secondly, rupture of intermodal cohesion may be a corollary of a specific contextual feature of crowdfunding project presentation rather than be inherent to advertising discourse in general. Specifically, a crowdfunding project, particularly one involving a tangible product, as in the case of the Technology category, is addressed to two target groups, i.e. (1) investors and (2) customers, with an aggregate of the two being both possible and common. In addition, other parties may be attracted to the project, for instance business rivals or media representatives, but these are not relevant to the rationale behind the rupture of intermodal cohesion.

With investors' interest in the product being differently motivated to that of customers, the project presentation may be expected to focus on these distinctive target groups alternately. This division is clearly seen, for example, in the Knocki presentation, not only in the promotional video but also in the main text interspersed with various visual elements. On the one hand, there are sections of relevance for potential customers and future users: a brief instruction manual (*The Basics*), followed by the step-by-step set-up procedure (*Setup is easy!*), a list of possible household contexts in which the device can be applied (*A Few of the Many Use Cases*) and a definition of the customer group (*Who is Knocki for?*). On the other hand, there are sections focusing on the company developing the device, containing data primarily significant to potential investors: the company's profile and history (*Our story*), its personnel (*Our team*) and a stage-by-stage history of the product's development so far (*Our timeline*), followed by short- and long-term goals for its upgrade (*Stretch goals*). Also, the standard legal clause concluding each Kickstarter project presentation, *Risks and challenges*, concerns investors rather than customers.

While all the above-listed sections are realized in modes produced and received one at a time, be it text or graphics, and hence customer-targeted content and investor-targeted content are presented alternately, the promotional video would have to demarcate the content intended for the two distinctive audiences differently. It is what I call "rupture of intermodal cohesion" that serves this purpose, exploiting the two modes unfolding in parallel, i.e. video and voice-over commentary, to present customer-targeted content and investor-targeted content. What is important is that for the purpose of target-audiences' demarcation the promotional video employs elements of two patterns of discourse organization unfolding simultaneously in two modes.

A relevant example is the opening 25-s sequence in the Knocki promotional video. The voice-over commentary takes the perspective of the potential customer, and the text delivered is structured as Problem–Solution. The Situation is first delineated (*We are surrounded by technology. It is entering our homes and helping us automate daily tasks*), and then followed by the statement of the Problem by a still invisible user (*But I find myself thinking there has to be a more natural and accessible way to control the devices around us. If the goal of automation is to simplify our lives, why does it feel so complicated?*). Only at this point is the speaker revealed to be Jake Beshernitzan, the company's co-founder. His business identity is of less importance to customers, but it is definitely vital to the product's marketing and its potential investors. The discourse pattern then progresses from the general Problem (of the anonymous, invisible everyman concerned with automatization of household devices' control) to the specific Solution, delivered by Beshernitzan's company.

However, the film content that unfolds in parallel does not reproduce the content of the voice-over commentary. Moreover, the images are not congruent with the primarily customer-oriented Problem-Solution pattern of the latter. Instead, when Beshernitzan outlines the Situation and then the Problem, the simultaneous scenes depict the work at the company's R-and-D laboratory, with takes being switched between different tasks performed (Example move of the General-Example pattern, starting *in media res*, with no General move): component printing, microscopic analysis, early drawings and computer designing. Jake Beshernitzan, the company's co-founder, is shown to be actively engaged in the R-and-D process. The company's activities and its mode of operation are not directly relevant to an average customer but they are certainly so for potential investors.

In consequence, the rupture of intermodal cohesion allows the company to address two distinct audiences at the same time: potential customers in the Problem–Solution structured voice-over content and potential investors in the (General-) Example structured video content. As a result, rupture of intermodal cohesion appears to be an advantage of multimodal genres that cannot be underestimated in the case of content-condensed genres of advertising discourse.

Moreover, it should also be noted that rupture of intermodal cohesion can also involve different discourse resources for addressing either of the target groups. As the Knocki promotional video illustrates, the voice-over commentary underlines the wide spectrum of the potential customers with inclusive first-person plural pronouns. The Situation thus construed refers to the general experience of modern society, being *"surrounded by technology [...] entering our homes and helping us automate daily tasks"*. The same pronominal forms are also used in the following Problem move, highlighting that the Problem is as much a shared experience as the Situation, and finding a Solution is construed as an urgent need in society.

By contrast, the Knocki video's film scenes, which represent the company's R-and-D laboratory, make use of quick alternation of shots, underlining the quick pace of work. These shots show how advanced equipment (e.g. 3D printing or CAD software) is used in the laboratory on the one hand, and how its employees are engaged in discussions over specific components on the other. These situations can be interpreted as depicting the company's business assets: advanced technology support and well-orchestrated teamwork. As such, it is the content primarily intended for potential investors, as much interested in the quality of the end product as in the company's business condition, its equipment base and work environment.

Finally, it is interesting that rupture of intermodal cohesion can co-occur with other phenomena identified in my analysis, in particular transfer of moves across modes. A relevant example in the Knocki promotional video is when the Problem is being identified in the voice-over commentary (*If the goal of automation is to simplify our lives, why does it feel so complicated?*), the simultaneous film scenes already show the Solution, namely the Knocki device being already developed by the company's engineers.

2.8 Conclusion

The study has shown that patterns of discourse organization are realized in multimodal discourses differently to how they are realized in monomodal texts which were originally analysed by Hoey (1983; 2001). This difference has been found in particular in multimodal discourses where content is simultaneously received from two or more modes. Taking as reference the genre of promotional video in crowdfunding project presentation, and drawing on the results of my earlier empirical case studies, I propose here an open classification of three types of interaction between patterns of discourse organization, their moves and parallel modes of expression: (1) transfer of moves across modes; (2) move-and-pattern overlap; and (3) rupture of intermodal cohesion. It should be noted, however, that despite these possible variations, patterns of discourse organization are instrumental to the structuring of the content in multimodal discourse as much as they are in monomodal discourse.

If communication nowadays is largely, if not exclusively, multimodal (Iedema 2003: 39; Kress 2010: 32), then there is a need for a relevant framework of analysis, multidimensional and dynamic, so as to thoroughly represent multimodal communication in both its complexity and its progression. Such a model should also pay due attention to discourse patterns, which have been shown here to act as signposts in the intricate semiotic landscape of multimodal communication. Identifying the three types of interaction between patterns of discourse organization, their moves and parallel modes of expression is a first step toward this comprehensive theoretical and methodological framework of analysis.

References

Barthes, Roland. (1964) 1977. *Image—Music—Text*. New York: Hill and Wang.

Bateman, John A. 2008. *Multimodality and Genre: A Foundation for the Systematic Analysis of Multimodal Documents*. London: Continuum.

Bateman, John A. 2014. *Text and Image: A Critical Introduction to the Visual / Verbal Divide*. New York: Routledge.

Bateman, John, Janina Wildfeuer, and Tuomo Hiippala. 2017. *Multimodality. Foundations, Research and Analysis. A Problem-Oriented Introduction*. Berlin: Mouton de Gruyter.

Bauman, Zygmunt. 2007. *Consuming Life*. Cambridge & Malden: Polity Press.

Bednarek, Monika. 2015. Corpus-assisted Multimodal Discourse Analysis of Television and Film Narratives. In *Corpora and Discourse Studies*, ed. P. Baker and T. McEnery, 63–87. London: Palgrave Macmillan.

Bednarek, Monika, and James R. Martin, eds. 2010. *New Discourse on Language: Functional Perspectives on Multimodality, Identity XE "Identity", and Affiliation*. London: Continuum.

Chapelle, Carol, ed. 2013. *The Encyclopedia of Applied Linguistics*. Oxford: Wiley-Blackwell.

Fina, De., and Anna, and Barbara Johnstone. . 2015. Discourse Analysis and Narrative. In *Handbook of Discourse Analysis*, 2nd ed., ed. D. Tannen, H. Hamilton, and D. Schiffrin, 152–168. Chichester: Wiley Blackwell.

Djonov, Emilia. 2013. Multimodality and Hypermedia. In *The Encyclopedia of Applied Linguistics*, ed. C. Chapelle. Oxford: Wiley-Blackwell. (on-line edition: https://doi.org/10.1002/978140519 8431.wbeal0826; pages unnumbered).

Djonov, Emilia, and Sumin Zhao, eds. 2016. *Critical Multimodal Studies of Popular Discourse*. New York: Routledge.

Dudley-Evans, Tony. 1994. Variations in the Discourse Patterns Favoured by Different Disciplines and their Pedagogical Implications. In *Academic Listening: Research Perspectives*, ed. J. Flowerdew, 146–158. Cambridge: Cambridge University Press.

Fairclough, Norman. 2003. *Analysing Discourse: Textual Analysis for Social Research*. London: Routledge.

Ferreira, Sidnéa Nunes., and Vivaine M. Heberle. 2013. Text Linguistics and Critical Discourse Analysis: A Multimodal Analysis of a Magazine Advertisement. *Ilha Do Desterro (UFSC)* 64: 111–133.

Flowerdew, Lynne. 2003. A Combined Corpus and Systemic-Functional Analysis of the Problem-Solution Pattern in a Student and Professional Corpus of Technical Writing. *TESOL Quarterly* 37 (3): 489–511.

Flowerdew, Lynne. 2008. *Corpus-based Analyses of the Problem-Solution Pattern*. Amsterdam: John Benjamins.

Grimes, Joseph E. 1975. *The Thread of Discourse*. The Hague: Mouton.

Halliday, Michael, and Alexander Kirkwood. 1978. *Language as a Social Semiotic: The Social Interpretation of Language and Meaning*. London: Edward Arnold.

Harvey, Anamaria. 1995. Interaction in Public Reports. *English for Specific Purposes* 14 (3): 189–200.

Hodge, Robert, and Gunther Kress. 1979. *Language as Ideology*. London: Routledge.

Hodge, Robert, and Gunther Kress. 1988. *Social Semiotics*. Cambridge: Polity Press.

Hoey, Michael. 1983. *On the Surface of Discourse*. London: George Allen & Unwin.

Hoey, Michael. 1994. Signalling in Discourse: A Functional Analysis of a Common Discourse Pattern in Written and Spoken English. In *Advances in Written Text Analysis*, ed. M. Coulthard, 26–45. London: Routledge.

Hoey, Michael. 2001. *Textual Interaction: An Introduction to Written Discourse Analysis*. London: Routledge.

Hoey, Michael, and Eugene Winter. 1986. Clause Relations and the Writer's Communicative Task. In *Functional Approaches to Writing: Research Perspectives*, ed. B. Couture, 120–141. London: Frances Pinter.

Iedema, Rick. 2003. Multimodality, Resemiotization: Extending the Analysis of Discourse as Multisemiotic Practice. *Visual Communication* 2 (1): 29–57.

Jewitt, Carey, ed. 2009. *The Routledge Handbook of Multimodal Analysis*. London: Routledge.

Jones, Rodney H. 2013. Multimodal Discourse Analysis. In *The Encyclopedia of Applied Linguistics*, ed. C. Chapelle. Oxford: Blackwell. (on-line edition: https://doi.org/10.1002/978140519 8431.wbeal0813; pages unnumbered).

Jordan, Michael P. 1984. *Rhetoric of Everyday English Texts*. London: Allen & Unwin.

Knox, John. 2013. Multimodality and Systemic Functional Analysis. In *The Encyclopedia of Applied Linguistics*, ed. C. Chapelle. Oxford: Wiley-Blackwell. (on-line edition: https://doi.org/10.1002/9781405198431.wbeal0836; pages unnumbered).

Kowalski, Grzegorz. 2017. Problem-Solution Text Pattern and References to Target Groups in Crowdfunding Projects' Presentations. In *Discourse Studies: Ways and Crossroads*, ed. K. Broś and G. Kowalski, 131–173. Berlin: Peter Lang.

Kowalski, Grzegorz. 2018. Problem–Solution Pattern in Internet Presentations of Local- and Global-Target Start-ups. *Rhetoric and Communications E-Journal* 34. http://rhetoric.bg/rhetoric-and-communications-issue-34-may-2018.

Kowalski, Grzegorz. 2019. Applicability of Text Organization Patterns in an Analysis of Multimodal Web Genres. In *Modern Developments in Linguistics and Language Teaching: The Problem of Method* [Soveremennyje Napravlenija v Lingvistike i Prepodavanii Jazykov: Problema Metoda], *III International Conference Proceedings, Penza, 24–27 April 2019, Vol. I Methods in Linguistics*, ed. T.V. Dubrovskaya, 125–129. Penza: Penza State University Publishing House.

Kress, Gunther. 2010. *Multimodality. A Social Semiotic Approach to Communication*. London: Routledge.

Kress, Gunther, and Theo van Leeuwen. 1996. *Reading Images: The Grammar of Visual Design*. London: Routledge.

Kress, Gunther, and Theo van Leeuwen. 2001. *Multimodal Discourse: The Modes and Media of Contemporary Communication*. London: Arnold.

Lemke, Jay L. 1998. Multiplying Meaning: Visual and Verbal Semiotics in Scientific Text. In *Reading Science*, ed. J.R. Martin and R. Veel, 87–113. London: Routledge.

Lemke, Jay L. 2002. Travels in Hypermodality. *Visual Communication* 1 (3): 299–325.

McCarthy, Michael. 1991. *Discourse Analysis for Language Teachers*. Cambridge: Cambridge University Press.

Machin, David. 2007. *Introduction to Multimodal Analysis*. London: Hodder Arnold.

Machin, David. 2009. Multimodality and Theories of the Visual. In *Routledge Handbook of Multimodal Analysis*, ed. C. Jewitt, 181–190. London: Routledge.

Machin, David, ed. 2014. *Visual Communication*. Berlin: Mouton de Gruyter.

Machin, David, and Theo van Leeuwen. 2007. *Global Media Discourse: A Critical Introduction*. London: Routledge.

Martin, James R., and Peter R. R. White. 2005. *The Language of Evaluation: Appraisal in English*. London: Palgrave.

Martinec, Radan, and Andrew Salway. 2005. A System for Image-Text Relations in New (and Old) Media. *Visual Communication* 4: 337–371.

Mitchell, William John Thomas. 1995. *Picture Theory*. Chicago & London: University of Chicago Press.

Norris, Sigrid. 2004. *Analyzing Multimodal Interaction: A Methodological Framework*. London: Routledge.

Norris, Sigrid. 2011. Three Hierarchical Positions of Deictic Gesture in Relation to Spoken Language: A Multimodal Interaction Analysis. *Visual Communication* 10 (2): 1–19.

Norris, Sigrid, and Rodney H. Jones. 2005. *Discourse in Action: Introducing Mediated Discourse Analysis*. London: Routledge.

Norris, Sigrid, and Carmen Maier. 2014. *Interactions, Images and Texts. A Reader in Multimodality*. Berlin: Mouton de Gruyter.

O'Halloran, Kay L. 2005. *Mathematical Discourse: Language, Symbolism and Visual Images*. London: Continuum.

O'Halloran, Kay L. 2011. Multimodal Discourse Analysis. In *Continuum Companion to Discourse Analysis*, ed. K. Hyland and B. Paltridge, 120–137. New York: Continuum.

O'Halloran, Kay L., and Bradley A. Smith. 2011. *Multimodal Studies: Exploring Issues and Domains*. New York: Routledge.

O'Halloran, Kay L., Sabine Tan, Bradley Smith, and Alexey Podlasov. 2010. Challenges in Designing Digital Interfaces for the Study of Multimodal Phenomena. *Information Design Journal* 18: 2–21.

O'Toole, Michael. 1994. *The Language of Displayed Art*. Rutherford, NJ: Fairleigh Dickinson University Press.

O'Toole, Michael. 2010. *The Language of Displayed Art*, 2nd ed. London: Routledge.

Page, Ruth, ed. 2011. *New Perspectives on Narratives and Multimodality*. New York: Routledge.

Paltridge, Brian. 1996. Genre, Text Type, and the Language Learning Classroom. *ELT Journal* 50 (3): 237–243.

Rohlfing, Katharina, Daniel Loehr, Susan Duncan, Amanda Brown, Amy Franklin, Irene Kimbara, Jan-Torsten. Milde, Fey Parrill, Travis Rose, Thomas Schmidt, Han Sloetjes, Alexandra Thies, and Sandra Wellinghoff. 2006. Comparison of Multimodal annotation tools: Workshop Report. *Online-Zeitschrift Zur Verbalen Interaktion* 7: 99–123.

Schiffrin, Deborah, Anna De Fina, and Anastasia Nylund, eds. 2010. *Telling Stories: Narrative, Language and Social Life. 2010.* Washington: Georgetown University Press.

Scollon, Ron. 2001. *Mediated Discourse: A Nexus of Practice*. London: Routledge.

Scollon, Ron, and Suzie Wong Scollon. 2004. *Nexus Analysis: Discourse and the Emerging Internet*. London: Routledge.

Seizov, Ognyan, and Janina Wildfeuer, eds. 2017. *New Studies in Multimodality: Conceptual and Methodological Elaborations*. London: Bloomsbury.

Stocchetti, Matteo, and Karin Kukkonen, eds. 2011. *Images in Use: Towards Critical Analysis of Visual Communication*. Amsterdam / Philadelphia: John Benjamins.

van Leeuwen, Theo. 2013. Critical Analysis of Multimodal Discourse. In *The Encyclopedia of Applied Linguistics*, ed. C. Chapelle. Oxford: Wiley-Blackwell. (on-line edition: https://doi.org/10.1002/9781405198431.wbeal0269; pages unnumbered).

Wildfeuer, Janina. 2014. *Towards a New Paradigm for Multimodal Film Analysis*. New York: Routledge.

Zhao, Sumin, Emilia Djonov, Anders Björkvall, and Morten Boeriis, eds. 2017. *Advancing Multimodal and Critical Discourse Studies: Interdisciplinary Research Inspired by Theo van Leeuwen's Social Semiotics*. New York: Routledge.

Chapter 3
Regulating Social Behaviour by Multimodal Public Signs: Semiotic Pragmatics of Prohibition

Evgeniy Kozhemyakin and Tatiana Dubrovskaya

Abstract Interaction in both institutional and everyday situations involves a range of resources. Apart from verbal means, social behaviour is regulated through various semiotic instruments that contribute to or specify verbally expressed meanings. While there is a vast body of scholarly studies focusing on multimodality in communication, the structure of multimodal texts needs refining. In this chapter, we draw upon public signs and notices to explore how different semiotic resources, such as words, fonts, frames, colours and images cooperate to produce the pragmatic effect of prohibition. We distinguish between the two groups of public signs with respect to the relation they bear to institutional discourse and the semiotic resources employed: public signs that retain the marks of official legal discourse and thus rely predominantly on verbal means; and naïve regulators, which are deprived of legal markers and reiterate legal norms through multimodal resources, offering a ready-made version of a social norm. Our findings imply that multimodal resources allow for a combination of legal and commonsensical meanings in everyday interactions.

Keywords Multimodality · Public signs · Public notices · Social behaviour · Semiotic resources · Prohibition

3.1 Introduction

Social behaviour in both institutional and everyday situations is communicational and discursive. By counting it as *communicational*, we mean that we use means of communication (such as speech and writing, gestures, images, postures, etc.) to act and interact socially, as well as to reflect and affect social interaction. Such affecting

E. Kozhemyakin (✉) · T. Dubrovskaya
Belgorod National Research University, Belgorod, Russia
e-mail: kozhemyakin@bsu.edu.ru

T. Dubrovskaya
Penza State University, Penza, Russia

© The Author(s), under exclusive license to Springer Nature Switzerland AG 2021   27
N. V. Sukhova et al. (eds.), *Multimodality, Digitalization and Cognitivity
in Communication and Pedagogy*, Numanities - Arts and Humanities
in Progress 20, https://doi.org/10.1007/978-3-030-84071-6_3

refers to a range of actions taken to maintain or reward acceptable or "normal" behaviour and to restrict or prohibit unacceptable or "abnormal" behaviour.

By saying *discursive*, we mean that people communicate in a certain discourse facet, i.e. in a certain way of language use. A discourse provides us with more or less appropriate semiotic means to express ideas and thoughts, transmit emotions and images, impact on others' actions and regulate their behaviour. The choice of such means is always free, but language possibilities, abilities of our receptors and social expectations and norms limit our choice of semiotic means. The social semiotic theory usually applies the terms *affordance* (Kress 2010) to mark basic potentialities and constraints of a mode, which are usually determined by their materiality, and *fitness* to indicate the appropriate way of using semiotic means in various social situations. We cannot (should not) express anything in a way that is not determined (afforded) by language, seems impossible to be produced or perceived physically, or in a way that contradicts (does not fit) generally accepted ethical standards and legal norms. Nor can we interact with others or coregulate our behaviour unless other people use the same communicational mode, share the same language and are aware of the very fact of communication. In principle, social behaviour is constructed in cooperative communication by means of discourses.

Normally, when we think about means of communication, discourse and language, we tend to take into account only verbal means, i.e. words. We often assume it to be norm that the main meaning transmitter is verbal language, while non-verbal means are used to specify verbally expressed meanings or provide some additional information. As Jakobson claimed in his work *On Linguistic Aspects of Translation* (1959), there are three ways of interpreting a verbal sign: intralingual translation, i.e. an interpretation of verbal signs by means of other signs of the same language; interlingual translation, i.e. an interpretation of verbal signs by means of some other language; and intersemiotic translation or transmutation, i.e. an interpretation of verbal signs by means of signs of nonverbal sign systems (Jacobson 1959: 233). Of all the three, the last one pertains to the topic of this chapter.

This complexity of interaction between various semiotic means or resources used in communication is generally expressed with the term *multimodality*. This term indicates the capacity of texts to convey meanings by various communicational modes, not a single one. If we call a printed text *multimodal*, it means that it involves words, colours, size, margins, fonts, etc. to render meanings as a whole. When an oral interaction is called *multimodal*, we should take into account all valuable means to communicate meanings: words pronounced, intonations, pauses, rhythms, tone and other non-verbal elements including gestures, postures, movements, etc.

Researchers have been focusing on multimodality in communication for almost 20 years (Kress and van Leeuwen 2001; Norris 2004; Baldry and Thibault 2005; Kress 2010; O'Halloran and Smith, 2012; Bateman and Wildfeuer 2014; Bateman et al. 2017; Jovanovic and van Leeuwen 2018), while the problem had not been new for linguists and semiologists previously. The general idea that underlies contemporary multimodality studies concerns the critical view of the role of verbal means as central elements for meaning transmission in communication systems (Danesi 2018; Djonov and van Leeuwen 2018; Hiippala 2018). Constructing the complexes of meanings enacts 'cooperation' between verbal and non-verbal—auditory, visual and proxemic—means of communication.

Among various descriptions of multimodality, there are several focusing on the interdisciplinary nature of multimodal studies. Thus, Kibrik shows that the term *multimodal*

> bases on the notion of modality accepted in psychology, neurophysiology and information sciences: modality is a type of the external stimulus perceived by one of the human receptors, mainly by sight and hearing. (Kibrik 2010: 135)[1]

It should be added that modality is also a specific object of study in semiotics, which predominately deals with visual (verbal and iconic) elements of communication. In this paper, we focus on the synthetic usage of verbal and visual resources in communication which are perceived by sight.

The features of multimodal communication comprise semiotic heterogeneity, simultaneous multichannel transmission of messages, complexity of reception and communicational combinativity. Multimodal texts simultaneously affect various receptor abilities of addressees when sending messages.

Interpreting communication phenomena as multimodal is very important, especially in terms of research into social regulation through communication, since establishing social order involves a whole range of means and resources. It would be an oversimplification to claim that we regulate our behaviour with words only. A glance, an intonation, a posture, a certain colour or an image often make a better and more valuable contribution to social regulation than words do. It means that people use various communicational modes to represent what is "normal" and what is not, and to make others behave according to the constructed order.

Numerous thoughtful findings concerning how social behaviour regulation is studied in the history of humanities and social sciences were thoroughly observed by Duncan (1962). While we are deeply aware of how we regulate social behaviour by means of words (Luria 1961; Hayes and Hayes 1992), as well as having deep and wide knowledge of how people use non-verbal (visual) means for organising social order (Schefflen and Schefflen 1972; Barry 1997; Lemonnier 2016), we cannot claim that we possess a systematic view of how words and non-words work together to set social matters in order.

Nevertheless, the problem is a focus in many research fields. Social semiotics (Kress 2010) and critical discourse analysis (Machin and Mayr 2012) take an avid interest in how individuals use semiotic resources to (re)produce social hierarchy and power, control social processes, represent socially charged phenomena, etc. In other words, researchers pay attention to how semiotic resources are used in social life. This consideration requires that a cross-disciplinary approach be taken to discursive phenomena and semiotic means of communication.

In this chapter, we concentrate on the structure of the multimodal texts used to regulate social behaviour in everyday situations. What attracts our interest is how different semiotic resources, such as words, fonts, frames, colours, elements

---

[1] Hereinafter, translations have been done by the authors.

of proxemics, images and size interact or cooperate to produce the pragmatic effect of regulation. We suppose that there are several types of such semiotic cooperation depending on which semiotic resource is central to meaning-making and attracting attention, and that there can be both verbally focused and mixed multimodal texts.

Another area of interest to us lies within the social aspects of semiotic resources use: we are concerned with how and why people use multimodal texts in everyday situations to regulate social behaviour while there is a large number of institutional restrictions and legal texts regulating social life. We label them as *institutional legal texts*, which as a whole constitute official legal discourse. Official legal discourse is produced by authorised bodies and establishes basic ideas, topics and typical linguistic patterns that characterise a given institutional sphere. Institutional legal texts are often referred to in notices and signs. As we can suppose at the start of our research, in everyday situations multimodal texts re-code institutional verbal texts into communicational modes that are more appropriate for everyday consumption since they make legal norms more comprehensible in the commonplace contexts of interaction and perception. In such contexts, normative influence is often realised through 'naïve regulators', whose formal facets (features) do not become established by official legal documents. Besides, naïve regulators can also pertain to the situations beyond the official legal rules.

We draw upon public signs and notices as a popular means employed to regulate social behaviour in everyday situations. They comply with our research goals and needs: they are multimodal, and they impact on our actions as well as enacting legal norms and restrictions on an everyday basis.

3.2 Multimodal Analysis: State-Of-The-Art Approaches

As Murray (2009: 3) indicates,

> Communication studies, and most of the history of rhetoric before it, has long accepted the fact that communication takes place through nonverbal means; the suggestion that rhetoric applies to more than just words is not a new one.

Yet, it seems that the monopoly of "pure" linguistic analysis has been overcome relatively recently, and the last two decades have witnessed a rocketing interest in multimodal communication and "a shift of focus in linguistic enquiry where language use is no longer theorized as an isolated phenomenon" (O'Halloran 2004: 1). A growing number of studies in multimodality rely on the assumption about "the simultaneous orchestration of diverse presentational modes" (Bateman 2008: 1) and explore various social practices as symbol-making practices that involve much more than verbal communication.

The variety of multimodal data discussed in scholarly papers is undeniable and embraces numerous types of semiotic complexes, including political cartoons and election posters (Artyomova 2002; Saduov 2012), media texts (Caple 2010; Kozhemyakin 2019), museum exhibitions (Pang Kah Meng 2004), print advertisements

(Yuen 2004; Kozhemyakin and Stupakova 2018), internet posts (Dubrovskaya 2019) and rap music (Caldwell 2010), as well as genres of academic discourse, such as biology textbooks (Guo 2004) and lectures (Khutyz 2016; Sorokina 2017) among the rest. This list is definitely non-exhaustive. It is obvious that the interpretation of such multimodal complexes or similar ones should imply attention to heterogeneous presentational modes such as visual resources, proxemics, kinetics, sounds and music, spatial positioning of inanimate objects, etc., which appear in different combinations in an infinite range of communicative situations. All of these modes are traditionally opposed to language as a verbal resource. Some scholars, however, point to the privileged position of discursive language (the term used in Murray 2009) and assume that the concept of language should expand its meaning:

> I would like to also suggest that the term 'language' include the symbol systems of music, film, sculpture, dance, et cetera. (Murray 2009: 1)

In a similar vein, O'Toole (2004) compares the meanings constructed by architectural components with the meanings constructed in language. Indicating a stunning similarity between the two, he uses the metalanguage of linguistics to discuss how architectural components are combined to make a coherent whole:

> As in language, the Collocational potential of architectural elements—their Conjunction in rooms and floors and buildings, their Reference to each other and to their environment—is what makes them into coherent and usable 'texts'. (O'Toole 2004: 11)

Even much more linguistic objects, such as written documents, are prone to pervasive multimodality, and Bateman (2008) indicates the necessity to define possible directions for their study. Among the reasons for the ascendancy of the multimodal document and its complexity is "the dramatic growth of the technologies by which such documents are produced, distributed and consumed" (Bateman 2008: 2). In the multimodal analysis, scholars also ascribe a greater semantic potential to multimodal complexes than verbal language alone while indicating explicitly that concentration solely on language "has resulted in rather an impoverished view of functions and meaning of discourse" (O'Halloran 2004: 1).

Going further along the path of multimodality, Norris suggests abandoning the term "non-verbal", which until now has been used to refer to modes like gesture, gaze or posture (Norris 2004). She explains that *non-verbal* implies being an element subordinate to language. However, as Norris insists,

> modes like gesture, gaze, or posture can play a superordinate or an equal role to the mode of language in interaction, and therefore, these modes are not merely embellishments to language. (Norris 2004: x)

At the same time, the problem is not purely terminological. While "proper" linguistics has developed rather efficient methodological tools and techniques to analyse the verbal side of communication, the heterogeneity of non-verbal modes and the infinity of communicative situations that employ such modes present a major methodological impediment. A reference to a distinct lack of methodology is a typical start for multimodal analysts:

There remain substantial gaps in our understanding of how investigation can proceed. (Bateman 2008: 2);

[…] while we all intuitively know that people in interaction draw on a multiplicity of communicative modes […] an analysis of such multimodal interaction brings with it many challenges. (Norris 2004: 2);

[…] we need a model of analysis that can deal with the material, and social practice-based nature of the forms of communication that we want to critically analyse. (Ledin and Machin 2019: 498)

Hence, developing an integral analytical model that would encompass both verbal and non-verbal modes has been set as a principal goal in multimodal studies.

Various analytical frameworks have been devised and used to explore how meanings are constructed through a combination of modes. In their paper on doing critical discourse studies (CDS) with multimodality, Ledin and Machin (2019) argue that most multimodal studies rest upon the core principles drawn from the systemic functional linguistics (SFL) of Halliday. This statement is easily validated by taking a look at some recent works on multimodality. In an introduction to a collection of research papers, O'Halloran explicitly states that

the theoretical approach informing these research efforts is Michael Halliday's (1994) systemic functional theory of language which is extended to other semiotic resources. (O'Halloran 2004: 1)

SFL is the approach taken by the authors of yet another collection on multimodality (Bednarek and Martin 2010). Bateman explains the popularity of and demand for SFL in multimodal studies by the applicability of functional domains (the representational domain, the interactional domain and the text-organisational domain) to units other than linguistic:

Systemic-functional approaches investigate how texts in general are articulated to show their appropriateness for particular situations of use, or contexts. Moreover, 'text' as such is construed as an essentially semantic unit, rather than one defined by its external appearance or surface realisation. It is this starting point that has made it natural to consider extensions of the framework to apply to semiotic artefacts more broadly. (Bateman 2008: 38)

However, Ledin and Machin take a rather sceptical approach towards using the same analytical model inspired by Halliday to "hugely different semiotic phenomena" (Ledin and Machin 2019: 498). Their main concern is whether the principles of SFL are suitable for such a problem-oriented approach as CDS. The conclusion they draw with respect to a systemic-functional approach is that it is "not suitable for carrying out problem-driven critical research" (Ledin and Machin 2019: 510), with two major obstacles standing in the way:

We cannot use a model that seeks context from within the text. Nor can we remove texts from their complexity at the macro and meso level, which links them into social practices […]. (Ledin and Machin 2019: 510)

Important for critical multimodal analysis are—for the scholars—

canons of use, laden with meanings that not only come from 'within' the semiotic artefact, but are taken for granted and deeply ideological. (Ledin and Machin 2019: 511)

Although it seems that the category of "canon of use" needs further clarification, we agree with Ledin and Machin in that multimodal analysis should be targeted at those semiotic aspects that are necessary for answering the research question.

Halliday's analysis, however, can hardly be underestimated in terms of multimodal research since it reveals several basic principles of synthetic interaction between different semiotic resources. Thus, researchers should carefully consider a concrete ensemble of means applied to accomplish a certain pragmatic function, i.e. to represent people, objects and situations or to regulate social behaviour, etc. In other words, when following the claims of Halliday, one should always keep in mind the resource integration principle.

Social, ideological and institutional aspects, which Halliday's framework lacks— thus causing Ledin and Machin's concern—are at the focus of social semiotics (Hodge and Kress 1988; Vannini 2007). As the researchers claim, multimodality contributes to understanding how language, conceived in a broader sense, functions in our representation and construction of social order. Language has an ideological basis common with social relationships; therefore, it is almost impossible to extract institutional, ideological or—wider—social context from the text. Nor is language isolated from ideology, institutions and society. It would be proper to claim that language can function as ideology in institutional terms to accomplish social functions. This means that social semiologists tend to seek the relations between language as a semiotic resource, ideology, institutions and society without mixing them into a single unity. As Kress (2010) remarks, communicational modes can be considered as relational tools.

Nevertheless, Norris (2004) argues that different communicative modes, such as language, gesture, gaze and material objects, are structured in significantly different ways. Norris defines her approach as interactional, because she is "*only* concerned with what individuals express and others react to" (Norris 2004: 3). She does not purport to decipher people's thoughts and feelings. And, what is important too, she is "*not* concerned with a person's intentionality, which sometimes may be different from what is expressed or different from what is perceived by others" (Norris 2004: 4). In other words, Norris refrains from any endeavours to dig into human cognition, which seems expedient since such an approach excludes any intuitive interpretations on the researcher's part.

This point corresponds with the basic principles of social semiotics, which aims at analysing representations and constructions but not intentions. Also crucial for our analytical position is the claim that textual analysis can only reveal how something is materially represented and constructed but not intended by an individual, or at least what possible interpretation or reaction is evident in concrete communication situations.

Therefore, the analytical framework for multimodal texts analysis will embrace such aspects as social (what is said), representational (how it is said) and pragmatic (what it is said for). At the empirical level these aspects comprise:

- the represented objects (people, things, situations, actions) and the focus of a representation. These refer to the social aspect;

- the structure of co-deployed semiotic resources (verbal and visual means), which corresponds to the representational aspect;
- the pragmatic function (informing, permission, prohibition, motivation, etc.), which denotes the pragmatic aspect of multimodal communication.

In what follows, we will apply this model to the cases under study.

3.3   Re-Examining Public Signs

Public signs constitute an essential part of cultural practices and a popular regulatory instrument in public communication. Hundreds of them are involved in the daily routine of any community member since all social spheres make use of public notices in diverse contexts and for various purposes. Places such as educational institutions, public transport, cinemas and theatres, hospitals, cafes, zoos, airports and open city spaces, to name but a few, are equipped with public signs that inform, warn, prohibit, request, instruct, etc. Public signs appear in and manifest recurrent typical situations that need to be controlled on a regular basis. However, as we indicated in another study on public notices, they

> do not only accompany people's various activities. They are not simply linguistic accompaniment to the physical environment: through language forms they construct our living environment, imposing certain forms of social behaviour and inculcating particular values in the community. (Dubrovskaya 2012: 303)

Now that we aim to explore public signs as multimodal ensembles, a correction should be made that a linguistic side of a public sign works in alignment with a non-verbal complex.

Thus, in this paper we take a public sign to be any publicly exposed sign or notice that combines verbal and non-verbal resources in order to regulate people's social behaviour in a specific recurrent situation over a lasting period of time. In what follows, we will review major trends in the study of public signs and indicate some basic assumptions for the current research.

A lot of scholarly works on public signs are *linguistically oriented*; that is, they focus on verbal elements while, at the same time, offering some *general analysis of multimodal components*. Specifically, linguists discuss public signs in terms of their illocutionary force, or communicative intention, and genre, often combining the two. In their study of the urban landscape, Kitajgorodskaya and Rozanova (2003) discuss what they define as "smaller written genres", including all kinds of public notices, advertising and non-advertising posters, graffiti, etc. The scholars distinguish between two types of such "smaller written genres": 1) posters by city authorities aimed at affecting people's behaviour, and 2) car stickers used by individuals to manage the emotional side of communication. While giving a rigorous treatment to the illocutionary force of both genres, Kitajgorodskaya and Rozanova also mention how the accompanying visuals interact with the verbal contents: a text deciphers a visual, the same text is illustrated with different visuals in different posters, symbolic visuals are added to the text, etc. Although the analysis is based on linguistic criteria, the observation made on the regulatory function of public signs and their difference in terms of institutionality might be relied on as a further point of reference in this study.

The classification of public notices in terms of genres and communicative intentions is offered in our own paper (Dubrovskaya 2012). There we also briefly discuss the role of pictorial elements in public notices and claim that a picture contributes to the meaning of a notice, makes up a stylistic unity with the text, and there might emerge sophisticated multimodal complexes in which a text, a picture and background knowledge of potential audience are inextricably intertwined.

A wider view of public signs and notices offers a key to understanding a social situation, which is made manifest through a linguistic landscape. Akindele (2011) considers public signage, including the language of street signs, advertising signs, building names, billboards, shop signs and informative signs as well as warning notices and prohibitions. The scholar diagnoses the social situation of Gaborone, Botswana, including "official language policies, prevalent language attitudes, and the long-term consequences of language contact" (Akindele 2011). The interrelation between the types of public signage and social life becomes an object of scrutiny in other studies on linguistic landscape, which uncover social realities and intergroup dynamics, language prevalence, the distribution of languages in different spheres of signs usage and cultural values (El-Yasin and Mahadin 1996; Meifang 2009; Kayam et al. 2012).

Unlike the approach that focuses on the linguistic side of public signs and notices, the *semiotic landscape approach* proposed by other scholars embraces all the diversity of components in multimodal texts. Therefore, it is characterised as "a more qualitative, broader perspective compared to the linguistic landscape approach" (Domke 2015: 2). Among the elements of multimodal texts, specifically prohibitions, Domke lists colour, pictograms, written and spoken language, sounds, different languages, using signs, posters, and mobile signs among others. Thus, she construes text widely "as a perceivable functional unit consisting of all semiotic resources which are used to fulfil a communicative action" (Domke 2015: 3). When examining signs of prohibition, she turns to their materiality and perception, time- and place-boundness, which places the discussion in a broader context of "the meaning making through the text's 'locatedness' and therefore social and communicative construction of space/place" (Domke 2015: 2).

Apart from discussing the meaning of street signs as a "ubiquitous type of everyday written text", Cook (2014) also categorises them based on the material (stone, metal, paper) and the type of writing (capitals and archaic letters, handwritten, printed and painted signs). When characterising her approach, Cook explains that it lies "within general study of material culture" since "written language is visible and tangible material in a way that spoken language is not" (Cook 2014: 81). Materials of notices are ascribed different degrees of durability, and thus notices have different functions (locating, informing, expressing ideas and conveying identity).

As is seen from this brief literature review, there exist two major trends in the analysis of public signage: one focusing on the linguistic side and communicative purposes of verbal texts, the other encompassing the diversity of multimodal elements and ascribing a context-building function to a sign. In Sect. 3.4 of this paper, we rely on the latter and explore public signage in terms of their regulatory function as well as some formal criteria.

3.4 Public Signs as Ancillary Regulators: Case Studies

In the analysis that follows, we suggest distinguishing between two groups of public signs with respect to the relation they bear to legal discourse and the semiotic resources employed:

(1) Public signs that retain more or less explicit marks of official legal discourse. Verbal means employed in them are essential and cannot be replaced with non-verbal means. However, multimodal resources may assist in translating legal norms to the public or in resemiotisation (Iedema 2001) or transmutation (Jakobson 1959) of original written (verbal) legal discourse into visuo-verbal public signs;

(2) Naïve regulators, which are deprived of legal markers. Legal norms constitute mental presupposition of what is claimed or required by the sign. These naïve regulators reduce the legal norm to a pure prohibition without providing any details on the legal origin of the prohibition or possible penalties for breaking the rule. Naïve regulators remind of and reiterate legal norms mostly through multimodal resources, offering a ready-made, standardised version of a social norm.

As has been mentioned above, we employ a fourfold scheme of analysis that involves a few aspects: 1. the represented objects, 2. the focus of representation, 3. the structure of co-deployed semiotic resources and 4. the pragmatic function.

These four dimensions refer to the main semiotic aspects of representation: semantic (reference or represented objects and the focus of representation), syntactic (interposition and interrelation of semiotic elements or the structure of semiotic resources) and pragmatic (functional and practical aspects of semiosis).

The first two dimensions of study can be defined as semantic. They embrace the represented objects (What is the reference of a sign or notice, i.e. what objects and relations of reality are represented in it?) and the focus of representation (Which objects or their parts are represented as central in meaning-making?).

The third dimension can be defined as syntactic, and it pertains to the structure of co-deployed semiotic resources interposition, i.e. interposition and interrelation of semiotic elements or structure of semiotic resources (How do semiotic resources correlate with each other? How is the hierarchy of meanings in the message constructed by the structure of the text?).

Finally, the pragmatic dimension involves functional and practical aspects of semiosis (How do various aspects and resources of the text correlate with the perception and behaviour of the reader? How do elements and affordance of the message impact the reader's mind?).

3.4.1   Translating Legal Norms: Power of the Verbal

The first type of public signs that we are discussing here includes the signs that represent legal knowledge (meanings) and are aimed at translating this knowledge to the general public. Unlike legislation itself, a verbally concise and visually attractive form of such public signs is not only informative, but it is also easily discernible and perceived by an average citizen.

Because this paper presents a few case studies, we do not think it is expedient to describe the data collection. Instead, we will explain the origin of specific public notices that are selected to illustrate each type of public signage.

The examples of legally induced public signs in our data collection include the public notices exposed in a liquor store in Perth, Western Australia. See Fig. 3.1, 3.2, 3.3. (The pictures were taken by one of the authors.)

These seven public notices were placed on the wall behind the counter, meaning the shop owners arranged the space in the way to make the notices visible to customers. In what follows, we will consider the verbal contents of the notices in relation to the multimodal resources involved.

Fig. 3.1   Notices 1 and 2 (from top to bottom)

Fig. 3.2 Notices 3 and 4
(from top to bottom)

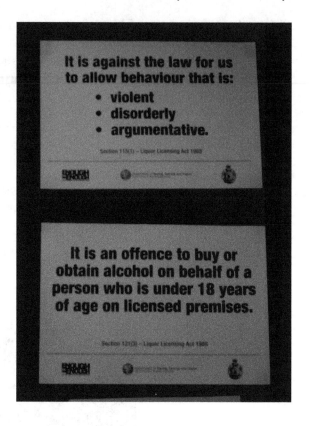

Five of the seven notices start with an explicit reference to legislation: *'It is against the law...'*. Also, all of the notices include indications of the two major legal acts that regulate the sale, supply and consumption of alcohol in Western Australia, including the Liquor Licensing Act 1988 and the Liquor Control Act 1988. (Hereinafter, these acts are abbreviated as LLA 1988 and LCA 1988 correspondingly and quoted in the versions applicable at the time of taking the photos [November 2012].) In the notices, references to the exact sections of the legislation are provided in smaller fonts as compared to the main contents, but their presence in the notices is essential since they point to the exact sources of the rules quoted:

"Section 121—Liquor Licensing Act 1988".

"Section 115(2)—Liquor Control Act 1988", etc.

Interestingly, the two legislation acts (LLA 1988 and LCA 1988) are rather lengthy documents: 214 pages and 322 pages, respectively. The question arises why some specific excerpts from legislation were chosen for public exposure. Apparently, these excerpts represent and regulate most typical social situations that a shop owner (or a licensee) has to deal with on an everyday basis. In the texts of the notices, we can identify a few recognisable situations in a liquor store (not only in Australia but also in most countries where alcohol is sold over the counter), which involve:

Fig. 3.3 Notices 5, 6, and 7 (from top to bottom)

- attempts of underage persons to buy alcohol, including with the help of other people (Notices 1 and 4. See Fig. 3.1 and Fig. 3.2);
- attempts of underage persons to buy alcohol through presenting a false ID (Notice 6. See Fig. 3.3);
- attempts of drunk persons to buy alcohol (Notice 2. See Fig. 3.1);
- disorderly behaviour of some customers, including their refusal to leave the store (Notices 3 and 7. See Fig. 3.2 and Fig. 3.3).

Thus, the notices appear to focus on the problematic aspects of relations between the owner (the licensee) and the customers, specifically those that may result in punishment for the owner or the customer. Four notices offer precise information on the penalties that are imposed in case of offences, depending on the status of a person.

Because these notices present naïve—simplified—versions of legislation, they maintain some features of legal discourse while at the same time explicating characteristics of less formalised communication. The notices employ some basic categories that are found in legislation: *licensed premises, to sell or supply, false or misleading ID, licensee, a drunk person, violent and disorderly behaviour.* It is important to note, however, that public notices function as mediators between the law and the general public. Thus, legal texts undergo certain transformations which remove details, extract most of the general principles and reformulate statements in a more comprehensible—naïve, so to speak—way.

Among the noticeable modifications are the following:

- *using more common lexemes* rather than legal terms: the term *"juvenile"* used in the legislation is replaced by the explanatory phrase *"a person under 18 years of age"*. This phrasing draws on the technical explanation of the term *"juvenile"* in LCA: *"juvenile means a person under the age of 18 years"* (LCA 1988: 5);
- *simplifying the contents of a legal concept.* Replacing the terminological *"liquor"* with *"alcohol"* is not an absolutely synonymous substitution. Compare Notice 1 (Fig. 3.1) and Sect. 121 of LLA, which the notice represents:

121. (1) Subject to this Act, where liquor is sold or supplied to a juvenile on licensed premises—

(a)   *the licensee;*

(b)   *the manager of the licensed premises;*

(c)   *any other person by whom the liquor is sold or supplied; and*

(d)   *any person who permits the sale or supply,*

   each commit an offence. (LLA 1988, Sect. 121)

While in this context *"alcohol"* in Notice 1 (Fig. 3.1) represents a general idea of alcoholic drinks that can be bought in a store, *"liquor"* is used in legislation terminologically and is defined in LLA as follows:

"liquor" means—

(a)   *a beverage which at 20° Celsius contains more than 1.15% ethanol by volume;*

(b)   *any other substance prescribed as being liquor for the purposes of this Act; and*

(c)   *any thing that, for the purposes of sale, is held out to be such a beverage or substance.* (LLA 1988, Interpretation);

- *summarising legal principles and presenting them in a more concise and comprehensible way.* This is often achieved through rephrasing and syntactic changes. See Notice 7 (Fig. 3.3), which embraces two different sections of LCA in one sentence;
- *transferring an abstract legal principle stated in legislation to a potential concrete situation.* A whole number of phrases with deictic elements, such as *at this venue, you are asked, to leave this venue, the premises, for us,* become incorporated in

the public notices to indicate the association between the law and reality. As the definition states,

‘deixis’ is generally understood to be the encoding of the spatiotemporal context and subjective experience of the encoder in an utterance. (Green 2006: 415)

The usage of determiners and personal pronouns, linguistic elements that are heavily context-dependent, turn universal legislation into rules for particular people in a particular spatiotemporal context.

Thus, the examples analysed demonstrate how legal norms are translated in a rather overt form to common public knowledge through verbal transformations of official legal discourse.

Public notices that are used to implement legally approved practices in everyday life may also rely on a combination of verbal and visual resources. In such cases, legal discourse retains its original form, so it helps to identify legal norms more or less easily. The interrelation between the verbal and the visual is not, however, linear. In the case that follows, we will show how a multidimensional regulative phenomenon is constructed.

Notice 8 (Fig. 3.4) was placed on an entrance door of an alcohol and tobacco mini-market in a Russian city. The text can be rendered from Russian into English as follows: "We undertake the obligation not to sell cigarettes to children". Although there is no explicit reference to legislation, the notice informs the customers of the store's respectful attitude to the law. Russian Federal Law No. 15-FZ entitled "Protecting the health of citizens from tobacco smoke impact and consequences of tobacco consumption" contains Article 20 that prohibits, among other issues, selling tobacco products to underage persons (Federal Law 2013).

Fig. 3.4 Notice 8

Apparently, in Notice 8 (Fig. 3.4) the legislation is undergoing similar transformations in order to convey the law to the public. The Russian legal terms "nesovershennoletnie" (the underage) and "tabachnaya produktsija" (tobacco products) have been replaced with the more common and less precise lexemes "deti" (children) and "sigarety" (cigarettes). The legal principle receives a very concise reformulation, which can be physically squeezed into the space of a door sticker and remain visible. In addition, the text establishes explicit institutional relations between the legislation and the mini-market through the deictic pronoun "my" (we).

The visual structure of the notice has two important elements. First, the sign has the shape of a red octagon framed with white, which is a commonly accepted and easily recognised "stop sign". In the present context, it gets a symbolic meaning of no access to the store for children. Although children can physically enter the store, they will not be able to receive service there.

Second, the part of the text in block letters НА СЕБЯ (na sebja) is part of the sentence as a whole, which informs people of the store's obligation not to sell cigarettes to children. However, taken in isolation, it means "Pull", giving a very utilitarian directive on how to open the door. Therefore, the words in larger block letters НА СЕБЯ are ambivalent: on the one hand, they are part of the legal prohibition, which is expressed verbally and reinforced through the visual pragmatics of the "stop sign", and on the other hand, they present a primitive instruction on using the door and belong to everyday routine. Thus, the combination of verbal and visual resources in Notice 8 (Fig. 3.4) serves two purposes simultaneously, and the sticker's meaning unfolds in two directions—legal and mundane. While verbal elements refer to the institutional (legal) discourse, visual resources transcode the institutional message to more common everyday behavioural situations, and thus they inculcate the legal meaning into the context of mundane life.

3.4.2 Naïve Regulators: Supremacy of Multimodality

As has been said, naïve regulators demonstrate little relation to codified institutional norms and rely on multimodal resources. It seems that in this type of notice, text duplicates meanings that are conveyed via visual forms. As an example, Notice 9 (Fig. 3.5) contains a few rules related to social conduct on a public beach in Western Australia. All the rules are conveyed to individuals iconically, i.e. through symbolic representations of undesirable activities, which are circled red and crossed with a diagonal red line. Removing the accompanying concise texts *(no glass, no alcohol, no dogs, etc.)* will result in a loss of only a small portion of meanings, such as the period of surfcraft prohibition and the details about lifeguards being on duty *(Lifeguards on duty when yellow and red flags are displayed)*. Meanwhile, the loss of pictures will considerably damage the meaning structure. Using capital letters for all prohibitions in all seven signs in Notice 9 (Fig. 3.5) might also be considered meaningful. Capitalising serves to emphasise the rules and make them more visually

Fig. 3.5 Notice 9

accessible as well as serving to draw a border between legal texts proper on the one hand and naïve representations of such legal texts on the other hand.

Similarly, Notice 10 (Fig. 3.6) prohibits individuals both verbally and visually from stepping on the ice on a public pond. While the text presents a direct prohibition

Fig. 3.6 Notice 10

(*Entering the ice is prohibited!*, which is a Russian equivalent of an English language warning "Danger! Thin ice."), the pictures reiterate the prohibition through the symbolically crossed picture of ice skates and the image of a break in the ice, which represents a possible dangerous consequence of violating the rule. The message will remain clear without the textual component since the narrative is rendered visually and is composed of visual communication through the ordinary means. These means are as follows:

- the reason and the consequence are arranged in a logical and temporal order from left to right. First comes the reason (skating) followed by the consequence (a break in the ice);
- the red cross indicates an undesirable but manageable thing, while a break in the ice, still being undesirable, is not crossed with red lines since it is not manageable. In other words, what is crossed is a matter of individual choice; what is not crossed is inevitable;
- the red frame indicates the general pragmatic genre of the message, specifically the one of prohibition and warning against danger;
- the iconic objects are represented graphically rather than being painted. Such a representation refers to a schematised instruction instead of a realistic depiction of the situation. Schematic rendering points to the universality of the prohibition. By contrast, a realistic depiction, e.g. a photo, may be interpreted as a specific instance and hence not have the regulatory power of prohibition applicable to everyone. Also, a schematic depiction is simple, and thus it can be read and interpreted more quickly than a detailed photo-realistic depiction. It can be inferred that the whole message does not construct a description; it constructs the behaviour.

The verbal elements co-deploy the meaning of prohibition, but they regulate a concrete situation rather than referring to a legal norm.

The legal norms underlying Notices 9 (Fig. 3.5) and 10 (Fig. 3.6) are probably restorable, but the rules are perceived as commonsensical and needing no legal justifications. A cursory web search for legislation on walking on the ice shows that in the absence of Russian federal legislation on the subject, there exist local legal acts regulating public behaviour in these circumstances. Thus, the legal background of such signs is not brought to the fore and remains tacit, while the notices place the emphasis on undesirable actions and their consequences and exemplify them through multimodal resources.

3.5   Conclusion

In everyday situations, individuals regulate social behaviour and prohibit undesirable actions by various means of communication, with public signs playing an important role in this process. From a naïve point of view, public signs and notices seem to only specify a legal norm; however, the pragmatics of their usage is much wider than that. The very fact that public signs and notices are generally multimodal makes us consider the implications of different semiotic resources that are used to construct a sign and convey meanings.

In the foregoing, we have revealed two groups of public signage used for prohibition: verbally focused (institutional regulators) and mixed (naïve regulators). (We also admit the existence of yet another group—visually focused regulators; however, their consideration falls beyond the scope of this paper.) These two types are distinguished based on the role of verbal elements. The removal of words might destroy the whole meaning structure (the case of institutional regulators), or, on the contrary, meanings can still be inferred in the absence of words (the case of naïve regulators).

Verbally focused messages rely mainly on words and tend to reproduce official legal discourse, i.e. they impact on behaviour directly by telling recipients what they must or must not do according to the law. In fact, verbal messages are part of legal prohibition, while iconic elements specify the core meaning or support it rhetorically. The pragmatics of prohibition in verbally focused signage refers strictly to the law. In other words, the law "speaks" to us through the medium of verbally focused signs and notices, which invoke legal discourse. However, visual elements of verbally focused signs can refer to everyday activities by transcoding a legal message to routine situations, and thus they contribute to embedding the law into mundane life.

Naïve regulators rely both on verbal and visual elements, and the meaning is co-deployed by them both. Signs of this type are free of legal markers and reiterate legal norms through multimodal resources, thus representing a convenient version of a social norm. A legal norm is still present in mixed signs and can be easily restored. The stress, however, is formally placed on norms as common sense, which does not need special legal justifications. The iconic rhetoric represents the reality as perceived by a recipient rather than institutions. These signs and notices emphasise undesirable actions and their consequences by exemplifying them through multimodal resources, and they regulate a typical situation rather than refer to a legal norm.

Thus, it might be inferred that there exist two aspects of social behavior regulation—legal and naïve. While the legal aspect is rendered through words and performs the directive functions of prohibition, the naïve aspect draws predominately on multimodal resources and performs the descriptive or explanatory functions of Prohibition. The law employs words to speak to individuals; however, words are not sufficient for common sense, hence the usage of iconic language.

We suppose that despite the universality of semiosis principles, multimodal codification of everyday situations is culturally determined. The forms and ways in which the words and non-words are used to regulate social behaviour might vary from culture to culture. Therefore, it is possible that data from other languages will cause revision of the proposed theory. Cross-cultural social semiotics is an area that requires further investigation.

Acknowledgements We express our sincere gratitude to our colleague Dr. Grzegorz Kowalski for his thoughtful comments on the initial version of the chapter. We are, of course, responsible for any remaining drawbacks.

References

Akindele, Dele Olufemi. 2011. Linguistic Landscapes as Public Communication: A Study of Public Signage in Gaborone Botswana. *International Journal of Linguistics* 3(1). https://doi.org/10.5296/ijl.v3i1.1157.

Artyomova, Evgenija. 2002. *Cartoons as a Genre of Political Discourse.* [Karikatura kak zhanr politicheskogo diskursa.] PhD thesis. Volgograd.

Baldry, Antony, and Paul J. Thibault. 2005. *Multimodal Transcription and Text Analysis.* London: Equinox.

Barry, Ann Marie. 1997. *Visual Intelligence: Perception, Image, and Manipulation in Visual Communication.* New York: State University of New York.

Bateman, John A. 2008. *Multimodality and Genre. A Foundation for the Systemic Analysis of Multimodal Documents.* New York: Palgrave Macmillan.

Bateman, John, and Janina Wildfeuer. 2014. A Multimodal Discourse Theory of Visual Narrative. *Journal of Pragmatics* 74: 180–208.

Bateman, John, Janina Wildfeuer, and Tuomo Hiippala. 2017. *Multimodality: Foundations, Research and Analysis–A Problem-Oriented Introduction.* Berlin: Walter de Gruyter GmbH & Co KG.

Bednarek, Monika, and Jim R. Martin, eds. 2010. *New Discourse on Language. Functional Perspectives on Multimodality, Identity, and Affiliation.* London, New York: Continuum.

Caldwell, David. 2010. Making Metre Mean: Identity and Affiliation in the Rap Music of Kanye West. In *New Discourse on Language. Functional Perspectives on Multimodality, Identity, and Affiliation,* eds. M. Bednarek and J.R. Martin, 59–79. London, New York: Continuum.

Caple, Helen. 2010. Doubling-up: Allusion and Bonding in Multisemiotic News Stories. In *New Discourse on Language. Functional Perspectives on Multimodality, Identity, and Affiliation,* eds. M. Bednarek and J.R. Martin, 111–133. London, New York: Continuum.

Cook, Vivian. 2015. Meaning and Material in the Language of the Street. *Social Semiotics* 25(1): 81–109.

Danesi, Marcel. 2018. *Understanding Media Semiotics.* London: Bloomsbury Academic.

Djonov, Emilia, and Theo van Leeuwen. 2018. Social Media as Semiotic Technology and Social Practice: The Case of ResearchGate's Design and its Potential to Transform Social Practice. *Social Semiotics* 28(5): 641–664.

Domke, Christine. 2015. Prohibition Signage in Public Places: On the Functional Organization of Different Media, Communication Forms, and Text Types. *10plus1: Living Linguistics.* Issue 1.

Dubrovskaya, Tatiana. 2012. Public Notices as Part of Linguistic Environment: Genre Analysis. In *Evolving Paradigms: Language and Applied Linguistics in a Changing World. Refereed proceedings of Applied Linguistics Association of Australia Annual Conference,* 302–324. Curtin: Curtin University.

Dubrovskaya, Tatiana. 2019. "Only Mother and Geländewagen 5.5 Deserve Love": Busters' Lyrics as a Genre of the Youth Internet Discourse ['Ljubvi dostojna tol'ko mat' i Gelendvagen 5.5': patsankaja lirika kak zhanr molodezhnogo internet-diskursa.] *Speech Genres* [Rechevyje zhanry] 1(21): 56–65. https://doi.org/10.18500/2311-0740-2019-1-21-56-65

Duncan, Hugh Dalziel. 1962. *Communication and Social Order.* New York: Bedminster Press.

El-Yasin, Mohammed K., and Radwan S. Mahadin. 1996. On the Pragmatics of Shop Signs in Jordan. *Journal of Pragmatics* 26 (3): 407–416. https://doi.org/10.1016/0378-2166(95)00017-8.

Federal Law. 2013. Federal Law No. 15-FZ as of 23.02.2013 (version as of 29.07.2018) Protection of Citizens' Health from Tobacco Smoke Impact and the Consequences of Tobacco Consumption (with changes and additions coming into force 01.03.2019) [Federalnyj Zakon No. 15-FZ Ob okhrane zdorovja grazhdan ot vozdejstvija okruzhajuschego tabachnogo dyma i posledstvij potreblenija tabaka (s izmenenijami i dopolnenijami ot 01.02.2019).] http://www.consultant.ru/document/cons_doc_LAW_142515/ Accessed 5 May 2020.

Green, Keith. 2006. Deixis and Anaphora: Pragmatic Approaches. In *Encyclopedia of Language and Linguistics*, ed. K. Brown, 415–417. London, Amsterdam: Elsevier. https://doi.org/10.1016/B0-08-044854-2/00328-X

Guo, Libo. 2004. Multimodality in a Biology Textbook. In *Multimodal Discourse Analysis. Systemic-functional Perspectives*, ed. K.L. O'Halloran, 196–219. London, New York: Continuum.

Halliday, Michael, and Alexander Kirkwood. 1994. Spoken and Written Modes of Meaning. In *Media Texts: Authors and Readers*, ed. D. Graddol and O. Boyd-Barrett, 51–73. Clevedon, Philadelphia, Adelaide: The Open University.

Hayes, Steven C., and Linda J. Hayes. 1992. Verbal Relations and the Evolution of Behavior Analysis. *American Psychologist* 47: 1383–1395.

Hiippala, Tuomo. 2018. *Structure of Multimodal Documents: An Empirical Approach.* New York and London: Routledge.

Hodge, Bob, and Gunther Kress. 1988. *Social Semiotics.* Cambridge, UK: Polity Press in association with Basil Blackwell, Oxford, UK.

Iedema, Rick. 2001. Resemiotization. *Semiotica* 137(1–4): 23–39.

Jakobson, Roman. 1959. On Linguistic Aspects of Translation. In *On Translation*, ed. R.A. Brower, 232–239. Cambridge, MA: Harvard University Press.

Jovanovic, Danica, and Theo van Leeuwen. 2018. Multimodal Dialogue on Social Media. *Social Semiotics* 28(5): 683–699.

Kayam, Orly, Tijana Hirsch, and Yair Galily. 2012. Linguistic Landscape: Investigation of Linguistic Representations of Cape Town. *International Journal of Linguistics* 4 (3): 71–77. https://doi.org/10.5296/ijl.v4i3.2197.

Khutyz, Irina. 2016. Multimodality in Academic Discourse as a Provision of Communicative Efficiency [Multimodalnost' akademicheskogo diskursa kak uslovije ego kommunikativnoj uspeshnosti.] *Bulletin of Adygey State University* [Vestnik Adugejskogo gosudarstvennogo universiteta]. *Series 2: Philology and Culture Studies* 1(172): 90–95.

Kibrik, Andrey A. 2010. Multimodal Linguistics [Multimodalnaja lingvistika.] In *Cognitive Studies – IV.* [Kognitivnyje issledovanija – IV], eds. Yu.I. Aleksandrov and V.D. Solovjev, 134–152. Moscow: IP RAN.

Kitajgorodskaya, Margarita, and Nina Rozanova. 2003. Modern Communication in the City: Types of Communicative Situations and their Actualization in Genres (Example of Moscow) [Sovremennoje gorodskoje obschenije: tipy kommunikativnykh situatsij i ikh zhanrovaja realizatsija (na primere Moskvy).] In *Modern Russian Language. Social and Functional Differentiation* [Sovremennij russkij jazyk. Sotsialnaja i funktsionalnaja differentsiatsija], ed. L. Krysin, 101–126. Moscow: Yazyki slavjanskoj kul'tury.

Kozhemyakin, Evgeny. 2019. Multimodal Semiosis in Mass Media: Several Remarks on Methodology. In *European Proceedings of Social and Behavioural Sciences. III PMMIS 2019 Post Mass Media in the Modern Informational Society "Journalistic Text in a New Technological Environment: Achievements and Problems"*, ed. M.V. Zagidullina, 18–25. London: Future Academy.

Kozhemyakin, Evgeny, and Alina Stupakova. 2019. Elite Code in the Contemporary Press Advertising Discourse: A Semiotic Aspect. [Elitarnyj kod v sovremennoj press-reklame: semioticheskij aspect.] In *Genres and Types of Text in Scientific and Media Discourse* [Zhanry i tipy teksta v nauchnom i medijnom diskurse], ed. A. Pastukhov, 68–81. Orel: OGIK.

Kress, Gunther. 2010. *Multimodality. A Social Semiotic Approach to Contemporary Communication.* London and New York: Routledge.

Kress, Gunther, and Theo van Leeuwen. 2001. *Multimodal Discourse: The Modes and Media of Contemporary Communication.* London: Edward Arnold.

Ledin, Per, and David Machin. 2019. Doing Critical Discourse Studies with Multimodality: From Metafunctions to Materiality. *Critical Discourse Studies* 16 (5): 497–513. https://doi.org/10.1080/17405904.2018.1468789.

Lemonnier, Pierre. 2016. *Mundane Objects. Materiality and Non-verbal Communication.* New York: Routledge.

Liquor Control Act. 1988. https://www.legislation.wa.gov.au/legislation/prod/filestore.nsf/Fil
  eURL/mrdoc_23628.pdf/$FILE/Liquor%20Control%20Act%201988%20-%20%5B07-e0-01%
  5D.pdf?OpenElement Accessed 5 May 2020.
Liquor Licensing Act. 1988. http://www.austlii.edu.au/au/legis/wa/num_act/lla1988540l1988236/
  lla1988540l1988236.pdf Accessed 5 May 2020.
Luria, Alexander. 1961. *The Role of Speech in the Regulation of Normal and Abnormal Behaviors.*
  New York: Liveright.
Machin, David, and Andrea Mayr. 2012. *How to Do Critical Discourse Analysis: A Multimodal
  Introduction.* New York: Sage.
Meifang, Zhang. 2009. Social Context and Translation of Public Notices. *Babel* 55 (2): 142–152.
  https://doi.org/10.1075/babel.55.2.03zha.
Murray, Joddy. 2009. *Non-discursive Rhetoric. Image and Affect in Multimodal Composition.*
  Albany: SUNY Press.
Norris, Sigrid. 2004. *Analyzing Multimodal Interaction. A Methodological Framework.* New York:
  Routledge.
O'Halloran, Kay L. 2004. Visual Semiotics in Film. In *Multimodal Discourse Analysis. Systemic-
  functional Perspectives*, ed. K.L. O'Halloran, 109–131. London, New York: Continuum.
O'Halloran, Kay L., and Bradley A. Smith, eds. 2012. *Multimodal Studies: Exploring Issues and
  Domains (Vol. 2).* N.Y.: Routledge.
O'Toole, Michael. 2004. Opera Ludentes: The Sydney Opera House at Work and Play. In *Multimodal
  Discourse Analysis. Systemic-functional Perspectives,* ed. K.L. O'Halloran, 11–27. London, New
  York: Continuum.
Pang Kah Meng, Alfred. 2004. Making History in *From Colony to Nation*: A Multimodal Analysis
  of a Museum Exhibition in Singapore. In *Multimodal Discourse Analysis. Systemic-functional
  Perspectives*, ed. K.L. O'Halloran, 28–54. London, New York: Continuum.
Saduov, Ruslan. 2012. *The Phenomenon of Barak Obama's Political Discourse. Linguistic,
  Cultural and Semiotic Analysis* [Fenomen politicheskogo diskursa Baraka H. Obamy: ling-
  vokul'turologicheskij i semioticheskij analiz.] Ufa: Bashkir State University.
Schefflen, Albert, and Alice Schefflen. 1972. *Body Language and Social Order. Communication as
  Behavioral Control.* Englewood Cliffs: Prentice-Hall.
Sorokina, Yulya. 2017. Notion of Multimodality and Issues of Multimodal Lecture Discourse Analysis [Ponyatije multimodalnosti i voprosy analiza multimodalnogo lektsionnogo diskursa.] *Philo-
  logical Sciences. Theory and Practice [Filologicheskije nauki. Vorposy teorii i praktiki]* 19(76.1):
  168–170.
Vannini, Phillip. 2007. Social Semiotics and Fieldwork: Method and Analytics. *Qualitative Inquiry*
  13(1): 113–140.
Yuen, Cheong Yin. 2004. The Construal of Ideational Meaning in Print Advertisements. In *Multimodal Discourse Analysis. Systemic-functional Perspectives,* ed. K.L. O'Halloran, 163–195.
  London, New York: Continuum.

Chapter 4
Methodological Problems in Analysing Non-verbal Arguments: The Case of Visual Argumentation

Igor Ž. Žagar

Abstract For the last twenty years (or so) the field of argumentation has been becoming more "flexible" and open to new approaches, to approaches that are not based merely on logic (of one form or another), not even just on language. This paper tackles (so-called) visual argumentation, more precisely, the impossibility of (pure) visual argumentation, its very vague methodology and epistemology. After a short overview of the history of visual argumentation, I concentrate on one of its most problematic theses: reasoning is seeing/seeing is reasoning. Following N. J. Enfield's groundbreaking work on *enchrony* (*The Anatomy of Meaning*, 2009), I then show that "visual" meaning is always composite and context-grounded; "visual" meaning should always be constructed through an interactive-recursive multimodal process (*enchrony*); and any meaning analysis should be conducted in terms of *enchronic analysis* and reconstructed as composite utterances.

Keywords Visual argumentation · Reasoning · Multimodality · Enchrony · Composite utterances

4.1 Introduction

In 1996, Argumentation and Advocacy published a groundbreaking issue devoted to visual argument. It was the first collection of essays on the subject. Twenty years later, we consider some of the doubts about the possibility of visual argument that were discussed in that first issue. We argue that these doubts have been answered by the last 20 years of research on visual argument, and we look at some of the key theoretical and applied issues that characterize this burgeoning subfield in the study of argument. (Groarke et al. 2016: 217)

This is how Leo Groarke, Catherine Palczewski and David Godden introduce a special, double issue of the journal *Argumentation and Advocacy*, dedicated to twenty years of "visual argumentation" (henceforth VA). In fact, in the past twenty years, the research on VA has started to burgeon, with authors like Groarke (1996, 2002, 2003,

I. Ž. Žagar (✉)
Educational Research Institute & University of Primorska, Ljubljana, Slovenia

N. V. Sukhova et al. (eds.), *Multimodality, Digitalization and Cognitivity in Communication and Pedagogy*, Numanities - Arts and Humanities in Progress 20, https://doi.org/10.1007/978-3-030-84071-6_4

49

2009, 2013a, 2013b, 2015), Gilbert (1994, 1997), Kjeldsen (1999, 2007, 2012, 2013, 2015), Roque (2010, 2012, 2015), Dove (2002, 2011a, 2011b), Godden (2013, 2015) and others, who mostly took VA and "visual arguments" for granted, never really doubted their position about visuals having argumentative potential or even force and never asked any serious methodological, let alone epistemological questions about VA.

The whole debate on the possibility of visual arguments in a way mirrors (and reformulates) the famous "debate on iconism", started by Umberto Eco at the end of the 60s (Eco 1968, 1975), and extending to the beginning of the new millennium (Calabrese 1977; Fabbrichesi Leo 1983; Groupe μ 1992; Eco 1997; Polidoro 2015). The debate dealt with the problem of reality and image perception, or more precisely with the status of *iconic signs*: are photographs, paintings and caricatures signs? And if they are, what makes them signs, in what manner they are signs, and how we are supposed to read them. Unfortunately, the VA authors seem to be unaware of this debate on iconism altogether.

All of the VA papers mentioned above are basically concerned with showing— using different visuals from different sources—that visuals can convey arguments; the questions what in the visual under examination can serve as a premise/argument and what as a conclusion/claim or how can we extract premises/arguments and conclusions/claims from a visual are rarely addressed with any systematic methodological rigour. It is only in his 2015 paper (i.e. almost twenty years after the "discovery" of VA!), "The Study of Visual and Multimodal Argumentation" (Kjeldsen 2015: 116), which served as an introduction to the thematic issue of the journal *Argumentation* on visual argumentation, that Kjeldsen announces an attempt "to take visual argumentation a step further in order to examine what visual and multimodal argumentation is and how it may work". One of the rare exceptions in this line of reasoning is David Godden's paper (Godden 2017: 395–431) "On the Norms of Visual Argument: A Case for Normative Non-revisionism", where he discusses the possible necessity of setting up different normative frameworks for verbal and visual arguments. But then the overall conclusion of his paper—namely, that every argument containing a visual should count as visual argument—is rather controversial and a step back in the discussion, while from an epistemological and methodological point of view, it should be scrutinized in its very essence. Which is not the aim of this paper.

On the other hand, there has been some criticism of visual argumentation from more "traditional" scholars in the field of argumentation (Johnson 2003, 2010; Patterson 2010) that was never seriously debated by the proponents of VA, and their objections (mostly that different norms and different criteria should indeed be established to evaluate visual arguments as arguments) were never systematically discussed, let alone rebutted.

In this paper, I want to concentrate on two "milestones" in the development of VA: 1) in the first part of the paper, I analyse the very first example of visual argument ("smoking fish"), showing that doubts about the possibility of VA have solid empirical, not only epistemological and methodological basis; 2) in the second part of the paper I show that claims about visual argumentation are becoming more and more bold and radical with time: from the "possibility of visual meaning" in 1996 (the "smoking fish" example), some proponents of VA (Groarke in particular) have come a long way to boldly claim that "seeing is reasoning" in 2013. To expose and analyse the conceptual underpinnings of this radical position, I will concentrate on Leo Groarke's 2013 programmatic paper "The Elements of Argument: Six Steps to a Thick Theory" (Groarke 2013).

Along the way, I also mention (without analysing in detail) some basic concepts VA is—in my view—lacking, but that should be incorporated in their conceptual framework to better explain the basic problems (not just epistemological and methodological but also rhetorical and hermeneutical) concerning VA: how visuals function—that is, how they get or catch the viewers, how the viewers break down the presented visuals—and how they reconstruct their meaning. In discussing these problems, central attention will be devoted to the (rather new) concept of *enchrony* (Enfield 2009).

Because stereotypes such as "knowing is seeing" and "seeing is knowing" are deeply rooted and widely used metaphors in (not just) Western culture, culminating in the ubiquitous cliché "a picture is worth a thousand words", the critical rhetorical analysis I'll be performing, borrowing the tools mostly from the interaction of multimodal analysis and anthropological linguistics (Enfield 2009), may significantly contribute to the somehow neglected methodological questions about how meaning and knowledge are extracted from visuals and, consequently, how visuals may generate meaning and knowledge.#

4.2 Twenty Years as a Dichotomy

Let us, therefore, start in 1996. The introduction to the double issue of *Argumentation and Advocacy* on VA, written by Birdsell and Groarke, is (understandably) still pretty cautious as to what visuals can do (all emphases, in italics, are mine):

- … the first step toward a theory of visual argument must be a better appreciation of both the *possibility* of visual meaning and the *limits* of verbal meaning. (Birdsell and Groarke 1996: 2);
- … we often clarify the latter (i.e., spoken or written words) with visual cues … (ibid.);
- Words can *establish a context of meaning* into which *images can enter with a high degree of specificity* while achieving a meaning different from the words alone. (ibid.: 6);
- … diagrams can *forward* arguments… (ibid.);
- The implicit verbal backdrop that allows us to *derive arguments from images* is clearly different from the immediate context created by the placement of a caption beside an image. (ibid.)

If we sum up: in 1996, visuals may have some argumentative or persuasive potential (there is a possibility of visual meaning, visuals can forward arguments, and arguments can be derived from visuals), but they are usually (always?) still coupled

Fig. 4.1 Smoking fish (taken from Birdsell and Groarke 1996). *Source*: U.S. Department of Health, Education, and Welfare, Public Health Service, 1970, NML Image ID A03279, http://resource.nlm. nih.gov/101581762, Public Domain

with the verbal, and can achieve these argumentative effects (only?) in combination with the verbal.

The *pièce de resistance*, the very first visual argument (or "visual argument") Birdsell and Groarke offer to illustrate the claims above (i.e. the possibility of VA), is an anti-smoking poster, published by the US Department of Health, Education and Welfare in 1976, that I would like to analyse in more detail. Here it is (Fig. 4.1):

In analysing the poster, the authors first admit that

> visual images can, of course, be vague and ambiguous. But this alone does not distinguish them from words and sentences, which can also be vague and ambiguous. (Birdsell and Groarke 1996: 2)

We can agree with that. They then qualify this poster as "an amalgam of the verbal and the visual" (ibid.), which, again, sounds quite acceptable. But then they unexpectedly conclude: "Here the argument that you should be wary of cigarettes because they can hook you and endanger your health is forwarded by means of visual images…" (ibid.: 3). Which is obviously not the case. Without the verbal part—"don't you get hooked!"—the poster could be understood (framed)[1] as a joke,

---

[1] The concept of frames, which I am using here, are frames that help us organize our everyday experience, frames as developed by sociologist Erving Goffman in his influential book *Frame Analysis: An Essay on the Organization of Experience* (1974). What are Goffman's frames? In his own words:

> When the individual in our Western society recognizes a particular event, he tends, whatever else he does, to imply in this response (and in effect employ) one or more frameworks or schemata of interpretation of a kind that can be called primary. I say primary because application of such a framework or perspective is seen by those who apply it as not depending on or harking back to some prior or "original" interpretation; indeed a primary framework

as a cartoon, where, for example, smoking is presented as such a ubiquitous activity that anglers even use cigarettes to catch fish. *Only when we add the verbal part* "don't you get hooked!" is the appropriate (intended) frame set: the poster is then, *and only then*, understood as an anti-smoking advert, belonging to an anti-smoking campaign. More specifically, "hooked" activates an associative chain or semantic frame of knowledge relating to this specific concept, which includes (among other meanings) "become addicted", being at the same time and within the same space juxtaposed with a visual representation of a hook with a cigarette on it.

Every argument is, of course, open to criticism and counter-arguments. I wanted to empirically (and experimentally) test both lines of reasoning and argumentation—Groarke and Birdsell's argument(ation) and my counter-argument(ation)—so I designed a pilot questionnaire, entitled "A Short Questionnaire on Understanding Visuals (Drawings, Pictures, Photographs…)," that consisted of three well-known visuals from Leo Groarke's work on VA, namely:

(1) The smoking fish (where—a very important point!—the text "Don't you get hooked" was removed from the picture; see Fig. 4.2)'

(2) the poster "UvA for Women"; and

Fig. 4.2 Smoking fish (taken from Birdsell and Groarke 1996, with text removed)

is one that is seen as rendering what would otherwise be a meaningless aspect of the scene into something that is meaningful. (Goffman 1974: 21).

Goffman distinguishes between natural and social frameworks. Natural frameworks "identify occurrences seen as undirected, unoriented, unanimated, unguided, purely physical" (ibid.: 22). Social frameworks, on the other hand,

provide background understanding for events that incorporate the will, aim, and controlling effort of an intelligence. […] Motive and intent are involved, and their imputation helps select which of the various social frameworks of understandings is to be applied. (ibid.: 24).

(3)   Jacques-Louis David's painting "La Mort de Marat" (The Death of Marat).

Each visual was preceded by a short necessary introduction, framing the visual (but not explaining the exact context), while below the visual two questions were asked. In the case of the smoking fish (the analysis of the other two visuals can be found in Žagar 2017), both questions read as follows:

> Introduction: The drawing below dates back to the seventies of the previous century. Please, take a good look at it, and then answer the two questions below.
>
> Question 1: What do you see in the drawing (how would you describe the "content" or "what is going on" in the drawing in the most correct and objective way)?
>
> Question 2: In your opinion, what could be the goal/purpose/meaning of the drawing? In other words, how would you interpret it (e.g. a joke, advertisement against smoking/cigarettes, advertisement in favour of smoking/cigarettes, advertisement in anglers' bulletin, caricature, other). Please, give reasons for your opinion.

This questionnaire, in the Slovenian language, was distributed to three different age groups, with different educational backgrounds, all European, with Slovenian citizenship. I planned a fourth one, a group of refugees living in Slovenia (mostly from Syria, Iraq and Afghanistan, some of them from North Africa), to show how cultural differences may influence the interpretation, but the refugee coordinator refused to participate for "ethical reasons". The survey took place between 29 May and 5 June 2017. Here are some of the characteristics of these groups:

- Group 1: STUDENTS (number: 26, age: 20–24, gender: 25 female, 1 male, education: completed high school, 2nd year of Educational Studies at the University of Primorska, Slovenia).
- Group 2: RESEARCHERS (number: 7/30,[2] age: 28–68, gender: 6 female, 1 male, education: PhD in Philosophy, Sociology, Psychology, Education Sciences, two PhD candidates, Educational Research Institute, Slovenia).
- Group 3: SENIORS (number: 3/12,[3] age: 69–86, gender: 2 female, 1 male, education: high school to university education, attendants of the University of the Third Age, Slovenia).

Of course, from the methodological point of view—and strictly statistically speaking—the samples vary too much and cannot be compared in an orderly quantitative fashion. But at this point, I was interested in qualitative data, and as a pilot study, even such disparate groups are adequate. More elaborate and varied testing is being planned, though. What did our pilot study show?

Group 1: 9 students out of 26 thought that the drawing "could have been/might have been/probably was/likely was" an anti-smoking advert (none of them straightforwardly answered that it was an anti-smoking advertisement).

There were another three answers that the visual was probably an advert against smoking, but two of them argued further that the anti-smoking intention was just an intermediate stage, while the main point of the advert was probably that, by smoking,

---

[2] 7/30 means that 30 questionnaires were distributed, but only 7 were returned.

[3] 12 questionnaires were distributed, only 3 were returned.

we are polluting the environment. One of the respondents opted for an anti-smoking advert because "the hook pulls the cigarette out of the fish's mouth, thus preventing it from smoking".

Interestingly, three students thought that the drawing was a representation of society in the seventies. One of them commented that "society realized that smoking was bad, but has already surrendered to destiny", while the other one thought that the drawing "represents people dissatisfied with the system".

What is even more interesting is the fact that most of the respondents substantiated their claims not by the maggot on the hook in the fish's mouth, but by the expression on the fish's "face". Here are some qualifiers they used to describe the expression of the fish's face in relation to the maggot on the hook (and further, the social situation at large):

- sad expression,
- indifferent eyes,
- bored and apathetic fish,
- bored and indifferent gaze,
- dead face,
- sad gaze,
- angry gaze,
- unsatisfied expression,
- boredom and discontent,
- not in a good mood,
- reluctant and angry,
- without emotions, and
- sad eyes.

This shifting of the focus from 1) the maggot on the hook to the 2) "facial expression" of the fish, while 3) keeping in mind the information from the instructions that the drawing is from the seventies, represents a perfect proof that the determination of the meaning of the drawing was reached/constructed through *enchronic analysis*, a concept I will be explaining in much more detail later in the paper. At this point, I offer just a short quote about what enchronic analysis is (emphases mine):

> Enchronic analysis is concerned with *relations between data from neighbouring moments*, adjacent units of behaviour in locally coherent communicative sequences. (Enfield 2009: 10)

In short, if we have a line of events A, B and C: what happens in B and how B is seen, depends on A, on what happened in A and how A was framed or conceptualized. Consequently, the interpretation of C, how it is seen, understood and conceptualized, narrowly depends on A and B. I'll say more about that later, when analysing the breadfruit example.

Now, let us return to the other answers from Group 1. Two of the respondents thought it was (some kind of) a joke, meaning/implying that smoking is so widespread nowadays that even fish have started to smoke. Another two thought the drawing was an advert in an angler's newsletter, its purpose being to alert readers against the pollution of waters.

One of the respondents thought it was a joke at the expense of non-smokers, another one that it was a teaser, a challenge to non-smokers (pleading in favour of cigarettes). Yet another one thought the drawing was a protest from the vegetarian viewpoint (emphasizing the feelings of a fish when it gets caught), somebody took it as a kind of allegory (in her own words): you can get hooked or you cannot (the choice is yours).

The remaining three respondents couldn't decide about the message.

Group 2 had much less to say about the appearance of the fish, for most of them it looked "sad and bored". As for the message, three of them answered that it could have been an anti-smoking advert; two of them emphasized it could be either a funny ad, a joke, or an anti-smoking advert; while one of them was reminded of the famous Rat Park Experiment; and one of the respondents thought the drawing looked like an illustration from a children's book.

From Group 3, we got the following three answers: (1) advertisement for the tobacco industry, (2) could be anything and (3) I really don't know.

The conclusion we can draw from all of these answers is pretty obvious, I think: Birdsell and Groarke's claim that the argument that you should be wary of cigarettes because they can hook you and endanger your health is forwarded by means of visual images *is clearly refuted*. It seems that, unless there is a clear verbal supplement (e.g. "don't you get hooked") interacting with the visual part, the interpreters' inference about the (intended) meaning of the drawing (let alone its possible argumentation potential, which may not be inferred at all) obviously depends on their historical, social, cultural and/or individual background, on the specifics of their education and/or their values.

But the smoking fish example dates back to 1996. As I explained at the beginning of the paper, in the last ten years or so, there has been a tendency to interpret visuals as directly and unambiguously offering arguments by themselves, without any intervention or help from the verbal (or any other code). Such an approach could be epitomized as "reasoning is seeing" or/and "seeing is reasoning".

As a case in point—exposing possible caveats as well as cul-de-sacs of visual argumentation in general – for the rest of the paper, I concentrate on Leo Groarke's radical proposal ("reasoning is seeing"), presented and conceptualized in his 2013 programmatic paper (Groarke 2013b).

4.3 The Reasoning is the Seeing. Is It?

Here is the photo Groarke takes as a starting point for his reasoning:

This is how he frames it (again, all emphases throughout the text that follows are mine):

> Consider a debate spurred by an unusual fruit I discovered during a kayak ride on the Detroit River. When my description ("nothing I recognize; a bumpy, yellow skin") initiated a debate and competing hypotheses on the identity of the fruit, I went back and took the photographs reproduced below. *On the basis of these photographs, the fruit was quickly identified as breadfruit.* (Groarke 2013b: 34–35)

This is how Groarke reconstructs the argument (actually the process of arriving from argument(s) to conclusion) in question (please, pay special attention to the part that is emphasized):

> The argument that established this conclusion *compared my photographs to similar photographs found in encyclopaedia accounts of breadfruit.* One might summarize the reasoning as: "The fruit is breadfruit, for these photographs are like standard photographs of breadfruit." But this is just a verbal paraphrase. *The actual reasoning—what convinces one of the conclusion—is the seeing of the sets of photographs in question.* Using a variant of standard diagram techniques for argument analysis, we might map the structure of the argument as:

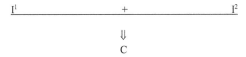

$$I^1 \qquad\qquad + \qquad\qquad I^2$$
$$\Downarrow$$
$$C$$

> where C is the conclusion that the fruit is a piece of breadfruit, I1 is the set of photographs I took, and I2 is the iconic photographs of breadfruit to which they were compared. (ibid.: 36)

Let me expose and emphasize the main part of the quote, the part we will be concentrating on, once more: "The actual reasoning … is the seeing of the sets of photographs in question".

4.3.1 Argumentation as Comparing Visuals

But, and this is a crucial question: could reasoning really be just seeing? Should (and does) reasoning really consist of just "the seeing of the sets of photographs in question"? Is just seeing and visually comparing photographs from different sources really enough for the reasoned, justified conclusion (in question)? And last but not least, let us not overlook Groarke's remark that "on the basis of these photographs, the fruit was *quickly* identified as breadfruit". Is the velocity of (visual or any other kind of) reasoning to be considered a virtue, a necessary and sufficient criterion for good argumentation?

To answer these questions, we will try to replicate Groarke's procedure and compare his photos of what he identified as breadfruit to the encyclopaedic photos of breadfruit.

Here are some photos of breadfruit I found in different encyclopaedias:

Fig. 4.3 Fruit found on the Detroit River I; photo by Leo Groarke, taken from Groarke 2013b

Fig. 4.4 Breadfruit at Tortuguero (Breadfruit, n.d.); photo by Hans Hillewaert/Wikimedia Commons, CC BY-SA 3.0

Fig. 4.5 The fruit of the breadfruit tree—whole, sliced lengthwise and in cross-section (Breadfruit, n.d.); courtesy of the USDA-Agricultural Research Service Tropical Plant Genetic Resources and Disease Research Unit, Hilo Hawaii

And here, again, I turn to Groarke's two photos: the one we have already seen (Fig. 4.6) and the one we haven't seen yet:

Fig. 4.6 Breadfruit (Health benefits of consuming bread fruit, n.d.)

Fig. 4.7 Fruit found on the Detroit River II; photo by Leo Groarke, taken from Groarke 2013b

Please inspect these photos carefully. Is there really such a resemblance between the two represented sets of fruits (Groarke's two photos and the photos of breadfruit from the internet) that we can quickly identify the fruit from the Detroit River as breadfruit?

Breadfruit, as we have seen from the encyclopaedic photos, has a kind of rough, knobbly skin with some kind of spines or hard hairs, patterned with irregular, 4, 5 to 6-sided faces, while in the centre there seems to be a kind of a cylindrical core. On the other hand, the skin of the fruit found in the Detroit River seems rather smooth, without spines or hairs, covered with smooth irregular bumps, not 4, 5 or 6-sided faces, and there seems to be no cylindrical core in the centre.

4.3.2 The Necessity of the Verbal

In such cases (where entities look alike, but are not quite the same), just "seeing" is obviously not enough, and it is wise, if not necessary, to consult other reliable sources, like *verbal descriptions*. Why verbal descriptions? Because in such cases (checking the photos in different encyclopaedias) there is not much else one can consult. On the other hand, language is still the only communicative "medium" that is (rather) linear, straightforward and sufficiently unambiguous; in combination with pertinent visuals, it is almost error-proof. And if, when consulting encyclopaedias or other relevant sources, *we don't just check the photos, but the text as well*, we find the following description of breadfruit (please, pay attention to emphases in italics):

> Breadfruit (*Artocarpus altilis*) is one of the highest-yielding food plants, with a single tree producing up to 200 or more fruits per season. *In the South Pacific*, the trees yield 50 to 150 fruits per year. *In southern India*, normal production is 150 to 200 fruits annually. Productivity varies between wet and dry areas. *In the Caribbean*, a conservative estimate is 25 fruits per tree. Studies in Barbados indicate a reasonable potential of 6.7 to 13.4 tons per acre (16-32 tons/ha).
>
> [...]
>
> Breadfruit, an *equatorial lowland species*, grows best below elevations of 650 meters (2,130 ft), but is found at elevations of 1,550 meters (5,090 ft). Its preferred rainfall is 1,500-3,000 millimeters (59-118 in) per year.
>
> [...]
>
> Breadfruit is a *staple food in many tropical regions*. The trees were propagated far outside their native range by Polynesian voyagers who transported root cuttings and air-layered plants over long ocean distances. (Breadfruit, n.d.)

In short, breadfruit is a tropical plant, usually found (and used) in tropical areas. It is, therefore, not very probable to find it in Ontario, in the Detroit River (though it is not completely impossible, of course, that a specimen of a breadfruit could find its way into the Detroit River from one of the local Caribbean restaurants or stores).

But, if relevant sources (encyclopaedias) were indeed amply consulted (or at least browsed through) and the point of departure in investigating the nature of the Detroit River fruit was not based on some kind of preconceived idea or an intuition that the found fruit looked very much like breadfruit, a neutral, objective and meticulous investigator should have easily found the following photos as well:

And once more, I turn to the two photos of a fruit found in the Detroit River (Fig. 4.3 and Fig. 4.7).

A close comparative observation between the encyclopaedic photos of this second fruit and those of breadfruit reveals that this second fruit *looks* much more like the

Fig. 4.8 Maclura pomifera (Maclura pomifera, n.d.a)

Fig. 4.9 Maclura pomifera (Maclura pomifera, n.d.b); photo by Jean-Pol Grandmont / Wikimedia Commons, CC BY 3.0

fruit found in the Detroit River: its skin seems smooth, without spines or hairs, and it is covered with smooth irregular bumps, not faces as in the bread fruit.

If we then consult the verbal part of the encyclopaedia, describing this fruit, as well, we find the following (once more, pay attention to emphases in italics):

> *Maclura pomifera*, commonly called Osage orange, hedge apple, horse apple, bois d'arc, bodark, or bodock is a small deciduous tree or large shrub, typically growing to 8–15 meters (26.49 ft) tall. It is dioecious, with male and female flowers on different plants. The fruit, a multiple fruit, is roughly spherical, but bumpy, and 7.6–15 centimeters (3–6 in) in diameter. *It is filled with sticky white latex. In fall, its color turns a bright yellow-green.*
>
> […]
>
> Osage orange occurred historically in the Red River drainage of Oklahoma, Texas and Arkansas and in the Blackland Prairies, Post Oak Savannas, and Chisos Mountains of Texas. *It has been widely naturalized in the United States and Ontario.* (Maclura pomifera, n.d.c)

As you can see for yourself, the verbal description of *Maclura pomifera* actually fits the Detroit River fruit much more accurately than the description of breadfruit. Because we also learn that Osage orange "has been widely naturalized in the United States and Ontario", it is much more probable to conclude that the fruit found in the Detroit River was an Osage orange (*Maclura pomifera*), and not a breadfruit (*Artocarpus altilis*).

4.4   Thousands of Words and a Single Picture

What can we learn from this? Above all, that sayings like "a picture is worth a thousand words" should be indeed taken seriously. But, to be (absolutely) sure which of those thousand words refer to that particular picture we have in front of us, in these particular circumstances, we have to cut down (on) those words considerably. On the other hand, *without any words at all, we can hardly identify the exact content of the picture*, as our Detroit fruit example clearly showed.

In other words, this reconstruction shows that there is no pure visual argumentation, relying on the epistemology of "reasoning is seeing" (as there are, probably, very few purely verbal arguments; if any at all). Instead of visual argumentation (or purely verbal argumentation, for that matter), we should (always) talk about multimodal argumentation and multimodal meaning (combining, in our case, primarily visual and verbal, but involving other semiotic modes, such as gesture and gaze, as well).

But multimodal meaning and multimodal argumentation require a different (expanded, at least) analytical framework, let us call it multimodal analysis, more particularly and with an important emphasis: *interactive-recursive* multimodal analysis or *enchronic* analysis. In relation to this very important distinction, I would like to emphasize a few points.

In cases where just "seeing" is not enough and we have to use verbal (or other) sources (and incorporate other types of signs, like gestures, gazes…), we should be talking of *enchronic analysis* (Enfield 2009). What is enchronic analysis (of which our analysis of the Detroit River fruit is a rather exemplary case, as we shall see a few paragraphs later)?

As we well know, mostly from linguistics, synchronic analysis gives us a horizontal cross section of investigated phenomena: it somehow freezes the actual state of things (in a certain domain). Diachronic analysis, on the other hand, gives us a vertical cross section of the investigated phenomena: it looks at how the state of things (in a certain domain) has changed through time and history.

Enchronic analysis, on the contrary, looks at (Enfield 2013) social interaction as a sequence of moves which occur as responses to other such moves, and in turn these moves give rise to yet further moves, shifting between different types of signs. We could say that enchrony *dynamically, interactively and recursively* combines synchrony and diachrony, that it opens synchrony to diachrony, that it injects diachronicity into synchronicity on a micro level, switching between different codes.

The Detroit River fruit example is a good example of enchronic analysis: from observation of the photos of the fruit taken at the river, we have to move to the observation of the photos in encyclopaedias and compare the two. To get more complete and accurate information (because the photos do not tell the whole story), we have to switch from the photos to the text and incorporate the textual information as well. Then, because the text opens up new questions/problems about the photos, we have to look for yet more photos, and from those, switch back to yet another text. Finally, we (have to) compare all of these again with the initial photo (of the fruit taken at the river).

When consulting encyclopaedias, we don't just check the photos, but the text as well, and then go and (re)check other available texts and photos, and compare them with the initial photo(s). The final result we arrive at after this *dynamic interaction* should be described as *composite meaning*, resulting in *composite utterances*, conceptualized as: "[…] a communicative move that incorporates multiple signs of multiple types" (Enfield 2009: 15).

For further illustration, here is a visual example of a composite sign (with composite meaning), Enfield himself uses:

Fig. 4.10 Willy Brandt in
Warsaw Ghetto; published in
Enfield (2009)

And this is his analysis (needless to say that emphases are mine):

While the kneeling posture may have an intrinsic, ethological basis for interpretation, this particular token of the behaviour has had a deeply *enriched meaning* for many who have seen it, because it was performed by this particular man, at this time and place. The man is Willy Brandt, chancellor of West Germany. Once you know this, the act already begins to take on *enriched meaning*. It is not just a man kneeling, but a man whose actions will be taken to stand for those of a nation's people. It is 7 December 1970, a state visit to Warsaw, Poland. These *new layers of information should yet further enrich your interpretation*. To add another layer: the occasion is a commemoration of Jewish victims of the Warsaw Ghetto uprising of 1943. [...] The body posture [...] is a *composite sign in so far as its meaning is partly a function of its co-occurrence with other signs*: in particular, the role being played by its producer, given the circumstances of its time and place of production. The behaviour derives its meaning as much from its position on these coordinates as from its intrinsic significance. (ibid.: 3–4)

We are dealing with several layers of meaning here, resulting in a complex amalgam of signs as a process and product of a sequence of meaning-making moves. Let us break this amalgam down, step-by-step (following Enfield's analysis in the previous quote):

- first layer, there is a kneeling posture as such, with its prototypical meaning;
- second layer, there is the presence of Willy Brandt, at that time the chancellor of Germany, with a variety of different meanings attached to him or his function;
- third layer, the chancellor of Germany is taking the kneeling position;
- fourth layer is provided by the information that this act of kneeling was part of Brandt's state visit to Warsaw; and
- fifth layer is provided by the information that Brandt's kneeling act was part of the commemoration of Jewish victims of the Warsaw Ghetto.

Speaking of the photo as such, it is these five layers of meaning that form an amalgam of signs, but even more layers of meaning could be added, depending on the 1) background knowledge of the observer and interpreter, as well as 2) the context in which the photo is being interpreted.

In view of all that has been said, let us return to the fruit found in the Detroit River. If, after checking and re-checking different photos, different texts and the two photos of a strange fruit found in the Detroit River, we finally point (and very probably gaze) at it, declaring "This fruit is not a bread fruit!", we have produced a composite utterance, enchronically (i.e. dynamically, interactively and recursively) embracing several—at least nine—layers of meaning-making moves:

(1) checking the photos of the Detroit River fruit,

(2) checking the photos of breadfruit in different encyclopaedias,

(3) checking the text that comments on those photos,

(4) checking the Detroit River fruit again,

(5) looking for more photos of similar fruits,

(6) checking the text that comments on those fruits,

(7) rechecking the Detroit River fruit again,

(8) finding out that the Detroit River fruit is not a breadfruit,

(9) making clear (voice, gesture, gaze) that the Detroit River fruit is not a breadfruit.

These nine layers belong to and are expressed by three types of signs that are enchronically combined in almost every one of the nine steps (conventional signs: words/text; non-conventional signs: photos, gesture, gaze; symbolic index-ical: demonstrative pronoun "this", linking the conventional and non-conventional signs).

4.5   Conclusion

As hopefully became clear in the analysis of the Detroit fruit example, *reasoning is not and cannot be just seeing, and just seeing is not and cannot be reasoning.* Consequently, there could be no "pure" visual, but only multimodal argumentation: at least verbal, and probably other codes, should be taken into consideration to reach sufficient, satisfying and complete meaning interpretation. This is not all. All of these codes *should be taken into consideration dynamically, not statically: in their recursive interaction*—that is, switching from one code to the other and back. Therefore, to gain analytic credibility and interpretive force, scholars working on VA would be much better off if they included enchrony in their conceptual framework and considered incorporating all of these intermediate recursive steps, as well as all of these interactively dependent codes and concepts into their framework. The final result they enchronically arrive at should thus be described as *composite meaning*, resulting in *composite utterances*.

But this final result, speaking of VA, really only opens the Pandora's box of argumentation, namely: what about "traditional", verbal argumentation? In light of enchrony, this dynamic, interactive and recursive multimodality, shouldn't we reconsider that as well?

References

Birdsell, David S., and Leo Groarke. 1996. Toward a Theory of Visual Argumentation. *Argumentation and Advocacy* 33 (1): 1–10.

Breadfruit. n.d., https://en.wikipedia.org/wiki/Breadfruit. Accessed 16 Oct 2020.

Calabrese, Omar. 1977. *Arti figurative e linguaggio*. Rimini & Florence: Guaraldi.

Dove, Ian. 2002. Can Pictures Prove? *Logique Et Analyse* 179–180: 309–340.

Dove, Ian. 2011a. Image, Evidence, Argument. In *Proceedings of the seventh international conference of the International Society for the Study of Argumentation*, eds. F.H. van Eemeren, B. Garssen, D. Godden, and G. Mitchell. Amsterdam: Sic Sat.

Dove, Ian. 2011b. Visual Analogies and Arguments. In *Argumentation: Cognition and community. Proceedings of the 9th international conference of the Ontario Society for the Study of Argumentation (OSSA)*, ed. F. Zenker, 1–16. Windsor: ON: University of Windsor.

Eco, Umberto. 1968/1983. *La struttura assente*. Milano: Bompiani.

Eco, Umberto. 1975/1976. *A Theory of Semiotics*. Bloomington and London: Indiana University Press.

Eco, Umberto. 1997. *Kant and the Platypus*. San Diego-New York-London: Harvest Book, Harcourt, INC.

Enfield, Nick J. 2009. *The Anatomy of Meaning*. Cambridge: Cambridge University Press.

Enfield, Nick J. 2013. *Relationship Thinking: Agency, Enchrony, and Human Sociality*. Cambridge: Cambridge University Press.

Fabbrichesi Leo, Rossella. 1983. *La polemica sull'iconismo*. Naples: Edizioni Scientifiche Italiane.

Gilbert, Michael. 1994. Multi-modal Argumentation. *Philosophy of the Social Sciences* 24: 159–177.

Gilbert, Michael. 1997. *Coalescent Argumentation*. Mahwah, NJ: Lawrence Erlbaum.

Goffman, Erving. 1974. *Frame Analysis: An Essay on the Organization of Experience*. London: Harper and Row.

Godden, David. 2013. On the Norms of Visual Argument. In *Virtues of Argumentation. Proceedings of the 10th international conference of the Ontario Society for the Study of Argumentation (OSSA)*, eds. D. Mohammed and M. Lewinski. Windsor: ON: University of Windsor.

Godden, David. 2015. Images as Arguments: Progress and Problems, a Brief Commentary. *Argumentation* 2 9 (2): 2 3 5–2 3 8.

Godden, David. 2017. On the norms of visual argument: A case for normative non-revisionism. *Argumentation* 31 (2): 395–431.

Groarke, Leo. 1996. Logic, Art and Argument. *Informal Logic* 18: 105–129.

Groarke, Leo. 2002. Towards a Pragma-Dialectics of Visual Argument. In *Advances in Pragma-Dialectics*, ed. F.H. van Eemeren, 137–151. Amsterdam: Sic Sat and Vale Press.

Groarke, Leo. 2003. Why Do Argumentation Theorists Find it So Difficult to Recognize Visual Arguments? In *Informal Logic at 25: Proceedings of the Windsor conference*, eds. H.V. Hansen, C.W. Tindale, J.A. Blair, and R.H. Johnson. Windsor, ON: University of Windsor.

Groarke, Leo. 2009. Five Theses on Toulmin and Visual Argument. In *Pondering on Problems of Argumentation*, ed. F.H. van Eemeren and B. Garssen, 229–239. Amsterdam: Springer.

Groarke, Leo. 2013a. On Dove, Visual Evidence and Verbal Repackaging. In *Virtues of Argumentation. Proceedings of the 10th international conference of the Ontario Society for the Study of Argumentation (OSSA)*, eds. D. Mohammed and M. Lewinski, 1–8. Windsor: ON: University of Windsor.

Groarke, Leo. 2013b. The Elements of Argument: Six Steps to a Thick Theory. In *What Do We Know About the World? Rhetorical and Argumentative Perspectives*, eds. B. Kišiček and I.Ž. Žagar, 25–43. Ljubljana: Educational Research Institute. https://www.doi.org/https://doi.org/10.32320/978-961-270-171-0. Accessed 16 Oct 2020.

Groarke, Leo. 2015. Going Multimodal: What is a Mode of Arguing and Why Does it Matter? *Argumentation* 29 (2): 133–155.

Groarke, Leo, Catherine H. Palczewski, and David Godden. 2016. Navigating the Visual Turn in Argument. *Argumentation and Advocacy* 52 (4): 217–235.

Groupe μ. 1992. *Traité du signe visuel*. Paris: Seuil.

Health Benefits of Consuming Bread Fruit. n.d. https://healthybenefits.info/the-health-benefits-of-consuming-bread-fruit%E2%80%8F/ Accessed 16 Oct 2020.

Johnson, Ralph H. 2003. Why "Visual Arguments" aren't Arguments. In *Informal Logic at 25: Proceedings of the Windsor conference*, ed. H.V. Hansen, C.W. Tindale, A. Blair, and R.H. Johnson, 1–13. Windsor, ON: University of Windsor.

Johnson, Ralph H. 2010. On the Evaluation of Visual Arguments: Roque and the Autonomy Thesis. [Unpublished conference paper, presented to] Persuasion et argumentation: Colloque international organisé par le CRAL à l'Ecole des Hautes Etudes en Sciences Sociales, 105 Bd. Raspail, 75006 Paris, Salle 7, 7–9 September 2010.

Kjeldsen, Jens E. 1999. Visual Rhetoric—From Elocution to Invention. In *Proceedings of the fourth international conference of the International Society for the Study of Argumentation*, eds. F.H. van Eemeren, R. Grootendorst, J.A. Blair, and C.A. Willard, 455–460. Amsterdam: Sic Sat.

Kjeldsen, Jens E. 2007. Visual Argumentation in Scandinavian Political Advertising: A Cognitive, Contextual, and Reception-Oriented Approach. *Argumentation and Advocacy* 43 (3–4): 124–132.

Kjeldsen, Jens E. 2012. Pictorial Argumentation in Advertising: Visual Tropes and Figures as a Way of Creating Visual Argumentation. In *Topical Themes in Argumentation Theory*, ed. F.H. van Eemeren and B. Garssen, 239–256. Amsterdam: Springer.

Kjeldsen, Jens E. 2013. Strategies of Visual Argumentation in Slideshow Presentations: The Role of Visuals in an Al Gore Presentation on Climate Change. *Argumentation* 27 (4): 425–443.

Kjeldsen, Jens E. 2015. The Study of Visual and Multimodal Argumentation. *Argumentation* 29 (2): 115–132.

Kjeldsen, Jens E. 2015. The Rhetoric of Thick Representation: How Pictures Render the Importance and Strength of an Argument Salient. *Argumentation* 29 (2): 197–215.

Maclura pomifera. n.d.a. https://www.actaplantarum.org/galleria_flora/galleria1.php?aid=463 Accessed 16 Oct 2020.

Maclura pomifera. n.d.b. https://commons.wikimedia.org/wiki/File:Maclura_pomifera_FrJPG.jpg Accessed 16 Oct 2020.

Maclura pomifera. n.d.c. https://en.wikipedia.org/wiki/Maclura_pomifera Accessed 16 Oct 2020.

Patterson, Steven W. 2010. A Picture Held Us Captive: The Later Wittgenstein on Visual Argumentation. *Cogency* 2 (2): 105–134.

Polidoro, Pero. 2015. Umberto Eco and the problem of iconism. *Semiotica* 206: 129–160.

Roque, Georges. 2010. What is Visual in Visual Argumentation? In *Argument cultures: Proceedings of OSSA 09*, eds. J. Ritola et al., 1–9. Windsor, ON: University of Windsor.

Roque, Georges. 2012. Visual Argumentation: A Further Reappraisal. In *Topical Themes in Argumentation Theory*, ed. F.H. van Eemeren and B. Garssen, 273–288. Amsterdam: Springer.

Roque, Georges. 2015. Should Visual Arguments be Propositional in Order to be Arguments? *Argumentation* 29 (2): 177–195.

U.S. Department of Health, Education, and Welfare, Public Health Service. 1970. NML Image ID A03279, http://resource.nlm.nih.gov/101581762, Public Domain.

Žagar, Igor Ž. 2016. Against Visual Argumentation: Multimodality as Composite Meaning and Composite Utterances. In *Argumentation and Reasoned Action. Vol. I: Proceedings of the 1st European conference on argumentation*, Lisbon 2015, (Studies in logic, vol. 62), eds. D. Mohammed and M. Lewinski, 829–852. London: College Publications.

Žagar, Igor Ž. 2018. Perception, Inference, and Understanding in Visual Argumentation (and Beyond). In *Argumentation and Inference. Vol. I, Proceedings of the 2nd European conference on argumentation*, Fribourg 2017, (Studies in logic and argumentation, vol. 77), eds. S. Oswald and D. Maillat, 439–469. London: College Publications.

Part II
Language Teaching Methodology for Digital Environments

Chapter 5
Video Games in the Development of Cognitive Skills Relevant for Language Learning: A Systematic Review

Lilia V. Bondareva and Tatiana V. Potemkina

Abstract The purpose of the study is to analyse the modern pedagogical context which demonstrates the possibilities of using video games to develop cognitive skills when learning a foreign language. Pedagogical theories recognize the importance of games as a method. The game context is entertaining and allows scholars and teachers to build a staged development of educational skills. The research is based on a systematic review and analysis of current use of computer games for cognitive skills development in foreign language learning. The analysis shows that video games are used to develop several related cognitive skills: vocabulary development, understanding the context to provide feedback when building a simple dialogue, accuracy in the word choice, speech strategies, and reading and writing skills development. Evidence reveals didactic ways of organizing training based on video games to positively affect the development of cognitive skills. However, results show that this impact is limited, because video games have a strict design and cannot effectively develop cognitive skills requiring a wide choice of speech means in the interactions between players. It is also unlikely that video games either stimulate the use of speech strategies in a situation of uncertainty or provide for extra linguistic factors.

Keywords Video game · Cognitive skills · Second language learning

5.1 Introduction

Digital technologies today are implemented globally in various fields, from banking and trade to tourism and transport. In the field of education there is also a growing interest in the use of these tools. With the Internet came a wide availability of digital educational technologies for all categories of students: children, university students, adults. These learning tools are global and international in nature. The implementation of these tools in the educational process opens up big possibilities not only for learning but also for teaching.

L. V. Bondareva (✉) · T. V. Potemkina
National University of Science and Technology 'MISiS', Moscow, Russia

The educational environment is also changing under the influence of digital technologies. Over the past 20 years, a common information space based on digital technologies has been created. The new opportunities bring solutions to problems previously unsolved: a common educational space; access to educational resources for all students regardless of their geographical location; expanding access to multiple sources, with books no longer being the ultimate carriers of information.

With digital tools, educational organizations have the opportunity to standardize the process of evaluating education outcomes (Collins and Halverson 2018), to build individual educational pathways for a significant number of students, as the Internet provides resources to customize materials for each student based on their individual needs (Childress and Braswell 2006). In addition, the use of digital technologies allows making the educational environment more engaging and less competitive (Collins and Halverson 2018).

Digitization has a direct impact on the learning process: this process now goes beyond the boundaries of the classroom. The learning support system available through the digital environment is able to respond to the choice of the student when performing educational tasks, provide an individual pace in mastering educational content, and help reduce emotional stress during tests (Olejniczak et al. 2020). Digital technologies are actively introduced into the practice of teaching both directly in the classroom and in extracurricular independent work of students (Collins and Halverson 2018; Pereira 2013).

The teacher's role is also changing. The teacher performs the supporting function for students online. Students have the opportunity to act autonomously, dealing with both content and methodology issues in a way that is convenient for them.

The full range of digital resources for education is yet to be researched. However, at the moment many ideas of using digital tools for learning purposes are not unanimously accepted by scientists and educators and have both supporters and opponents.

Some researchers argue that over the last few years of studies into digital didactic tools their impact on the effectiveness of learning has not been conclusively determined. Hattie conducted a comparative analysis of the impact of different learning tools on student scores and presented data that indicate insignificance (less than 20%) of the "effect size" of various Internet resources on student scores in online learning (Hattie 2009). Säljö also points to the lack of evidence-based information that could indicate the advantages of digital learning tools over traditional ones (Säljö 2010). All this suggests that the degree of effectiveness of the organization of the educational process with the use of digital means in comparison with traditional visual means is either negligible or completely indistinguishable (Grimshaw and Cardoso 2018; Hattie 2009; Säljö 2010).

In addition, expert and research communities have widely discussed the occurrence of various emotional and cognitive disorders in children who are involved in the digital environment. For example, the World Health Organization (WHO) has recognized a new mental illness in children and adolescents known as "gaming disorder", which is caused by the passion for online games (Billieux et al. 2020). Recently, there have also been studies that document the negative impact of video games on development, including the impact on students' affection and on changes in their prosocial behaviour (Blumberg et al. 2019).

It is no coincidence that researchers of digital education more and more often note dissatisfaction of adults with the introduction of digital means in education, and there are straightforward calls for "turning off technology" and "preserving our humanity—obviously with deep fears about losing it" (Prensky 2019).

These data raise concerns about the feasibility of using digital resources as a training tool.

At the same time, along with a pronounced negative position in relation to the active spread of digital tools in the educational environment, there is a directly opposite point of view in the scientific and professional community.

Proponents of the active inclusion of digital means in the educational process maintain that the virtual online world provides opportunities for using augmented reality, which significantly expands the educational space and enhances students' experience in exploring scientific phenomena. Digital technologies provide remote open access to a variety of educational content. Anyone interested in science, regardless of where they live, can access the resources of the world's leading libraries.

The optionality of presence in the classroom allows students to freely manage their time, feel more liberated, make greater use of cooperation, and add opportunities to "customize" the content of training to their needs (Childress and Braswell 2006: 187–196). For example, playing video games for a reasonable time reduces anxiety in students (Grimshaw and Cardoso 2018: 159–175), increasing the motivation to learn the skills the game is aimed at. At the same time, the problem of mental and intellectual health may be helped with a conscious attitude toward digital technologies and to the age-specific development of children and adolescents through the construction of a safe digital educational environment.

New trends in education have shifted the design of all educational tools, including digital, to the individual needs of students in their skill development. Students more and more often formulate their own requirements for the size and content of the necessary knowledge, demonstrating interest in obtaining professionally important competencies (Yusof and Adnan 2019).

The use of digital tools in the educational process is associated not only with the educational effects that can be obtained through their use. The need to use digital technologies in education is caused by the general transformation of the living environment of young people.

All this dictates the need to explore the educational possibilities of existing and emerging digital learning tools.

5.2 Literature Review

This study is dedicated to one of the most actively implemented and still developing digital learning tools in the online environment: video games.

Pedagogical theories recognize the importance of gaming as a way of learning. The game creates an informal learning environment. The context of the game is usually entertaining, and therefore it has different means of involving students in the educational gaming space (Casañ Pitarch 2017), allowing educators to build a sequential development of educational skills. "Game mechanics" creates a structured environment for learning an educational skill (Brown 2008; Rabah et al. 2018).

Video games are a relatively new form of gaming. An analysis of the use of video games in education shows that

> gamification of learning is most effective when the principles of gaming and learning are shared, aligned or even equivalent and operationalized through game mechanics. (Rabah et al. 2018)

Video games are an actively developing educational resource. Recent studies in the field of gamification indicate an increase in the number of games made for educational purposes. The developers offer different ways of presenting educational content, such as simulations and story games.

According to a survey of US teachers, up to 80% of respondents use digital games. However, to date, the educational potential of this tool has not been studied, and the practical value of their application has also been little studied (Blumberg et al. 2019).

The inclusion of computer video games in education is most often associated with the need of teachers to expand the ways of involving students in the development of educational skills (Pozo Sánchez et al. 2020). Teachers are confident that the gaming interest, informal environment, and the opportunity to cooperate will increase the motivation of students to learn, reduce the level of their anxiety during tests and quizzes (Abrams and Gerber 2013), and contribute to the development of a non-conflict environment for communication.

Pereira analysed different approaches to deploying video games as a learning tool and made the obvious conclusions about the dynamics of change in relation to a video game: from a form of entertainment, the purpose of which is fun and a meaningless pastime, to a method of organization of educational space, which mainly performs the functions of engagement in learning, increasing the motivation of students and promoting the development of skills of different types (motor, cognitive, communicative; Pereira 2013).

Over the past few years, systematic reviews have been conducted, which presented different areas of study of computer games for education: the effectiveness of the use of computer games in mastering medical educational content (Ijaz et al. 2019), the impact of computer games on motivation in learning (Jabbar and Felicia 2019; Flores and Figueroa 2015; Bernhard-Skala 2019), the principles of usability assessment for mobile educational games (Gao et al. 2019), and the influence of computer games on the increase in speed and attention when teaching mathematics (Mahmoudi et al. 2015).

There are a number of studies that focus on the use of computer games in the development of cognitive skills. Cognitive skills are connected with areas such as the ability to solve various intellectual problems in the field of natural sciences, the development of memory, the special aspects of speech formation, and the development of critical thinking mechanisms.

Interactive games include skills such as active learning, critical thinking, and problem solving (Soyoof 2018).

Homer and his colleagues put forward arguments that lead to conclusions about the effectiveness of computer games in mastering executive function, which involves interrelated cognitive planning and control skills to achieve a goal (Homer et al. 2019).

Computer games, together with other digital tools for online learning, can, among other things, make learning content accessible to people with cognitive disabilities (Flogie et al. 2020; Cinquin et al. 2019). These games are aimed at acquiring basic, complex skills, the ability to focus attention, the formation of calculus skills, etc.

One of the most recent large-scale studies carried out by a group of scientists from different universities (Blumberg et al. 2019) is dedicated to the analysis of the impact of video games on the development of various cognitive skills. The authors provide data on the successful use of video games in the educational process at school in order to develop such cognitive skills as spatial abilities, skills of solving problems with rotation, and skills of choosing effective mathematical strategies for solving problems.

However, a number of authors believe that research on the beneficial or harmful aspects of video games for the cognition or teaching of school-age children is clearly insufficient (Ibid). Despite the diverse interest in the study of the use of video games in the educational process, in research practice there is some bias towards identifying the advantages of this tool. The negative impact of video games on children's development remains under-researched.

Despite numerous studies to date on the use of computer games in learning a foreign language (Peterson 2010; Rankin et al. 2006; Butler 2015; Um and de Haan 2005; Flores and Figueroa 2015), there is no available research that provides a systematic overview of the previous studies, determines the effectiveness of the use of computer games in the development of cognitive skills in the process of learning foreign languages, or generalizes effective didactic techniques.

5.3   Research Method

The research is based on the methodology of systematic review (Petticrew and Roberts 2006), which is based on the study of literature on this problem collected over the past five years. This analysis was undertaken using three databases: Google Scholar, ERIH plus, and SCOPUS. The focus was on publications that explore the use of video games in the study of foreign languages.

Here we present a systematic review of recent research on the problem of the application of computer games for the development of cognitive skills in foreign language studies. This will allow us to carry out an analysis of the application of computer games, to define the efficiency of this digital tool. It will reveal features of the application of the gamification approach for the development of these skills.

In total, 43 sources directly devoted to the use of video games for the development of cognitive skills in the study of foreign languages were analysed.

The study has a number of limitations. The interests of the authors of the article are concentrated on the pedagogical aspect of the use of video games, namely on the identification of pedagogical solutions for the use of video games for language teaching and cognitive skills development.

When choosing sources, the authors did not take into consideration neurobiological and psycholinguistic studies, which present the results of various biological and medical experiments.

5.4   Discussion

In order to learn a foreign language, both games for entertainment and serious games that are aimed at solving educational problems could be used.

Games for entertainment function as a language learning environment. Players learn vocabulary and speech patterns during the game. Learning a foreign language in the context of such a game is not the goal. The player's interest is mainly focused on the game's plot. Game developers, as a rule, offer standard, repetitive speech models, and vocabulary is limited to a given story—the content of the game. Learning a foreign language is not systematic. However, researchers note the educational potential of such games:

> motivation, classroom interaction, social interaction in the game, tangential learning, grades, complementary material, vocabulary, repetitive written content, plenty of written content, need for text interpretation, audio, and text in audio. (Savonitti and Mattar 2018)

Studying the impact of the multiplayer game World of Warcraft on foreign language learning, one group of scholars concludes that this game resource contributes to the study of a foreign language (Rama et al. 2012), as it involves communication between players through voice options.

Unlike entertainment games, educational video games solve problems that are directly related to learning a foreign language. And the ultimate goal of this game is to acquire a specific language skill: vocabulary development, grammar practice, reading skills, etc.

The analysis of the existing research allows us to conclude that video games are used in the process of learning a foreign language for the development of several related cognitive skills: vocabulary development, understanding the context to provide feedback when building a simple dialogue, accuracy in the choice of words in speech, and speech strategies.

Among video games for learning languages (educational games), the most common are those that address vocabulary development (Yudintseva 2015). A number of studies indicate that vocabulary work is based on several cognitive tasks which include memorizing the sound and letter complex of a word, understanding its meaning, holding it in memory, and reproducing it orally or in writing (Kosmas et al. 2018; Chen and Hsu 2019; Turgut and Irgin 2009; Yudintseva 2015).

Researchers and teachers believe that recognizing the sound and letter appearance of a word and understanding its meaning is one of the main cognitive skills for mastering foreign languages.

Due to the fact that the process of memorizing words requires regular repetition, which, from the point of view of students, makes the learning process demotivating (Soyoof 2018), the use of traditional teaching methods for these purposes may be ineffective. Automating the memorization process in a video game allows activating the process. However, repeated actions without providing feedback in the form of answers to questions, clarifying the context of using the word, or online tests do not lead to the desired outcome. Long-term retention of the target vocabulary does not occur.

The main advantages of using video games for these purposes are their following properties: practice and feedback, learning by doing, and learning from mistakes (Peterson 2010), which enhances the learning effect. Combining these properties with the narrative character of video games and colourful design makes the monotonous process of memorization more fun, and increases the involvement of students in the learning context.

No less important is the process of activating the word in speech. The development of this skill occurs through repetition, memorization of words, and their reproduction. The most difficult task for video game developers is to create conditions for the development of oral speech, audio reproduction of the word to students, and phonetic correction of the spoken word.

It is obvious that vocabulary largely determines the further success of students, affecting the development of communication skills. At the same time, an important factor in the development of communicative competence is the formation of active, passive, and potential vocabulary. The inclusion of tasks in the learning process that are aimed at understanding the meaning of a word, statements by context, and recognition of the root of a word all create conditions for the development of cognitive skills and allow students to advance in the development of a foreign language.

At the same time, the analysis of using video games for vocabulary development revealed different levels of their effectiveness: from high (retention of more than 60% of the target vocabulary) to low (no differences between those who learned vocabulary in the traditional way and those who memorized words using video games; Yudintseva 2015).

The success of learning new words will be determined by such aspects as the design features of the video game, the degree of involvement of participants, and the target settings of players (entertainment or training).

The pedagogical design of the didactic support system can also influence the quality of word acquisition. For example, using different methods to activate a word in speech (post-game questionnaire, chat-message game observations, interview, post-vocabulary assessment, etc.) allows the developer to systematize the educational process (Yudintseva 2015).

McGregor et al. (2019) studied vocabulary development among college students using the educational game Vocabulary.com. The obtained results indicate the inherent capabilities of this game in the accumulation of vocabulary. However, the researchers found a relationship between the pace of the game and the quality of vocabulary building: the effectiveness decreases if its intensity increases. As a result of video game training, students were not able to significantly improve their test results. This allows us to conclude that the ability to study new words more intensively in games encounters limitations of a physiological nature—the property of memory to hold the phonetic and semantic form of several new words for a long time.

Educators and video game creators are looking for the most effective ways to organize the game space. For these purposes, serious games include additional game components that are not directly related to the development of cognitive skills. The Lexis computer game includes physical activities—physical exercises, which, according to the authors, strengthen cognitive processes when learning a language. The results show a positive trend, as

> the visual help of the word facilitates the acquisition of new words [...] children find the appropriate word immediately, [...] children spell the word correctly. (Kosmas et al. 2018: 59–74)

Blumberg et al. (2019) point to the effectiveness of using video games that involve learning cognitive skills using physical exercise. The link between games and physical activity as a factor that enhances the process of memorization is included in games for different categories of students.

Experimenting with multi-player games shows that the number of players involved does not affect the number of vocabulary items learned. Research describes an experiment that records observations of the speech behaviour of players participating in a game (Soyoof 2018). The results obtained show uneven development of cognitive language skills by different participants.

Game strategies influence skill development. A description of the behaviour of players in a group video game shows that some participants choose words that expand their vocabulary and are new to them, while others choose words that are not new and do not require memorization (Rama et al. 2012). This strategy does not help to enrich vocabulary.

An analysis of the use of video games in second language learning by adults is presented by Andersen (2019). Observations show that as a result of playing together, students have an increased vocabulary, improved understanding of the text, and more accurate use of words in given speech situations. However, only one of the players showed significant dynamics. According to the researcher, this is due to the fact that the second player was less motivated and more loaded with other intellectual activities. This allows us to conclude that the use of the game in training requires the same systematic approach (step-by-step development of the material, regularity of access to training tasks, repeatability) as other digital and non-digital ways of mastering the educational content (Ibid).

Understanding context is a basic cognitive skill that influences the development of all types of speech activity when learning a foreign language (listening, reading, writing, speaking). This process is based on the ability to read, as well as to establish a semantic connection between the components of the statement while connecting familiar words to new ones.

The authors of several studies (Andersen 2019; Pereira 2013; and others) believe that designing a "digital game-based learning" (environment), which is aimed not only at understanding the meaning of a word but also developing the skills of understanding the meaning of a statement, is possible with the use of resources that a video game possesses. In this case, the virtual design of the game performs the function of building up the semantic space. Players can guess the content of the statement by the behaviour of the game's characters, by prompts based on the feedback received, etc.

Reading as a cognitive process involves recognizing and understanding individual words and statements. When learning to read, an important condition is the correct recognition of the graphic appearance of the word and the pronunciation of the word. This is a compulsory component of the game space. Repeated listening and viewing of individual words and statements (replicas of the game's characters, voicing the word when it is presented) obviously contribute to memorizing the graphic image of the word, developing reading skills and pronunciation.

Video game resources also allow developing writing skills (Manalastas 2020). Researchers give an example of games in which students play with the teacher. During games they write down words, sentences which are repeated by students afterwards (Stanley and Mawer 2008).

Video games include tasks that enhance cognitive processes and involve reading text, solving puzzles, and non-linear collaborative storytelling. An example is the interactive fiction type of video games (Pereira 2013). An entertaining story creates a space that encourages players to solve educational problems.

A significant advantage of learning a foreign language online is the provision of conditions for communication between players and within the video game based on the mechanisms provided by the game.

This analysis of video games that are used to develop cognitive skills when learning foreign languages is not exhaustive, but it allows drawing the following conclusions: video games can act as a training tool provided that game components act as training methods.

Table 5.1 features educational resources of video games that are used for the development of cognitive skills in foreign language learning.

The list of pedagogical methods of organizing the game space presented in Table 5.1 is not exhaustive, because games are improved and new features appear. In this regard, continuous research is required to fully understand the educational potential of a video game.

Table 5.1 Didactic methods of cognitive skill development in online games

Cognitive skills	Didactic methods	Source
Vocabulary development (word memorization and reproduction)	Interaction through negotiation for meaning; providing language materials to explain challenging vocabulary and grammatical features either directly in the game or through supplemental material	Andersen (2019)
	repetitive exposure to the target words (i.e., more than six times)	Turgut and İrgin (2009)
	Visual aid facilitates the acquisition of new words	Chen and Hsu (2019)
	Post-game questionnaire; chat messages; game observations; interview; post-vocabulary assessment	Kosmas et al. (2018)
	Pre-game vocabulary assessment; post-test assessment; post-project; survey questionnaires; reflection paper; self-report; pre-test; post-test	Yudintseva (2015)
	Prompts; clarification of meaning	McGregor et al. (2019)
More accurate use of words in speech	Clarification of meaning during feedback	Andersen (2019)
Text interpretation	Interaction among students; focus on the subject; audio chat for communication between players	Savonitti and Mattar (2018)
Text comprehension	Questions to find out what to do next; working with someone from a different group, then writing the walk-through or cheat for the game	Stanley and Mawer (2008)
	Reading and/or listening to information provided by the game, which gives back story; details of various game-specific statuses or clues towards immediate goals	Pereira (2013), Rama et al. (2012)
	Dialogues and discussions of players	Peterson et al. (2020)
Reading	Reading and listening to the characters controlled by the game	Savonitti and Mattar (2018)
Writing	Watching the teacher play the game and writing the main words and short phrases that a particular task within the game needs	Stanley and Mawer (2008)

(continued)

Table 5.1 (continued)

Cognitive skills	Didactic methods	Source
Language interaction	Interaction between players in a game	Peterson (2010), Rama et al. (2012)

5.5 Conclusions

Any learning process is aimed at developing cognitive skills. The level of cognitive skills largely determines the success of any training. The development of cognitive skills is increasingly the focus of teachers' attention, as practitioners are constantly searching for better teaching methods. Digital tools, as well as their availability, versatility, and broad capabilities, may have an important educational potential. The variety of ways that video games provide for organizing the game space makes it possible to include tasks for developing cognitive skills in the game design.

The analysis of the existing research has shown that video games are already actively used in the development of cognitive skills in the process of learning foreign languages.

Video games engage students in learning, thus affecting their motivation (Savonitti and Mattar 2018; Peterson 2010). Motivation issues are considered by all researchers as the main feature of a video game that has a significant impact on learning a foreign language.

Our study showed that video games are most often used to reduce stress, since they make the repetitive process less monotonous, so it is natural to use video games when developing cognitive skills related to improving students' vocabulary. At the same time, the ability to study new words more intensely in games has limitations of a physiological nature, including the property of memory to hold the phonetic and semantic form of several new words for a long time.

The study of foreign languages involves the development of cognitive skills that are associated with the development of memory, in particular with such speech-making operations as memorizing and reproducing words and phrases in a foreign language, understanding the context based on the establishment of semantic connections between components of a statement, and choosing and using exact words to construct a statement in a foreign language in a given speech situatison.

Skills development is based on a system of tasks that include different ways to activate cognitive processes: recognizing and reproducing a word, including it in a given context, reconstructing the text, and creating a dialogue mode.

The obvious positive effects of using a video game for educational purposes occur when the following conditions are met: games must have educational goals and a special pedagogical design, and they must perform educational tasks, contain different types of tasks, and assume different speech strategies.

Factors that influence the development of students' cognitive skills include creating conditions that stimulate cognitive activity. These conditions include additional physical activity in the video game.

The analysis of research that focuses on the use of video games in learning foreign languages for the development of cognitive skills shows that the impact of video games on the development of cognitive skills is limited, as

the game does not inherently provide the target language, but promotes language use around game-play. (Pereira 2013: 24)

An important condition for using games is to follow age restrictions both when choosing the level of speech complexity of the game and when choosing its content.

Restrictions are also related to the fact that video games have a strict algorithm of rules limiting the variation of speech means for player interaction and the use of speech strategies in a situation of uncertainty.

The interest of teachers in video games as a way of shaping the educational space is constantly increasing. However, at present the use of video games in modern pedagogical practice is often chaotic and unregulated, which opens good prospects for further investigation in this new field.

References

Abrams, Sandra Schamroth, and Hannah R. Gerber. 2013. Achieving through the feedback loop: videogames, authentic assessment, and meaningful learning. *The English Journal* 103 (1): 95–103.

Andersen, Tonje. 2019. *Learning by playing: A case study of second language acquisition in the online roleplaying game world of warcraft*. MS thesis, University of Oslo.

Bernhard-Skala, Christian. 2019. Organisational perspectives on the digital transformation of adult and continuing education: a literature review from a German-speaking perspective. *Journal of Adult and Continuing Education* 25 (2): 178–197.

Billieux, Joël, Marc N. Potenza, Pierre Maurage, Damien Brevers, Matthias Brand, and Daniel L. King. 2020. cognitive factors associated with gaming disorder. *Cognition and addiction. A Researcher's guide from mechanisms towards interventions*. Chapter 16: 221–230, Academic Press.

Blumberg, Fran C., Kirby Deater-Deckard, Sandra L. Calvert, Rachel M. Flynn, C. Shawn Green, David Arnold, and Patricia J. Brooks. 2019. Digital games as a context for children's cognitive development: research recommendations and policy considerations. *Social Policy Report* 32 (1): 1–33.

Brown, Harry J. 2008. *Video games and education*. ME Sharpe.

Butler, Yuko Goto. 2015. The use of computer games as foreign language learning tasks for digital natives. *System* 54: 91–102.

Chen, Hao-Jan Howard., and Hsiao-Ling. Hsu. 2019. The impact of a serious game on vocabulary and content learning. *Computer Assisted Language Learning*. https://doi.org/10.1080/09588221. 2019.1593197.

Childress, Marcus D., and Ray Braswell. 2006. Using massively multiplayer online role-playing games for online learning. *Distance Education* 27 (2): 187–196.

Cinquin, Pierre-Antoine., Pascal Guitton, and Hélène. Sauzéon. 2019. Online e-learning and cognitive disabilities: A systematic review. *Computers & Education* 130: 152–167.

Collins, Allan, and Richard Halverson. 2018. *Rethinking education in the age of technology: The digital revolution and schooling in America*, 2nd ed. Teachers College Press.

Flogie, Andrej, Boris Aberšek, Metka Kordigel Aberšek, Cecilia Sik Lanyi, and Igor Pesek. 2020. Development and evaluation of intelligent serious games for children with learning difficulties: Observational study. *JMIR Serious Games*, 8 (2). https://doi.org/10.2196/13190.

Flores, Jorge Francisco, and Figueroa. . 2015. Using gamification to enhance second language learning. *Digital Education Review* 27: 32–54.

Gao, Xiao Wen Lin, Braulio Murillo Véliz, and Freddy Paz. 2019. A systematic literature review of usability evaluation guidelines on mobile educational games for primary school students. *International Conference on Human-Computer Interaction*. Cham: Springer.

Grimshaw, Jennica, and Walcir Cardoso. 2018. Activate space rats! fluency development in a mobile game-assisted environment. *Language Learning and Technology* 22 (3): 159–175.

Hattie, John A.C. 2009. *Visible learning: A synthesis of over 800 meta-analyses relating to achievement*. London and New York: Routledge: Taylor and Francis Group.

Homer, Bruce D., Jan L. Plass, Maya C. Rose, Andrew P. MacNamara, Shashank Pawar, and Teresa M. Ober. 2019. Activating Adolescents' "Hot" executive functions in a digital game to train cognitive skills: The effects of age and prior abilities. *Cognitive Development*, 49 (January–March): 20–32.

Ijaz, Aneeqa, Mhammad Yasir Khan, Syed Mustafa Ali, Junaid Qadar, Maged N. Kamel, and Boulis. . 2019. Serious games for healthcare professional training: A systematic review. *European Journal of Biomedical Informatics* 15 (1): 14–30.

Jabbar, Azita Iliya Abdul, and Patrick Felicia. 2019. How game-based learning works and what it means for pupils, teachers, and classroom learning. *Design, motivation, and frameworks in game-based learning*. IGI Global, 1–29.

Kosmas, Panagiotis, Andri Ioannou, and Panayiotis Zaphiris. 2018. Implementing embodied learning in the classroom: effects on children's memory and language skills. *Educational Media International* 56 (1): 59–74.

Mahmoudi, Hojjat, Mohsen Koushafar, Javad Amani Saribagloo, and Gasem Pashavi. 2015. The effect of computer games on speed, attention and consistency of learning mathematics among students. *Procedia-Social and Behavioral Sciences* 176: 419–424.

Manalastas, Jared Parba. 2020. Digitalized instructional materials in creative writing based on technological pedagogical content knowledge. *Journal of Humanities and Education Development* 2 (2): 119–128.

McGregor, Karla K., Brooke A. Marshall, Samantha K. Julian, and Jacob Oleson. 2019. Learning while playing: A randomized trial of serious games as a tool for word mastery. *Language, Speech, and Hearing Services in Schools* 50 (4): 596–608.

Olejniczak, Karol, Kathryn E. Newcomer, and Sebastiaan A. Meijer. 2020. Advancing evaluation practice with serious games. *American Journal of Evaluation*. https://doi.org/10.1177/109821402 0905897.

Pereira, Joe. 2013. Video game meets literature: language learning with interactive fiction. *e-Teals: An E-journal of Teacher Education and Applied Language Studies*, 4: 19–45.

Peterson, Mark. 2010. Massively multiplayer online role-playing games as arenas for second language learning. *Computer Assisted Language Learning* 23 (5): 429–439.

Peterson, Mark, Jeremy White, Maryam Sadat Mirzael, and Qiao Wang. 2020. A review of research on the application of digital games in foreign language education. *New technological applications for foreign and second language learning and teaching*. IGI Global: 69–92.

Petticrew, Mark, and Helen Roberts. 2006. *Systematic reviews in the social sciences: A practical guide*. Blackwell Publishing.

Pitarch, Casañ, and Ricardo. . 2017. Gamifying content and language integrated learning with serious videogames. *Journal of Language and Education* 3 (3): 107–114.

Prensky, Marc. 2019. *What the world needs from education*.

Rabah, Jihan, Robert Cassidy, and Robert Beauchemin. 2018. Gamification in education: Real benefits or edutainment. In *17th European Conference on e-Learning, Athens, Greece*, 489–497.

Rama, Paul S., Rebecca W. Black, Elizabeth Van Es, and Mark Warschauer. 2012. Affordances for second language learning in world of warcraft. *ReCALL: The Journal of EUROCALL,* 24 (3): 322–338.

Rankin, Yolanda, Rachel Gold, and Bruce Gooch. 2006. Evaluating interactive gaming as a language learning tool.In *Proceedings for ACM SIGGRAPH Conference.*

Säljö, Roger. 2010. Digital tools and challenges to institutional traditions of learning: Technologies, social memory and the performative nature of learning. *Journal of Computer Assisted Learning* 26 (1): 53–64.

Sánchez, Pozo, Jesús López. Santiago, Arturo Fuentes Belmonte, and Cabrera, and Juan Antonio López Núñez. . 2020. Gamification as a methodological complement to flipped learning—an incident factor in learning improvement. *Multimodal Technologies and Interaction* 4 (2): 12. https://doi.org/10.3390/mti4020012.

Savonitti, Gabriel, and Joao Mattar. 2018. Entertainment games for teaching english as a second language: Characteristics and potential. *International Journal for Innovation Education and Research* 6 (2): 188–207.

Soyoof, Ali. 2018. Video games: A springboard for enhancing students' L2C. *International Journal of Pedagogies and Learning* 13 (2): 137–151.

Stanley, Graham, and Mawer Kyle. 2008. Language learners & computer games: From space invaders to second life. *Teaching English as a Second or Foreign Language* 11 (4): 1–12.

Turgut, Y.ıldız, and Pelin İrgin. 2009. Young learners' language learning via computer games. *Procedia-Social and Behavioral Sciences* 1 (1): 760–764.

Um, Eunjoon, 'Rachel', and Jonathan William deHaan. 2005. How video games can be used as an effective learning environment for cognitive apprenticeship theory-based learning. In *Annual Proceedings—Orlando,* 2: 499–505.

Yudintseva, Anastassiya. 2015. Game-enhanced second language vocabulary acquisition strategies: A systematic review. *Open Journal of Social Sciences* 3 (10): 101.

Yusof, Ahmad Ariffuddin, Airil Haimi Mohd Adnan, Nurul Nadiah Mustafa Kamal, Muhammad Anwar Mohd Kamal, and Muhamad Khairul Ahmad. 2019. Education 4.0 immersive learning with spherical videos (360) and virtual reality (VR) Experiences. In *Proceedings of the International Invention, Innovative & Creative (InIIC) Conference, Series*: 52–60.

Chapter 6
Language Acquisition in Virtual Worlds Versus Traditional Classroom Environments: A Comparative Overview Between the United States and Russia

Jasmin B. Cowin and Dana S. Saulembekova

Abstract The development of virtual worlds (VWs) in the field of language education evolved from purely text-based environments to two- and eventually three-dimensional spaces. VWs date back to the adventure games and simulations of the 1970s. Unlike traditional classroom settings, which are anchored in brick-and-mortar buildings, VWs give language learners the opportunity to practice languages in simulated, visually rich settings. Collaborative and communicative learning opportunities in VWs, together with the ubiquitous growth of online learning platforms and online degrees, raise questions on the long-term outlook for language teaching and learning in the Fourth Industrial Revolution. Although both the Russian Federation and the United States have a multitude of programmes, education degrees and certifications with specific competency requirements for future language teachers and higher education faculty, are there common long-term concerns about domains and respective definitions in technology, multicultural education and language acquisition? To shed light on these questions, the authors analysed US and Russian national missions and second language teaching standards for communication study teacher preparation programmes.

Keywords Virtual worlds · Digital environments · Traditional classroom environments · Second language acquisition · Russia · US

J. B. Cowin
Touro College and University System, New York, USA

D. S. Saulembekova (✉)
National University of Science and Technology 'MISiS', Moscow, Russia

6.1 Introduction. The United States and Russia. Brick-and-Mortar Buildings: Recollections from the Field

Dr. Cowin's field recollections. Stepping into my first high-stakes course assignment for my first college teaching experience in the US, I could just as well have traveled back to the 1980s. Entering the college classroom sparked a feeling of déjà vu related to my school experiences as a child, teen and college student. Nothing much had changed, apart from a computer precariously stationed on a movable desk. The decor consisted of four walls in a questionable shade of mustard yellow, a teacher's desk at the front of the classroom, tablet chairs, and a whiteboard plus blackboard. My first executive decision as a faculty member was to arrange the rows of chairs into a circle to promote group discussion. This seating arrangement created a front-row experience for all students, with the added advantage of less furtive cell phone use.

Fast forward to a second language workshop several years later at an institution of higher education in Russia. Again, here was an environment conceived in the 1980s, with the space and setup firmly anchored in teacher-centred teaching traditions. In one instance, a Russian workshop attendee informed me that "moving furniture was against university rules". Nevertheless, all tables were moved to the walls and chairs set up in a circle without any ill effects to the workshop attendees, tables, chairs or other university property. Instead, a lively discussion evolved on traditional classroom environments, the communicative language teaching approach and its implications for targeted language acquisition. The discussion centred on the importance of the physical setup, since experiential activities require presentations in a situation or context.

Brick-and-mortar classrooms in both Russia and the US often focus on information processing, which is firmly anchored in common cultural traditions of nineteenth-century teaching that feature the teacher at the front of the classroom delivering information for students to learn. Students in this model are often passive participants, sitting in chairs, following the directions of their faculty. For second language acquisition (SLA), the grammar-translation method, the direct method and the oral approach were (and still are) common to both the US and Russia. Classroom configurations, with slight variations, are identical in both cultures.

These first discoveries of the similarities of the use of classroom space spurred the authors to further investigate the similarities, boundaries and cultural differences in education between the US and Russia. In his chapter "Universal Categories of Culture", US anthropologist Clyde Kluckhohn argued that there should be universal categories of culture:

> All cultures constitute so many somewhat distinct answers to essentially the same questions posed by human biology and by the generalities of the human situation. (Kluckhohn et al. 1961: 317–318)

Awareness of cultural transformation is especially relevant when it comes to Generation Z (Gen Z), those born between 1997 and 2010, who make up the majority of the student body in universities today. According to the latest surveys, Gen Z has a specific profile (see Fig. 6.1).

Given the current internationalization of education, curriculum integration, student migration and online learning resources, experts are already dealing with this new generation of learners. When one unbundles the survey results in the report *Gen Z: A Look Inside Its Mobile-First Mindset* (Think with Google), the following picture emerges (see Table 6.1).

Gen Z members worry about having the right soft skills and experience for the workforce. Dell Technologies surveyed 12,000 secondary and postsecondary Gen Z students and found that 52% are more confident they have the tech skills employers

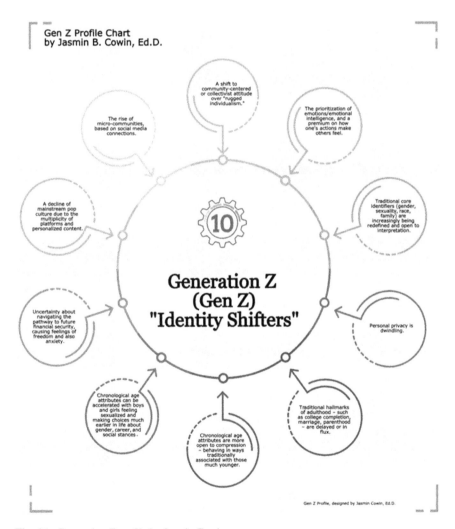

Fig. 6.1 Generation Z profile by Jasmin Cowin

Table 6.1 Generation Z
(Generation Z is defined as
youth ages 18–24 Google
2016) preferred technology
use

Technology	Percentage
Smartphone	87
Laptop	86
Television	66
Gaming console	43
Tablet	41

want than non-tech skills. On a related note, just over half (57%) think that their education has prepared them well for a future career (Dell Technologies 2019). Gen Zers also understand that technology is changing the workplace. The majority (59%) do not think their current jobs will exist in the same form twenty years from now. In terms of learning style, Gen Z learners prefer a fully self-directed and independent approach to learning (see Fig. 6.2).

Next, we looked at how the national systems of education and government initiatives in Russia and the United States are responding to the needs of the new generation of digital natives.

6.2 National Missions and Competencies: Similarities Rule

The mission of the US Department of Education is "to promote student achievement and preparation for global competitiveness by fostering educational excellence and ensuring equal access", as stated on the US Department of Education official website. In 2018, the Russian Government initiated a five-year national project *Obrazovaniye* ("Education") with the aim of becoming one of the ten leading countries in terms of quality of general education. Maximizing the competitive position of leading Russian universities in the areas of education, scientific research and innovation is another major goal, as stated by the Head of Project, Vasilyeva Olga, Minister of Education of the Russian Federation (2018).

Russia, like the United States, strives for competence-based, results-oriented and more measurable higher education. Special reforms and ratings are being introduced to boost competitiveness among universities in the global academic and professional markets. As part of the Soviet legacy, the majority of institutions of higher education (78%) are fully or partially funded by the federal government (Makeeva 2018). Therefore, the implementation of new initiatives and directives is highly centralized. To date, Russia has launched multiple projects to support industry sectors, regional universities, and science and research sectors. The Academic Excellency Project 5–100, launched in 2014, focuses on high-ranking Russian universities to improve their international ratings, including the Quacquarelli Symonds (QS) World University Rankings and Times Higher Education (THE). A number of other government-funded social and educational programmes help universities reach newly articulated

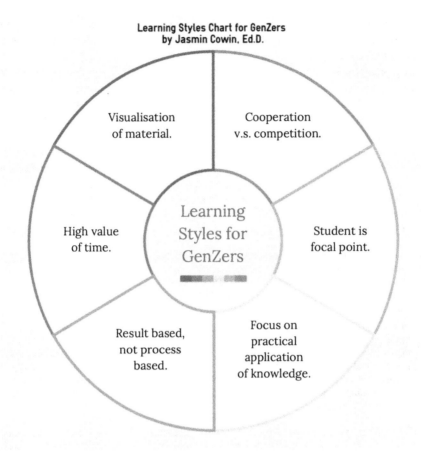

Fig. 6.2 Generation Z learning styles by Jasmin Cowin

goals, including 'Flagship Universities', 'University 20.35' and others (Agency of Strategic Innovations n.d.; Ministry of Science and Higher Education 2018).

In Russia, as in the US, language teacher qualification standards for schoolteachers, including language teachers, are more formalized than standards for university faculty. In the United States, institutions of higher education operate with considerable independence and autonomy. Compared to most other higher education systems around the world, the US system is largely decentralized and independent of regulation by the federal government. The Carnegie classification system divides all accredited degree-granting institutions by factors like the highest degree granted or special fields of study offered. Organizations such as the American Association of State Colleges and Universities are crucial in the development of national guidelines and directions. Institutions in this association award approximately 65% of public, four-year Bachelor's degrees in education each year. In Russia, as of 2018, two government bodies regulate national standards, develop education strategies and perform accreditation and supervision: the Ministry of Education, which is responsible for schools; and the Ministry of Science and Higher Education of the Russian Federation, which is responsible for universities.

The guidelines and professional standards for Russia's higher education teachers include general non-disciplinary skills and qualifications that are required in order to be hired. However, Russia has no unified system of vocational training for foreign language teachers. At universities, it is often up to the administration and management to establish and implement their own standards. English language teachers who are engaged in international or language-focused programmes commonly adhere to European frameworks of professional standards, such as the Cambridge English Language Assessment, Teaching English Continuing Professional Development, English as a New Language Standards (National Board for Professional Teaching Standards), or Standards for ESL/EFL Teachers of Adults Framework (Teachers of English to Speakers of Other Languages). According to Muzafarova et al. (2015):

> One of the most probable reasons for this situation is the lack of a unified (at the country level) system of vocational training for foreign language teachers, which would take into account the experience of leading domestic and foreign experts in EFL and which would contribute to the development of practical skills in applying modern teaching methods among future teachers.
>
> In addition, there are no uniform qualification requirements for EFL teachers as regards hiring, giving a promotion or extending an employment contract, especially at the level of higher education. In order to be employed in a university, the only condition in most cases is the formal availability of a document on specialized higher education, not necessarily pedagogical, but most often philological or linguistic. Each institution of higher education has its own regulatory documents governing certification procedures for teachers. (Muzafarova et al. 2015: 2, translation DS)

Therefore, for the purpose of comparing professional competencies for language teachers, the authors refer to the Federal State Standards of Higher Education for Skills and Competencies in Linguistics for Russia and the National Board for Professional Teaching Standards in the US.

The US Department of Education has historically provided oversight of the post-secondary accreditation system through its review of all federally recognized accrediting agencies. Accreditation is a practice in which nongovernmental, peer evaluation of educational institutions and programmes takes place to ensure a basic level of quality. The Secretary of Education determines which accrediting agencies are reliable authorities on the quality of education or training provided by institutions of higher education. The Department holds accrediting agencies accountable by ensuring that they enforce their accreditation standards effectively (US Department of Education 2019). Therefore, American educational institutions can and do vary widely in the character and quality of their programmes.

Both Russia and the US are currently reviewing their national teaching standards. As discussed previously, a centrally guided system sets standards in Russia and steers the education system to address society's needs and the country's ambitions for the coming decade. In contrast, in the US, multiple stakeholders—both national stakeholders and individual states—specify education policies and competencies (see Table 6.2).

Of great interest is that both nations have competencies for an equitable and culturally responsive practice that values students' cultural and linguistic resources.

Table 6.2 Russian and US language teaching standards (From the National Board for Professional Teaching Standards 2010, Federal State Standards of Higher Education in the subject of 'linguistics' 2016)

Russia: Professional skills and competencies for language teachers	United States: English as a new language standards
Communicative or Linguistic Competence Knowledge of the basic theoretical provisions about the language as a social phenomenon, its relationships with the mentality and culture of the people who speak it, and understanding of the etymology and development of the language. It also includes professionally oriented knowledge of a foreign language	*Standard IV:Knowledge of the English Language* Accomplished teachers have deep knowledge of the domains of language—listening, speaking, reading, writing and visual literacy—in order to assess their students' English language ability and effectively address their linguistic needs in school settings Accomplished teachers have a strong background in the components of language—phonology, vocabulary, grammar and discourse—and know how to facilitate English language learners' effective use of these components
Methodological or Linguo-Didactic Competence Knowledge of age-related features of the language acquisition process, awareness of physical and mental development processes and methods of teaching best suited to the target audience. Good grasp of a general theory of teaching and methods of teaching specialized disciplines as part of the main educational programme; the ability to use modern educational technologies in practice Willingness to use the achievements of the Russian and international methodological heritage, a good grasp of modern theories and approaches in teaching foreign languages; willingness to apply modern technologies in evaluating students' achievements with the aim of increasing their intellectual and personal development and forming intercultural communicative competence at all levels and stages of linguistic education; the ability to adjust the goals and learning content, to develop the curriculum and teaching materials, to determine the level of language skills and to assess the results achieved by students	*Standard I:Knowledge of Students* Accomplished teachers of English language learners apply their knowledge of students' language development, cultures, abilities, values, interests and aspirations to facilitate their students' linguistic, academic and social growth

(continued)

Table 6.2 (continued)

Russia: Professional skills and competencies for language teachers	United States: English as a new language standards
Sociolinguistic Competence Knowledge and ability to adequately use various functional styles in accordance with the communication situation, being aware of the national and cultural characteristics of the country of the target language, as well as possessing background knowledge of the culture, behaviours and rules that language learners are required to master	*Standard V: Knowledge of English Language Acquisition:Culture and Sociolinguistic Variables* Accomplished teachers evaluate cultural and sociolinguistic variables that affect students' language development. In identifying and responding to instructional needs of students, for example, teachers differentiate between the needs of native English speakers and the needs of English speakers from countries such as India, Liberia and Jamaica, who are learning academic language. Teachers know that cultural backgrounds create contexts in which students build frameworks for understanding English, which, in turn, facilitate English language development
Language and Information Competence The ability to work with global information search networks, internal and external professional systems and data visualization tools; awareness of syntactic and morphological analysis, automatic speech synthesis and recognition, lexicographic information processing and automated translation, automated identification and verification systems; knowledge of methods of formal and cognitive modelling of a natural language and methods of creating metalanguages; mastery of the basic mathematical and statistical methods of processing linguistic information, taking into account the elements of programming and automatic processing of linguistic corps; knowledge of standard methods of solving common types of task in the field of linguistic support in terms of information and other applied systems	*Standard IX:Professional Leadership and Advocacy* Accomplished teachers of English language learners contribute to the professional learning of their colleagues and the advancement of knowledge in their field in order to advocate for their students Accomplished teachers know and understand statistical data and research findings related to English language learners and can disseminate this information effectively. Teachers, for instance, can analyse and discuss disaggregated data including graduation rates, attendance reports, standardized test scores, and grades in content classes. They understand the implications for their instructional settings
Life-Long Learning Ability to adapt to new social and professional environments, and to acquire the new professional and personal skills required for a successful educational environment	*Standard VIII:Teacher as Learner* Accomplished teachers of English language learners are passionate about their field and consistently engage in the process of professional growth. Teachers thoughtfully evaluate their learning and apply it in their practice to maximize student success

In both nations, national and cultural characteristics are viewed as capital to build on rather than as barriers to learning. The revised Russian competencies represent a turning point, as they both reflect the importance of the traditional theory-intensive background knowledge required of new language specialists and propagate current global trends in education, such as student-centeredness, digital skills, competence-based learning, intercultural education and a global outlook. Russia's new focus on incorporating new technologies and life-long learning into education is vital if it wants to succeed in the transformative environment of disruptive change brought on by information and communications technology (ICT).

6.3 ICT, Visions and Competencies

In both nations, competencies are the bridge between traditional credit-hour measures of student achievement and the learning revolution. The authors define competency in line with the report 'Defining and Assessing Learning: Exploring Competency-Based Initiatives' as "a combination of skills, abilities, and knowledge needed to perform a specific task" (National Center for Education Statistics 2002: vii). Specific articulations of competencies inform and guide subsequent assessments at the course, programme and institutional levels. Defining competencies gives faculty and students across national boundaries, as well as other stakeholders, a common understanding of the specific skills and knowledge that learners should master. In both Russia and the US, higher education institutions and faculty use formal processes to obtain feedback on the definitions of competencies. In both nations, specific competencies provide directions for designing learning experiences and assignments to help students gain practice applying these competencies in different contexts and from country-specific cultural perspectives. Although teacher education programmes in Russia and the United States differ substantially in course descriptions and sequences, certain domains and competencies show commonalities.

Russia's federal project Digital Education Environment specifies that by 2024 Russia should create "a modern and safe digital educational environment providing high quality and accessibility of all types and levels of education" (Ministry of Science and Higher Education 2018: 1, translation DS).

New skills sets in teaching, administration and organization management are required to achieve those goals, and so are substantial funding and government support. In particular, as regards ICT skills, the Federal State Standards of Higher Education provide that future teachers obtaining Master's degrees in Foreign Languages are capable of solving communicative tasks in a foreign language communication using ICT, using ICT tools for analysis and joint creation of foreign-language media products, and using ICT tools for organizing network interaction for the purpose of foreign language communication. Some researchers are venturing even further and suggest a more fine-tuned classification of ICT skills:

Professional Competence-1 (PC): ability to use telecommunications facilities and social internet services in various communicative situations in compliance with the rules of network etiquette;

PC-2: ability to contribute critically to a collaboration; evaluate and select the content of media products in a foreign language; use media technologies to create foreign-language media products and integrate media products in a learning process;

PC-3: ability to use ICT tools for networking interaction between teachers and students, perform network project management, communicate and collaborate as part of the network community in a foreign language, select and create electronic educational resources in a foreign language, manage content and provide informational and methodological support for teaching a foreign language in an information and education environment. (Petrova 2020: 13, translation DS)

However, the general computer literacy level among Russian faculty and teachers is still far from the required level of competence which would ensure full-fledged implementation of the government initiatives at all levels of education. According to a 2017 survey by Russian Minister of Education Olga Vasilyeva, 84% of schoolteachers in Russia have low computer literacy skills (RIA News 2017). There is little official information about computer literacy among university faculty. A similarly bleak picture emerges in the United States. In 'Long Road Ahead for Digital Literacy in Higher Ed', Ravipati (2016) writes that "higher education institutions today face an increasingly pressing challenge: advancing digital literacy among students and faculty, according to a new report from the New Media Consortium" (Ravipati 2016: para 1).

One factor affecting the difficulty of implementing technology could be that faculty across national boundaries began their careers before the dawn of the Fourth Industrial Revolution and belong to the ageing Baby Boomer generation. Years ago, faculty advancement in Russia and the United States was driven by scientific input and academic publications. Digital competency was not required of Baby Boomer university faculty. Consequently, a shortage of tech-savvy professors in the humanities and social sciences has emerged.

US Secretary of Education Betsy DeVos called for educators to "rethink" school at the 2018 State Education Technology Directors Association conference. "Learning is really dynamic and spontaneous," she said (Johnston 2018: 4). "Wider use of technology can make classrooms more nimble and active, and empower students to take more control of their learning pathways."

Russia requires English teachers and faculty in both schools and universities to upgrade their teaching qualifications on a regular basis and provide certificates from state and non-state educational institutions as part of their personal professional portfolios. This requirement differs significantly from requirements in the US. Whereas US schoolteachers are subject to a teacher certification test and must amass continued professional education credits, higher education faculty do not have such obligations.

In Russia, training of university faculty members is mostly done internally based on the current needs and standards of the particular institution. Similarly, some US institutions offer internal training to faculty depending on institution-centric learning management systems or other continuing education needs. In both nations, subject matter content is gradually being adapted to digital media, including learning management systems such as Canvas, Moodle and other platforms.

Recently, more and more intercity conferences are being organized with a focus on providing peer-experience sharing and/or best-practice sharing. In 2017, the four-day conference 'The University of Tomorrow—Past, Present and Future' at Plekhanov Russian University of Economics was dedicated to the use of new technology in higher education and SLA in Russia. The Department of Foreign Languages and Communication at the National University of Science and Technology 'MISiS' organized an onsite intensive training programme in 2018 with the aim of upgrading the teaching qualifications of all faculty members. The five-day programme included workshops and seminars on course design in digital environments, and the efficient use of Canvas and other digital tools to enhance the quality of students' learning and upskill faculty.

These examples represent two different approaches to organizing teacher development training in Russia. The former was mostly aimed at raising awareness in academic circles of general trends and universal practices that often receive little or no follow-up or application within home institutions. The reasons for this may include a lack of resources or administrative support, insufficient financing, or inadequate ICT skills in general. The training session at the National University of Science and Technology 'MISiS' was planned and designed to meet the department's actual needs. The goal was to integrate innovative language teaching practices into the 2019 launch of a new Master's degree programme.

> A general trend can be traced—the emphasis on research and development as the main indicator of professional growth and little consideration of the quality of teaching in making personnel decisions. In all universities there is a formal requirement of the need to complete [continuous professional development] on a regular basis, but it is up to the teacher to decide on a topic or area for development and the means of achieving it. Moreover, the system of teacher training in universities often does not take into account the specifics of a foreign language as a subject that requires a special approach to teaching, and secondly, most of the short-term continuing education programmes do not include a practical component, being for the most part theoretical. Often such programmes are quite general and formalistic. (Muzafarova et al. 2015: 2, translation DS)

In the United States, professional teacher development is a large expenditure. According to the US Department of Education (n.d.b.),

> Nearly half of $3.0 billion in federal funding under Title II, Part A, and billions more in other federal funds goes to the professional development of teachers and leaders in our schools.

The Department's Office of English Language Acquisition provides national leadership to help ensure that English learners and immigrant students attain English proficiency and achieve academic success. Of great value and unique to the United States is the NCELA Resource Library, a searchable database of more than 20,000 items, including research articles, literature reviews, reports, classroom materials, curricula, fact sheets, multimedia products and more to help stakeholders learn about and advance their English learner education (National Clearinghouse for English Language Acquisition n.d.).

From a meta-perspective, large national US conferences with a focus on computer-assisted language learning (CALL) have become commonplace. Realities360 hosts massive conferences with industry professionals focused on exploring augmented reality and VR for training and education. Hands-On Learning BYOD (Bring Your Own Device) provides unique opportunities to apply new techniques by following an instructor step by step. Russia is still in the implementation stage, with a push to feature developing technologies not only for language acquisition, but for other academic fields.

6.4   Computer-Assisted Language Learning (CALL): Past, Present and Future

CALL encompasses a range of processes and tasks that engage computers in the teaching and learning of a new language. CALL may be defined as the search for and study of applications of the computer in language teaching and learning (Levy 1997: 1). Although the field of immersive technologies has changed significantly since 1997, educational institutions, language teachers and learners are still in the process of adapting and integrating ever-changing and evolving technologies into their traditional classrooms, online courses and augmented digital reality technology environments.

Before the advent of virtual reality (VR), augmented reality and mixed reality, CALL programs and materials were limited to those shown in Table 6.3. Before the development of affordable three-dimensional (3D) immersive learning spaces,

Table 6.3 Past computer-assisted language learning programs and materials

Programs and materials	Description
Software applications	Language learning software applications designed to develop and facilitate language learning, such as CD-ROMs, web-based interactive language learning exercises and quizzes
Web-based learning programs	Web-based learning programs, such as online dictionaries, online encyclopaedias, online concordances, news and magazine sites, e-texts, WebQuests, web publishing, blogs, wikis and so on
Generic software	Generic software, such as word-processors (Word); presentation software, such as e-books, Prezi and PowerPoint
Computer-mediated communication programs	Computer-mediated communication programs: synchronous online chat, video conferencing, asynchronous email, discussion forums, message boards, and so on

CALL activities were either one or two dimensional, often centred on activities with predetermined answers such as multiple choice or true/false quizzes, fill-in-the-blank cloze exercises, matching, sequencing, crossword puzzles, games, writing and word-processing, WebQuests, Web publishing, and synchronous or asynchronous online communication. These language teaching and acquisition activities were the same in both Russia and the United States, closely mirroring traditional classroom drill work. In addition, the technology did not require the dense bandwidth or hardware necessary for current 3D immersive environments.

Since then, the definition of educational technology and its application has changed together with the landscape of immersive learning. The Association for Educational Communications and Technology (2018) stated:

> Educational technology is the study and ethical application of theory, research, and best practices to advance knowledge as well as mediate and improve learning and performance through the strategic design, management and implementation of learning and instructional processes and resources [e.g., digital, adaptive and assistive technologies] ("The Definition and Terminology Committee").

The US Department of Education report *Evaluation of Evidence-Based Practices in Online Learning: A Meta-Analysis and Review of Online Learning Studies* stated:

> Online learning can be enhanced by giving learners control of their interactions with media and prompting learner reflection. Studies indicate that manipulations that trigger learner activity or learner reflection and self-monitoring of understanding are effective when students pursue online learning as individuals. (US Department of Education 2010: xvi)

In the United States, 48 states and the District of Columbia currently support online learning opportunities that range from supplementing classroom instruction on an occasional basis to enrolling students in full-time programmes. Although some online schools or programmes are homegrown, many others contract with private providers or other states to provide online learning opportunities. In addition, there are full-time online schools in which students are enrolled on a full-time basis. Students enrolled in these schools do not attend a brick-and-mortar school; instead, they receive all of their instruction and earn all of their credits online.

In Russian public schools there is a growing shift towards the use of digital technologies such as VR and augmented reality, which can significantly complement traditional methods and provide more profound immersion for SLA. An ambitious Russian project, the Moscow Electronic School, integrated all 555 schools in Moscow into a unified e-portal with digital resources, next-generation 3D equipment and shared educational media. Sergei Richert, senior methodologist and history and social science teacher at School No. 1788, described the Moscow Electronic School as follows:

> It is not about applications and gadgets replacing textbooks or class work with a teacher for students. It is about modern technologies, such as virtual and augmented reality, which can significantly complement traditional methods and provide a more profound immersion in the subject of study... The Moscow Electronic School is a unique combination of traditional education and digital technologies, which makes it possible to teach and learn in new ways. Two or three months ago, for trial purposes, [Moscow Institute of Open Education] presented virtual reality glasses and video content to our school. (Burlakova 2018: 1, translation DS)

Modern technologies, such as virtual and augmented reality represent the burgeoning field of 3D virtual spaces for teaching and learning. In the 1990s, the internet pioneered elements of innovation using technologies for education with an exponential growth trajectory centring on student experience, classroom management and assessment. Transitional phases shifted content delivery from face-to-face teaching to online teaching centred on distance learning through text- and video-based massive open online courses. The expansion of VR and augmented reality technology into virtual educational spaces has the potential to foster learning through simulations, digital kiosks, live virtual events, live interactivity, instructor-facilitated learning, robots driven by artificial intelligence, and hyper-realistic experiences. According to Zinchenko et al. (2010),

> Thus virtual reality systems make it possible to imitate visual, tactile and acoustic images simultaneously, which is unlikely to accomplish within the traditional paradigm of experimental psychology and which reinforces the 'truthfulness' of virtual reality environment (Zinchenko et al. 2010: 15).

6.5   Teaching, Technology and Transformation

Ray Clifford of the Defense Language Institute stated succinctly: "Computers will not replace teachers. However, teachers who use computers will replace teachers who don't" (quoted in Teachers of English to Speakers of Other Languages, Inc. 2008: 2). Both Russia and the US are undergoing major transformation in many areas, including education in general and higher education in particular. The increasing speed of development in haptics, computer simulations and VR technology "differs from the classical methods in allowing total control of the viewer's attention" (Zinchenko et al. 2010: 13). Across cultural boundaries, virtual spaces

> encourage meaning-making in situ, manipulation of virtual objects within places, and coordination among students, the relationships between design, learning, and translanguaging for learners. (Zheng et al. 2017: 107)

According to Virtual Worlds Best Practices in Education (2020):

> A virtual world is an online community that takes the form of a unique environment through which users can interact with one another and use and create ideas irrespective of time and space. Virtual worlds can be either 2D or 3D. They may be co-located or distributed. The core aspect that defines a virtual space is that a virtual environment provides a uniquely shared space for emerging relationships and serves as a foundation for the development of knowledge creation and sharing.

Place is a critical component of language acquisition; however, classrooms lack the contextual factors required for eco-dialogical translanguaging to emerge. Learners can only pretend to be where the target language is spoken, whereas in VR learners experience and remember those environments as real spaces. Classroom activities based on presence usually cannot allow the manipulation of material artefacts or collaboration with second language speakers (Velleman 2007).

Virtual worlds appear to appeal to a large segment of the population. Educators can take advantage of interest in this medium to enhance creativity in their students. (Bradford 2012: 6)

Virtual world examples include Second Life, OpenSim, Unity, Facebook, LinkedIn, Twitter, Pinterest, World of Warcraft, Eve Online and many others. These virtual environments are characterized by an open social presence where the direction of the platform's evolution is manifest in the community. This is unlike systems such as WebEx, Sococo, VenueGen and other platforms which are focused on more utilitarian goals to a closed audience.

3D simulations enable users to move freely in a simulated environment, to interact with objects, to examine elements up close at their own pace, and to explore in a fully immersive environment. When it comes to language learning and teaching, VR can tap into the physicality of language expression to enhance students' experience and interaction with their target language. Christian David Vázquez Machado, a research assistant in the Fluid Interfaces Group and a Learning Fellow in the MIT Media Lab, stated:

Due to its immersive nature and body-tracking capabilities, VR can allow learners to do kinesthetic activities in an environment that is able to track and understand their movements, provide real-time feedback, and engage them in activities within novel contexts that strongly relate to their physical actions. (Machado n.d.: 3)

3D environments also lend themselves to the implementation of all seven affordances of e-learning: ubiquitous learning, active knowledge making, multimodal meaning, recursive feedback, collaborative intelligence, metacognition, and differentiated learning with robust pathways for immersive communicative approaches in SLA.

Practical implementation of VR and AR with student-centred activities could include:

- Student created campus tours with the language objectives: using English for specific purposes and practising descriptive language.
- Creating community content maps for the local area with the language objective: writing and reading reviews using the target language in authentic contexts.
- Scavenger hunts with augmented reality experiences attached to physical locations with the language objective: understanding context clues, practising listening comprehension and procedural language.
- Augmented field trips placed at physical locations by using GPS coordinates with the language objective: giving or decoding directions.

6.6 Conclusion

Although Russia and the US have vastly different education systems and cultural dimensions, there are common denominators as both nations prepare for the advent of the Fourth Industrial Revolution and a globally competitive, twenty-first century workforce. Specifically, SLA and ways of educating tomorrow's teachers in face-to-face and online environments share great similarities. For both nations, content for language acquisition in brick-and-mortar higher education institutions is similar in terms of both delivery and presentation. Also, both nations have created ambitious directives with a focus on online and virtual environments coupled with robust implementation in degree-granting programmes. In terms of saturation and level of technology, the US implementation is more developed. However, directives from both the Russian Ministry of Education and the Ministry of Science and Higher Education clearly show a vigorous push not only to include computer skills in educational institutions, but also to advocate the use of modern educational technologies in professional teaching practice.

Global competitiveness directives in both nations might be forced to accelerate their focus on VR environments, specifically 3D virtual spaces for teaching and learning. VR technology might provide viable alternatives to the high cost of maintaining campus spaces and appeal to the Gen Zers' fluid and flexible approach to learning. For faculty specializing in language acquisition, VRs might become more common teaching arenas than traditional classroom environments.

Gen Zers are characterized by their fluency in multiple media, their preference for learning based on collectively seeking experiences rather than individually locating and absorbing information from a single best source (Bradford 2012). As the world grows more complex, with more access to more learning opportunities than at any previous time, technology provides ubiquitous opportunities in online and virtual environments. Information technology has expanded learning paths that do not lead solely to postsecondary institutions (National Center for Education Statistics 2002: 5). A growing interest in learning anywhere, any place and any time will challenge traditional educational delivery systems. Along with having expanded access, potential students are maturing into more sophisticated consumers and will grasp the concept of acquiring skills and competencies through diverse means, such as virtual or augmented environments and non-traditional micro credentials. The Wingspread Group on Higher Education noted that

> putting learning at the heart of the academic enterprise will mean overhauling the conceptual, procedural, curricular, and other architecture of postsecondary education on most campuses. (Johnson Foundation 1993: 14)

In conclusion, language study programmes, communication studies and teacher preparation programmes for second language acquisition must adapt to changing local and global marketplaces that demand agile thinking, life-long learning, and recognition of knowledge half-life. Unique technological factors such as the creation of 3D spatial representations, multisensory channels for user interaction, and intuitive interaction through natural manipulations in real time enable more holistic teaching and learning experiences. However, the field is still developing and working to adapt full online immersion teaching spaces for general use in education. Creating novel tech experiences in 3D environments promises to prepare students and institutions across national boundaries for the Fourth Industrial Revolution, which, according to Klaus Schwab, Chair of the Economic World Forum (2017), is characterized by a range of new technologies that are fusing the physical, digital and biological worlds, impacting all disciplines, economies and industries, and even challenging ideas about what it means to be human.

References

Agency of Strategic Innovations. n.d. What is University 20.35. https://2035.university/en/. Accessed 2 July 2019.

Association for Educational Communications and Technology. 2018. The definition and terminology committee. https://aect.org/aectnews.php. Accessed 16 Nov 2019

Bradford, Linda. 2012. *The viability of virtual worlds in higher education: can creativity thrive outside the traditional classroom environment?* 29012 Brigham Young University BYU Scholars Archive. https://scholarsarchive.byu.edu/cgi/viewcontent.cgi?article=4238&con text=etd. Accessed 29 Nov 2019.

Burlakova, Daria. 2018. *Virtual reality has come to school.* https://tass.ru/obschestvo/ 5000093. Accessed 3 July 2019.

Dell Technologies. 2019. *Research: The gen Z effect.* https://www.delltechnologies.com/en-us/per spectives/gen-z.htm. Accessed 18 Nov 2019.

Google. 2016. *Gen Z: A look inside its mobile-first mindset.* https://www.thinkwithgoogle.com/ interactive-report/gen-z-a-look-inside-its-mobile-first-mindset/#dive-deeper. Accessed 15 Nov 2019.

Johnson Foundation. 1993. *An American imperative: higher expectations for higher education. an open letter to those concerned about the American future. Report of the Wingspread Group on Higher Education.* Racine, WI: Johnson Foundation.

Johnston, Ryan. 2018. *DeVos: Technology enables educators to 'rethink' school.* https://edscoop. com/devos-technology-can-allow-educators-to-rethink-school/. Accessed 11 Nov 2019.

Kluckhohn, Florence R., Fred L. Strodtbeck, and John M. Roberts. 1961. *Variations in value orientations.* Evanston, IL: Row Peterson.

Levy, Michael. 1997. *Computer-assisted language learning: context and conceptualization.* New York, NY: Oxford University Press.

Machado, Christian David Vázquez. n.d. *Kinesthetic language learning in virtual reality.* https:// www.media.mit.edu/posts/kinesthetic-language-learning-in-virtual-reality/. Accessed 10 Nov 2019.

Makeeva, Anna. 2018. *Half of universities expelled in Russia.* https://www.kommersant.ru/doc/354 0086. Accessed 1 Aug 2019.

Ministry of Science and Higher Education. 2018. *The national project 'education'.* https://www.min obrnauki.gov.ru/common/upload/library/2019/07/NP_Obrazovanie.htm. Accessed 1 Aug 2019.

Ministry of Science and Higher Education. 2015. *On approval of the federal state standards of higher education in the subject of 'pedagogy'.* http://fgosvo.ru/uploadfiles/fgosvob/440301.pdf. Accessed 12 July 2019.

Ministry of Science and Higher Education of the Russian Federation. 2018a. *5–100 Russian Academic Excellence Projects.* https://5top100.ru/en/. Accessed 23 July 2019.

Ministry of Science and Higher Education of the Russian Federation. 2018b. *Support universities RF.* http://flagshipuniversity.ntf.ru/universities. Accessed 2 July 2019.

Muzafarova, Anna D., Tatiana P. Rasskazova, and Natalya O. Verbitskaya. 2015. *Comparative analysis of international standards for teaching a foreign language in the context of competencies of a modern specialist.* https://www.science-education.ru/pdf/2015/3/571.pdf. Accessed 3 July 2019.

National Board for Professional Teaching Standards. 2010. *English as a New Language Standard.* https://www.nbpts.org/wp-content/uploads/ECYA-ENL.pdf. Accessed 26 Sept 2019.

National Center for Education Statistics. 2002. *Defining and assessing learning: exploring competency-based initiatives (NCES 2002–159)*. Washington, DC: National Center for Education Statistics.

National Clearinghouse for English Language Acquisition. n.d. *Resource library*. https://www.ncela.ed.gov/resource-library. Accessed 01 Nov 2019.

Petrova, N. V. 2020. *The methodology of forming ICT competency for future master degree students with a major in foreign languages on the basis of social constructivist approach*. http://research.sfu-kras.ru/sites/research.sfu-kras.ru/files/Avtoreferat_Petrova.pdf. Accessed 3 July 2020.

Ravipati, Sri. 2016. *Long road ahead for digital literacy in higher education*. https://campustechnology.com/articles/2016/11/08/long-road-ahead-for-digital-literacy-in-higher-ed.aspx. Accessed 19 Oct 2019.

RIA News. 2017. *Vasilieva: Only 16% of teachers have good computer skills*. https://sn.ria.ru/20171222/1511515019.html. Accessed 22 Sept 2019.

Schwab, Charles. 2017. *World economic forum*. https://www.weforum.org/about/the-fourth-industrial-revolution-by-klaus-schwab. Accessed 12 Nov 2019.

Teachers of English to Speakers of Other Languages, Inc. 2008. *TESOL technology standards framework*. https://www.tesol.org/docs/default-source/books/bk_technologystandards_framework_721.pdf. Accessed 15 Oct 2019.

US Department of Education. n.d.b. *Teacher professional and career development*. https://www.ed.gov/oii-news/teacher-professional-and-career-development. Accessed 22 Sept 2019.

US Department of Education. 2010. *Evaluation of evidence-based practices in online learning: A meta-analysis and review of online learning studies*. https://www2.ed.gov/rschstat/eval/tech/evidence-based-practices/finalreport.pdf. Accessed 18 Nov 2019.

US Department of Education. 2019. *Accreditation in the United States*. https://www2.ed.gov/admins/finaid/accred/accreditation.html#Overview. Accessed 15 Oct 2019.

Velleman, David J. 2007. Bodies selves. *SSRN Electronic Journal* 2019. https://doi.org/10.2139/ssrn.1006884.Accessed22Sept.

Virtual worlds best practices in education. 2020. https://www.vwbpe.org/about-vwbpe. Accessed 22 April 2020.

Zheng, Dongping, Matthew M. Schmidt, Ying Hu, Min Liu, and Jesse Hsu. 2017. Eco-dialogical learning and translanguaging in open-ended 3D virtual learning environments: Where place, time, and objects matter. *Australasian Journal of Educational Technology* 33. https://doi.org/10.14742/ajet.2909.

Zinchenko, Yuri P., Galina Y. Menshikova, Yuri M. Bayakovsky, Alexandr M. Chernorizov, and Alexander E. Voiskounsky. 2010. Technologies of virtual reality in the context of worldwide and Russian psychology: Methodology, comparison with traditional methods, achievements and perspectives. *Psychology in Russia: State of the Art* 1: 11–45.

Digital Literacy Resources

Association of College and Research Libraries Information Literacy Competency Standards for Higher Education (go.nmc.org/alainfolit). The Association of College and Research Libraries provides a framework for assessing and developing information on pedagogical practices for literacy in postsecondary education.

Common Sense Media: Copyright and Fair Use (https://www.go.nmc.org/commsense).

Digital Pedagogy Lab (go.nmc.org/digpedlab). The Digital Pedagogy Lab offers new approaches to teaching with technology and professional development.

Jisc Digital Capability Codesign Challenge Blog (go.nmc.org/digcapa). This blog has a wealth of resources for helping build digital literacies, specifically with regard to leadership, pedagogy and efficiencies.

Open University of British Columbia: Open Education Accessibility Toolkit (go.nmc.org/openubc). This Open Educational Resources Accessibility Toolkit offers suggestions for creating accessible content for educators.

Wikimedia Foundation: What is Creative Commons? (go.nmc.org/wikifound). This short video overview with related resources explains and models how to share creative works using a Creative Commons license.

Chapter 7
Corpus Technologies in Teaching English to Speakers of Other Languages

Natalya Koshkarova

Abstract This paper examines the ways in which corpus technologies may be used while teaching English to speakers of other languages. It indicates the advantages and disadvantages of using national corpora in the language classroom. The author indicates the factors affecting the application of corpus technologies, including the level of a teacher's proficiency, the native language of the students, the relevance of the internet-based instruments to the needs of those who study a foreign language, and the current situation in lessons. The author employs the following scientific mechanisms: literature review, analysis of the study guides created on the basis of the language corpora, overview of the exercises constructed with the help of the corpus, and suggests for a system of tasks and instructions to be used in the language classroom. Information and communication technologies (ICT) in teaching English as a foreign language can be used not only at the initial stage (level A1, A2), but also at more advanced levels (B1, B2, C1, C2). The author distinguishes the different areas of the corpus pedagogy, describes three approaches to creating corpus-based exercises, and provides the samples of exercises created on the basis of the Michigan Corpus of Upper-Level Student Papers. The author comes to the conclusion that corpus technologies can serve not only linguistic but also linguo-didactic goals.

Keywords Corpus technologies · Teaching English · Speakers of other languages · Internet-based instrument · Corpora dissemination

7.1 Introduction

There is enormous and wide scope for using language corpora by those who study and teach language: on the one hand, linguists have a great opportunity to study the usage of various speech phenomena by native speakers, and on the other hand corpora can be used as a valuable tool of empirical character and for pedagogical purposes. If we speak about corpus linguistics as a separate branch of linguistics,

N. Koshkarova (✉)
South Ural State University, Chelyabinsk, Russia
e-mail: nkoshka@rambler.ru

© The Author(s), under exclusive license to Springer Nature Switzerland AG 2021
N. V. Sukhova et al. (eds.), *Multimodality, Digitalization and Cognitivity in Communication and Pedagogy*, Numanities - Arts and Humanities in Progress 20, https://doi.org/10.1007/978-3-030-84071-6_7

then the metalinguistic description of the phenomena presented in the corpus should be taken into account. With this aim, an author's search query should be as accurate as possible, and scientists should pay attention to the semantic differences between search words, and differentiate between the cultural and semiotic parameters of the terms used to study different phenomena with the help of the corpus. Curzan (2012: 11) singles out the following levels at which a scientist can exploit the language corpora: corpus linguistic methods.

> ...could help identify texts worthy of investigation now that so much is online; they could help provide systematicity to the cataloguing of linguistic features; and they could potentially reveal new patterns of co-occurrence.

It should be noted that corpus linguistics is not limited to the study of the discursive implementation of axiologically marked phenomena. Another important area of corpora application is in teaching foreign languages (for example, English as a foreign language, Russian as a foreign language, etc.). McEnery and Wilson (1997: 7) acknowledge the necessity of using national corpora while teaching foreign languages. The authors point out that in the corpus-based classroom there has been a.

> ...shift of emphasis away from the didactic pedagogue towards the fellow researcher, which has been so prevalent in higher education for several decades.

The role of national corpora while teaching and learning English and other foreign languages can hardly be overestimated. According to Alqadoumi (2013: 247),

> ... corpus linguistics grants access to real or authentic linguistic data, it allows teachers to design materials and educational activities that are considered very important to language learners.

Those who advocate introducing corpus technologies into the process of language teaching describe numerous areas of corpora dissemination in a foreign language classroom. Römer (2011: 205–210) lists the following spheres of pedagogical corpus applications: (1) syllabi design; (2) examining "language items in actual language use" and comparing "the distributions and patterns found in general reference corpora (of speech and/or writing) with the presentations of the same items in teaching materials (course books, grammars, and usage handbooks)"; (3) designing reference works and teaching materials; and the (4) direct application of corpus, or data-driven learning-DDL.

The problem of data-driven learning has garnered substantial attention from scholars recently. Scientists discuss the advantages and disadvantages of this approach from the pedagogical perspective (Boulton 2012; Lee 2011), describe this technique as a method of improving language proficiency (Chen et al. 2019; Talai and Fotovatnia 2012), and analyse data-driven learning in teaching different aspects of the language (Luo and Zhou 2017; Marinov 2015; Nugraha et al. 2017). The issue of implementing corpora technologies has been rather comprehensively investigated and scrutinised. There are still some drawbacks and limitations to using national corpora in the process of teaching languages. Römer (2011: 206) evaluates the correlation between the theory and practice of using corpus technologies; the scholar is.

> …hesitant to say that corpora and corpus tools have been fully implemented in pedagogical contexts … [and she] … would argue that much work still remains to be done in bridging the gap between research and practice.

One question that needs to be asked is how to introduce corpora technologies into a language classroom, taking into account the level of the teacher's proficiency, the native language of the students, the relevance of the internet-based instruments to the needs of those who study a foreign language, and the current situation of the lesson.

The aim of the present paper is to give an overview of the ways in which corpus technologies can be and are used in the process of teaching English to speakers of other languages, endeavour to create a system of corpus-based exercises to be used in the English classroom and to outline future directions for implementing corpus methods.

7.2 Data and Methodological Approach

The goal of this research is to offer possible ways to implement corpus technologies while teaching English and to justify the validity of these methods in the process of second language acquisition. The most suitable approach is through a literature review, analysis of the study guides created on the basis of the language corpora, overview of the exercises constructed with the help of the corpus, and introduction of a system of tasks and instructions to be used in the language classroom. The validity and reliability of this methodology is justified by the need to fill a gap which was created due to insufficient elaboration of the system of corpus-based methods in teaching English to Russian speakers. The following language corpora were used, with the intention of promoting corpus technologies in the Russian educational environment: *British National Corpus* (BNC), the *Corpus of Contemporary American English* (COCA), the *Michigan Corpus of Academic Spoken English* (MICASE). The initial assumption is that the national corpus of any language is a kind of guide for the language being studied. Students can find spelling and punctuation rules in the corpus, the lexical meaning of the word and its compatibility, the stylistic norms of a particular register, the language norms of a certain historical era, idioms, collocations, phrasal verbs, and so on.

Any language corpus can be treated as a kind of language environment, the main characteristics of which (representativeness, balance, significant size, electronic form of existence, annotation) make it possible to use it as an effective tool for forming language skills in the process of teaching. A novel step in the present research is the attempt to help teachers be at ease with the corpus tools, and guide them in compiling exercises based on the corpus. Providing a solid and valid description of the corpus technologies and their practical implications will ensure that the process of teaching

English to speakers of other languages will be closer to real life, reflect the true-to-life usage of language phenomena, and enhance student interest in studying English.

7.3 Results and Discussion

Corpus technologies can be seen as a type of information and communication technology (ICT) and "considered as an effective tool for developing practical skills in mastering a foreign language when organizing students' independent work" (Bazarova 2015: 88). ICT in teaching English as a foreign language can be used not only at the initial stage (level A1, A2), but also at more advanced levels (B1, B2, C1, C2). The following points can be distinguished among the advantages of using ICT in lessons of English as a foreign language:

- the availability of electronic educational content in the public domain during the educational process of students;
- providing feedback to teachers and students, as well as between students;
- exchange of knowledge between teachers and students, as well as between students;
- mobile access for receiving all types of digital services anywhere in the world and at any time;
- creation, formation, consolidation and development of a new type of knowledge, skills, abilities and competencies;
- creating a smart environment which is in many aspects similar or identical to natural intelligence;
- flexible individualised learning in an interactive educational environment;
- comprehensive modernisation of all educational processes, teaching methods and technologies;
- management of the formation of new knowledge, skills, abilities and competencies in the educational information environment (Khromov et al. 2015: 76–77).

National language corpora are freely available, and anyone studying a foreign language can easily take advantage of the huge array of relevant speech material which is presented in the corpus. Secondly, the corpus provides a unique opportunity to compile a wide range of exercises based on authentic material which can be used for practical and linguo-didactic purposes, not only by the teacher but also by the student. Thirdly, the corpus allows teaching all types of speech activity, providing the transfer of knowledge and skills from one type of speech behaviour to another (i.e. from reading to listening or from writing to speaking). National language corpora can also meet the needs of modern students, who are the product of "global computerisation". Finally, corpus technologies present a unique opportunity to overcome the perennial problem of textbooks and teaching materials—the obsolescence of teaching material content.

The following areas are distinguished in the corpus pedagogy:

- compilation of teaching materials on the basis of national language corpora;
- compilation and analysis of learner corpora;
- the use of the corpora as educational material.

We are strongly convinced that compilation of teaching materials on the basis of national language corpora in the methodology of teaching English should be given the highest priority since the creation of a teacher's own exercises should be based on the fundamental principles of corpus linguodidactics. This principle includes a review of the existing experience and adapting the skills being acquired to the specific needs and interests of students. Teachers of English are well acquainted with the textbooks designed on the basis of corpus technology. The grammar manual *Longman Grammar of Spoken and Written English* first published by Longman in 1999 should be singled out as a descriptive English grammar, written by Biber et al. (1999). The *Cambridge Grammar of English* (Carter and McCarthy 2007) is a manual which was also compiled based on the corpora and contains some seven thousand examples of grammatical phenomena from spoken and written English.

These manuals were both published several decades ago and have already passed the test of time. Recent manuals created on the basis of the corpus include the *Grammar and Beyond* textbook published by Cambridge University Press (Reppen and Vrabel 2011). This manual consists of four levels, each of which contains examples of real usage of the language, since the Cambridge English Corpus was used as the basis for compiling the textbook. Another advantage of this textbook is that students learn to correct mistakes, since the second corpus resource used in the design of this manual was the Cambridge Learner Corpus, which contains real English learner mistakes. The Cambridge Learner Corpus served as the basis for a long-term research programme, the English Profile Programme (The English Profile Programme URL) (Profile and Programme 2019). The use of such corpus materials (learner corpus—corpus of student texts, student corpus) helps to understand.

> …what grammatical topics are simple for all learners of a particular language, and what remains difficult even for those who speak the language as a second mother tongue. (Kopotev 2014: 103)[1]

Despite the use of the word 'grammar' in the title of the textbook *Grammar and Beyond*, it is aimed at developing all four language skills: reading, listening, speaking, and writing. For this purpose the manual contains a large number of exercises to help students grasp grammar constructions in the process of completing assignments for the development of a written skill, which is then improved by performing interactive exercises online.

The author of the course "Introduction to Corpus Linguistics" (Introduction to Corpus Linguistics 2018) A.I. Levinson notes that there are three approaches to creating corpus-based exercises: the easy way, the hard way, and data-driven learning (DDL).

Let us offer a step-by-step description of each of these methods.

"Easy way"

---

[1] Hereinafter the translation from Russian into English is done by the author.

1. The teacher selects the group of texts in which they will search, according to pre-selected criteria, for the language phenomena to be mastered in the process of teaching.
2. The teacher sets the appropriate search parameters in the corpus, such as a certain subcorpora, grammar criteria, etc.
3. The teacher chooses a number of examples as a basis for making exercises for use in the class-room.
4. The teacher simplifies the examples, excluding information that is not relevant to the solution of a particular linguo-didactic problem.
5. The teacher presents the selected examples in the form of exercises which are then used in lessons to develop a specific skill.

"Hard way"

1. The teacher formulates a question, the answer to which can be found in the corpus.
2. The teacher invites the students to follow the steps which the teacher has already completed:

   – set a search query;
   – select examples;
   – draw conclusions.

3. The teacher evaluates the student's work depending on how accurately they repeated the actions and conclusions of the teacher.

Data-Driven Learning (DDL)

1. The teacher sets the student a task that requires research using corpus data. The student may choose material for research on their own.
2. The teacher offers the student a detailed research plan.
3. The student begins to collect material.
4. The student processes the data received and formulates their own conclusions which may differ from those proposed by the teacher.
5. The results of the analysis are presented in the form of a mini-study.

The first way of using corpora in the process of teaching English to the speakers of other languages seems to be the most beneficial, since it (1) enhances a student's awareness of how words and grammar phenomena "work" in context; (2) provides miscellaneous examples of authentic language usage; (3) expands understanding of how language units function in the process of speech production, taking into account their form and meaning; (4) lets the students master their language skills by spotting errors in language usage by native speakers and those who study it as foreign speakers; (5) enables those who study a foreign language to differentiate between prescriptive speech phenomena and occasional variants.

The "Easy Way" of using corpus technologies is thus advantageous and is widely used in the practice of compiling textbooks, dictionaries, and other educational materials. However, any teacher of a foreign language (English, for instance) has the opportunity to develop their own materials based on the national corpus for use in classroom work depending on their level of training, professional orientation, and the skills being formed. Linguists and teachers of English widely use the *British National Corpus (BNC)*, the *Corpus of Contemporary American English (COCA)*, and the *Michigan Corpus of Academic Spoken English (MICASE)* (*MICASE* 2019). Such representative corpora can form the basis for each teacher to compose a subject corpus which includes not only a verbal, but also a multi-media component (video, image, sound).

It's worth noting the algorithm or the steps an ESL teacher should take while creating exercises based on the language corpora. One way to employ corpus technologies is to use 'raw' corpus as described by Hunston (2002: 172), but it requires much effort and proficiency on the part of a teacher to be able to develop exercises based on such material. It means that no preparatory work is done and the teacher gives students a task to be fulfilled using the corpora. The teacher should be experienced enough to formulate a task that can be accurately understood and performed by the students.

It is better to do some planning and preparatory work, however, which includes selecting a part of the corpus relevant to the topic; formulating research questions based on the section of the selected corpus which is relevant to, and coherent with, the teaching task and acquired skills and qualifications; retrieving and presenting the speech material on the basis of which the educational and training needs will be met; compiling the exercises based on the chosen concordance lines; introducing the exercises to the students and giving instructions; controlling the task; evaluating the students' fulfilment of the exercises and giving meaningful comment and feedback.

In spite of the plethora of advantages of corpus technologies, using computer-based techniques in the ESL classroom should have a greater purpose: providing knowledge about the authentic usage of a language and empowering students with the tools to work with large amounts of information.

Let us examine some of the exercises which can be developed with the help of *the Michigan Corpus of Academic Spoken English (MICASE)* (Fig. 7.1).

The MICASE corpus is a spoken language corpus of approximately 1.7 million words (nearly 200 h) focusing on contemporary university speech within the microcosm of the University of Michigan, in Ann Arbor, Michigan. This is a typical large public research university with about 37,000 students, approximately one-third of whom are graduate students. The speakers represented in the corpus include faculty, staff, and all levels of students, and native, near-native and non-native speakers (MICASE Manual 2003). It would seem that the corpus includes only those speech events that are somehow connected with the academic sphere: those associated with scientists and professors, scholars and people of letters. In the case of the Michigan Corpus of Academic Spoken English the term 'academic' is interpreted more widely and broadly: the corpus includes a large number of speech events that take place on campus. These events include small and large lectures, public interdisciplinary or departmental colloquia, student presentations, discussion sections, seminars, undergraduate lab sessions, office hours, study groups, lab groups and other meetings such as advising consultations.

Fig. 7.1 Michigan corpus of academic spoken English (MICASE)

The MICASE corpus also meets other requirements that should be taken into account when analysing speech phenomena: speech events include monologues and dialogues; students and faculty members; native, near-native, and non-native speakers of English; and male and female speakers.

There are two modes for exploring the MICASE corpus on-line: 'Browse' and 'Search'. When the teacher is looking for some type of language they can make a query according to the following criteria (Browse Mode): speech event parameters (type of event, academic division, academic discipline, participant level, and discourse mode); characteristics (gender, age, academic position/role, and native language) of any speaker participating in the event; and/or a word or phrase of interest (Fig. 7.2).

In the search mode of the MICASE corpus a teacher must first specify a word or phrase of interest. Teachers can also specify the attributes of the speech event (type of event, academic division, academic discipline, participant level, and discourse mode) in which the utterance occurs, characteristics of the speaker (gender, age group, academic position/role, and native language) uttering the key word or phrase, and/or a word or phrase that must appear within a specified proximity to the search word(s) (Fig. 7.3). As seen from the description, both modes have some similarities and many differences. In both modes a teacher can: (1) select more than one item in a speech event or speaker attribute category; and (2) view the entire transcript.

The following exercise was designed on the basis of the MICASE corpus.

1. Look at the sentences and say what part of speech the word *subject* belongs to:

*… even a conservative tracer though, will be **subject** to some other sorts of processes, that will create, a pathway that will be slightly different than the the average water flow …*

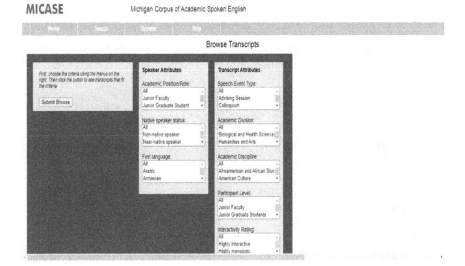

Fig. 7.2 Browse mode of MICASE

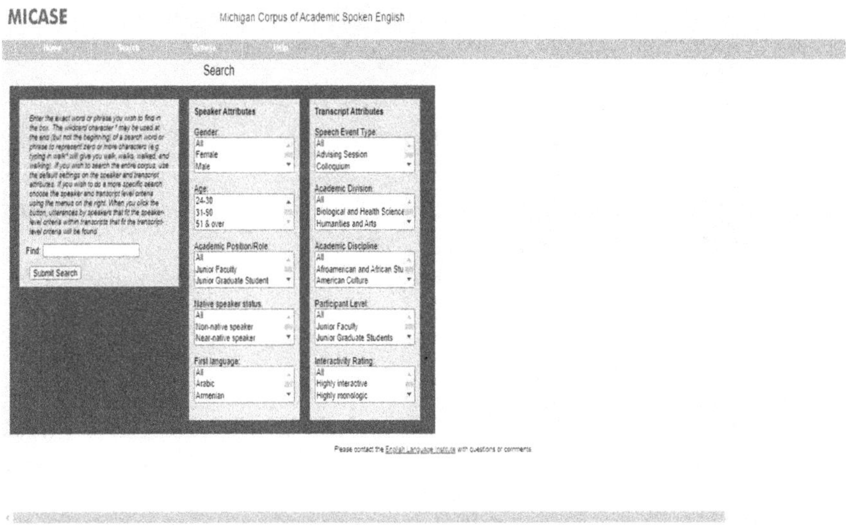

Fig. 7.3 Search mode of MICASE

… well let's back it up once, if i see Hysperides erant, i know i've got my **subject** *and my verb right?*

… well those kinds of things and this? actually Jeffery, Burks and i'm, doing a study about, indirectness in in communication what we did, was to give **subject***, a vague, verbal evaluation, and we asked subject to, translate that verbal evaluation*

into scales. and we found that Americans student tend to take that verbal evaluation directly at face value, so they made errors. because they couldn't see he didn't …

2. Look at the following concordance lines for the word 'subject' and match the meaning of each use with definitions 1, 2, 3, 4 and 5:

Meaning 1: a person or thing that is being discussed, described, or dealt with

Lines: ……………………………………………………………………………………

Meaning 2: the person or thing that performs the action of a verb, or is joined to a description by a verb.

Lines: ……………………………………………………………………………………

Meaning 3: a branch of knowledge studied or taught in a school, college, or university.

Lines: ……………………………………………………………………………………

Meaning 4: likely or prone to be affected by (a particular condition or occurrence, typically an unwelcome or unpleasant one).

Lines: ……………………………………………………………………………………

Meaning 5: cause or force someone or something to undergo (a particular experience or form of treatment, typically an unwelcome or unpleasant one).

Lines: ……………………………………………………………………………………

a   *…now of course, this is **subject** to change because once the agents receive these price quotes, they may want to submit new bids.*

b   *… but there's a lot of suspicion that grows there, and the target with a **subject** to a given threat or is su- **subject** to to suppression …*

c   *it might be **subject** to that because um, one of my best friends is actually taking this class.*

d   *…no you know we we don't want to get involved in this we don't want to, be subject to Iraqi aggression …*

e   *was working for Exame and i was writing for Exame this same kind of subject.*

f   *…think of a straight line, is, the shortest distance between two points. a straight line is your, **subject**, shortest distance between two points is your predicate. is the predicate already in the **subject**?*

g   *for those of you who know French as you know modern French, the use of the **subject** pronoun is obligatory you cannot drop the subject pronoun …*

h   *… so if there're no distortions externalities taxes, uh we should be getting this, maximized, **subject** to the constraints… well, the aggregate production function …*

i   *…. and, another problem is, that he's often misrepresented and simplified, by both folks who… are Marxist or claim to be Marxist and by folks who, oppose Marxism. it's a very political, **subject**.*

j *...any loads carried on asperities, is **subject**to the considerations of you know of dry wear or something like that the Archard type of wear.*

k *...the airplane has two processors on it and that's not **subject**to expansion so we certainly have computational resource limits.*

l *no and the election was like so close that, they would have voted for Nader then the election was so close as it is, that this is like a, sticky **subject**.*

m *now, even a conservative tracer though, will be **subject**to some other sorts of processes, that will create, a pathway that will be slightly different than the the average water flow.*

n ***subject**to the EC's agreement, we intend to set up an enterprise zone in the area.*

One more corpus was developed at the English Language Institute. It is *the Michigan Corpus of Upper-Level Student Papers (MICUSP)* (Michigan Corpus Of Upper-Level Student Papers 2020) which is a collection of around 830 A grade papers (roughly 2.6 million words) from a range of disciplines across four academic divisions (Humanities and Arts, Social Sciences, Biological and Health Sciences, Physical Sciences) at the University of Michigan (Fig. 7.4).

In order to compile an exercise based on *the Michigan Corpus of Upper-Level Student Papers (MICUSP)* a teacher might select a student level (which ranges from senior undergraduate to third year graduate), the student's self-identification of their native English speaker status (native English speaker vs. non-native English speaker), textual features (abstract, definitions, discussion of results, literature review,

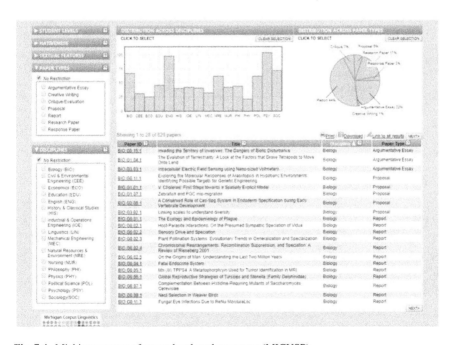

Fig. 7.4 Michigan corpus of upper-level student papers (MICUSP)

methodology section, problem-solution pattern, reference to sources, tables, graphs or figures), paper types (argumentative essay, creative writing, critique or evaluation, proposal, report, research paper, response paper), or disciplines (Biology—BIO, Civil and Environmental Engineering—CEE, Economics—ECO, Education—EDU, English—ENG, History and Classical Studies—HIS, Industrial and Operations Engineering—IOE, Linguistics—LIN, Mechanical Engineering—MEC, Natural Resources and Environment—NRE, Nursing—NUR, Philosophy—PHI, Physics—PHY, Political Science—POL, Psychology—PSY, Sociology—SOC).

As seen from the above-mentioned criteria, any user of *MICUSP* is offered a great variation across disciplines, paper types and student levels. A teacher might target any discipline and any paper type in the process of designing exercises based on the corpus. For instance, if we search for collocations of the word *education* then we obtain two graphs showing the distribution of the lexical unit's usage across disciplines and across paper types (Fig. 7.5). Then we can click to select the connection of two parameters restricting the query to a definite discipline (e.g., English) and a type of paper (e.g. argumentative essay) (Fig. 7.6).

MICUSP offers a great variety of opportunities to compile assignments for use in the process of teaching different aspects of English as a foreign language: grammar, speaking, academic writing, and so on. For instance, the purpose of academic writing as part of teaching ESL might be the formation of a learner's skills using a foreign language in the professional sphere, as well as obtaining, expanding, and deepening knowledge about the language. To achieve this goal, it is necessary to carry out

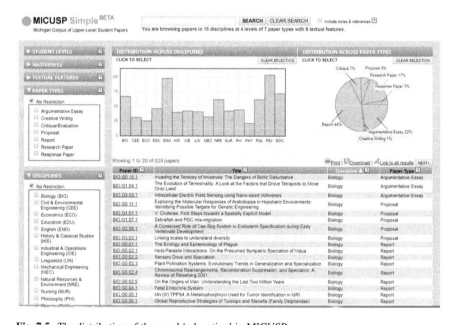

Fig. 7.5 The distribution of the word 'education' in MICUSP

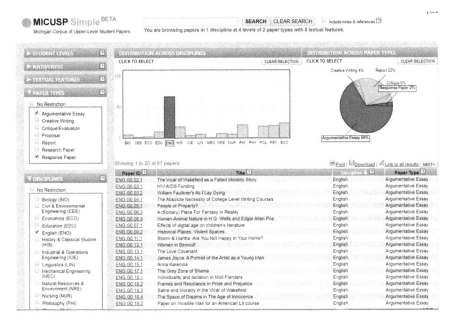

Fig. 7.6 The restriction of a query to a discipline and a type of paper

tasks aimed at developing appropriate cultural and professional competencies among students. The acquired competencies will enable graduates:

- to perceive and process the information in a foreign language obtained from printed, audiovisual and electronic sources of information within the framework of the socio-political sphere and doing business;
- to conduct a conversation in a foreign language, participate in discussions, speak publicly on topics within the professional sphere of communication, use speech etiquette correctly;
- to successfully conduct negotiations in a foreign language;
- to perform the functions of a translator and an interpreter;
- to continue professional training and carry out professional activities in a foreign language environment.
- Although *MICUSP* is corpus of written texts, not oral speech the affinity of all types of speech activity (reading, writing, listening, and speaking) mean that the language corpus under discussion enables teachers and students to become proficient not only in producing written texts but in speaking as well.

Below are examples of the exercises that can be compiled on the basis of *MICUSP*.

1.   Find the mistakes in the sentences.

Therefore, by investigating the relationship between the educations of women aged 41–64 and their fertility behavior I could possibly answer whether or not China would be left in this economic growth.

The phrase, the moral of the story, has arose from a tradition of using stories to teach morals.

His wife seems more conniving that pious.

This could be due to the rising importance of the marriage market within the middle class, however it is cited many times within the book that the woman are able to read, and that this fact improves their worth.

Generally, principals are highly qualified people who have a vast amount of knowledge about problems that arise in schools.

2.   Choose the correct option.

*A similar **effect/affect** can be observed in environmental systems: we are in danger of losing our global biodiversity to a monotonous fate.*

*Certainly, of course, the fish could have merely come up to the surface to **breath/breathe** air and survived that way, but as Sayer and Davenport (1991) pointed out, many modern-day fish do leave anoxic waters.*

*The convergence of continents would decrease the amount of coastlines and lower global **sea/see** level.*

*Finally, in certain cultures, particularly in India, it is sinful to harm rats, so they are often **allowed/aloud** entry or habitation in dwellings, making plague infections much more likely.*

*It's like this –let's say you don't know how to drive a car and I'm gonna teach you. I can say, 'Well, you're gonna have to do this, you're gonna have to press down on the **break/brake**, and throw it in drive,' but after a while, I can't do too much more talking. You're gonna have to get behind the wheel and do it yourself.*

3.   Correct the word in bold type.

*According to her, the employees wasted paper and hence as a cost cutting measure, she decided to take charge of the office **stationary**.*

*Furthermore, in reality colleges tend to admit more applicants than they actually expect will **except** their offers.*

*Later a policy will be formulated to support the new technology and to **insure** that full benefit of the technology is utilized.*

*Within a five **weak** period in late August and September, over 38,000 people were killed, and by February 1666 close to 100,000 were dead in London alone (Gregg, 1985).*

*There are many wild reservoir hosts of plague, but only a few will be discussed **hear**.*

4.   Fill in the blanks with the correct word.

habitat/habitant

This intense competition would have been a strong evolutionary push for tetrapods to find another suitable ....

reach/rich

The evolution of terrestrial tetrapods has certainly sparked much discussion over the years, and deservedly so, for a ... terrestrial vertebrate fauna of about 360 million years is contingent on this event.

passed/past

Although one male dolphin may not mate with the female, some of his genes will be ... on to the next generation if a close relative mates with her.

addition/edition

In ..., they explore the implications of ecosystem alterations and the threat of extinction on the more specialized mutualists.

wait/weight

The Commission's report highlights many of the challenges that face higher education today and in the near future and provides recommendations to combat these issues rather than ... for their arrival.

The examples of exercises compiled on the basis of the language corpora show that it can serve not only linguistic but also linguo-didactic purposes, combining functional and onomasiological aspects in the study of a foreign language. Corpus technologies allow teachers and students to consider not only normal but also contextual usage of various language phenomena, their correlations and representations in real language usage. English teachers should understand how the knowledge of different language phenomena is implemented in various types of discourse and how it relates to the native language system of the students who are exposed to a foreign language. English language students' cognitive and cultural patterns acquire special importance in modern educational circumstances when it is necessary to develop methods of teaching English to foreign students from different nations and cultures.

7.4   Conclusion

Using corpus technologies in teaching English to speakers of other languages breaks new ground as it gives the teachers an opportunity to develop materials based on real language usage, makes the process of teaching more effective, and facilitates the cognitive abilities of the teacher and the students. In this paper we presented examples of exercises compiled by an English teacher for use in the classroom. It should be noted, however, that corpus can also be effectively used by the students themselves providing them with the opportunity to search for specific word forms, word forms by lemmas, groups of word forms, and their morphological characteristics. Language corpora data also provides information about the origin and type of the text, its length and author, and various lexico-grammatical statistics. Corpus technologies are indispensable in the sense that they give students the opportunity to carry out linguistic analysis of the text providing the most objective, representative and comprehensive metatextual information about the language phenomena. The corpus is a kind of linguistic environment, the main characteristics of which (representativeness, balance, significant dimension, electronic form of existence, annotation) make it possible to use it as an effective tool for the formation of language skills in teaching a foreign language. At the same time the teacher should be able to master the corpus technologies and be at ease with the process of using corpus technologies in the classroom, compiling exercises based on the corpus and making this type of teaching material an integral part of the teaching process. If using corpus technologies becomes a seamless element of the learning environment, then students are expected to acquire a command not only of the studied language but of research skills as well.

References

Alqadoumi, Omar Mohamed. 2013. Using Corpus Linguistics as a Tool for Reform in English Language Teaching and Learning: The Case of Public Schools in Arab countries. In *Fourth International Conference on E-Learning "Best Practices in Management, Design and Development of e-Courses: Standards of Excellence and Creativity"* (7–9 May 2013). https://ieeexplore.ieee.org/document/6745550. Accessed Sept 25 2019.

Bazarova, Bayarma. 2015. Corpus linguistics and teaching foreign languages [Korpusnaja lingvistika i prepodavanie inostrannyh jazykov.] *Bulletin of the Buryat State University* 15: 88–92.

Biber, Douglas, Stig Johansson, Geoffrey Leech, Susan Conrad, and Edward Finegan. 1999. *Longman Grammar of Spoken and Written English*. Harlow, Essex: Longman.

Boulton, Alex. 2012. What Data for Data-driven Learning? In *The EUROCALL Review. Proceedings of the EUROCALL 2011 Conference* 20: 23–27.

Carter, Ronald, and Michael McCarthy. 2007. *Cambridge Grammar of English*. London: Longman.

Chen, Meilin, John Flowerdew, and Anthony Lawrence. 2019. Introducing In-service English Language Teachers to Data-driven Learning for Academic Writing. *System* 87: 1–12.

Curzan, Anne. 2012. The Electronic Life of Texts: Insights from Corpus Linguistics for all Fields of English. *Language & Computers* 76 (1): 9–21.

Hunston, Susan. 2002. Corpora and Language Teaching: General Applications. In *Corpora in Applied Linguistics*, ed. S. Hunston, 170–197. Cambridge: Cambridge University Press.

Introduction to Corpus Linguistics [Vvedenije v korpusnuju lingvistiku.] https://openedu.ru/course/hse/CORPUS/. Accessed 1 Oct 2018.

Khromov, Sergey, Nadezhda Guljaeva, Valerij Apal'kov, and Nina Nikonova. 2015. Information and Communication Technologies in the Teaching of Russian as a Foreign Language at the Initial Stage (level A1, A2) [Informacionno-kommunikacionnye tehnologii v prepodavanii russkogo jazyka kak inostrannogo na nachal'nom jetape (uroven' A1, A2).] *Open Education* 2: 75–81.

Kopotev, Michail. 2014. *Introduction to Corpus Linguistics* [Vvedenie v korpusnuju lingvistiku.] Prague: Animedia Company.

Lee, Hsing-chin. 2011. In Defense of Concordancing: An Application of Data-driven Learning in Taiwan. *Procedia Social and Behavioral Sciences* 12: 399–408.

Luo, Qinqin, and Jie Zhou. 2017. Data-driven Learning in Second Language Writing Class: A Survey of Empirical Studies. *International Journal of Emerging Technologies in Learning* 12 (3): 182–196.

Marinov, Sanja. 2015. Vocabulary Data-driven Learning in English for Specific Purposes: The Case of Students' Vocabulary Files. *Strani Jezici* 44: 82–109.

Michigan Corpus of Academic Spoken English (MICASE). http://micase.elicorpora.info/. Accessed 1 Jan 2019.

Michigan Corpus of Upper-Level Student Papers. https://micusp.elicorpora.info/. Accessed 1 Feb 2020.

McEnery, Tony, and Andrew Wilson. 1997. Teaching and Language Corpora. *ReCALL* 9 (1): 5–14.

MICASE Manual. The Michigan Corpus of Academic Spoken English. 2003. Michigan: The University of Michigan.

Nugraha, Sidik Indra, Fauzi Miftakh, and Kelik Wachyidi. 2017. Teaching Grammar through Data-driven Learning Approach. *Advances in Social Science. Education and Humanities Research (ASSEHR)* 82: 300–303.

Reppen, Randi, and Kerry S. Vrabel. 2011. *Grammar and Beyond. Level 1. Student's Book and Workbook.* Cambridge: Cambridge University Press.

Römer, Ute. 2011. Corpus Research Applications in Second Language Teaching. *Annual Review of Applied Linguistics* 31: 205–225.

Talai, Touraj, and Zahra Fotovatnia. 2012. Data-driven Learning: A Student-centered Technique for Language Learning. *Theory and Practice in Language Studies* 2 (7): 1526–1531.

The English Profile Programme. http://vocabulary.englishprofile.org/staticfiles/about.html. Accessed 7 Nov 2019.

Chapter 8
Improving Lexicography Teaching: A Practical Approach

Raluca Sinu

Abstract The aim of this chapter is to investigate the way a practical approach to teaching lexicography to master's students may complement their theoretical training in this field, raising awareness of the challenges of dictionary compilation. Our assumption is that involving students in practical projects affords them the opportunity to apply their previously acquired theoretical input in the field of (meta)lexicography. In the first part, the chapter will discuss the controversy surrounding the status of lexicography from the perspective of its dual nature (theory and practice), and its impact on teaching lexicography. Then, it will focus on the workflow of two projects (LEXICA-Admin and an English–Romanian Dictionary of Lexicography) designed to involve master's students in each stage of dictionary-making, in an attempt to underline the difficulties they faced, and the potential contribution of these projects to their lexicographic training. It will be argued that, even though these activities are not specifically meant to prepare future lexicographers, the insight gained as part of their lexicographic training can help improve students' dictionary consultation skills and their ability to critically assess a dictionary, turning them into more competent dictionary users.

Keywords Teaching lexicography · Dictionary compilation · Metalexicography · Lexicographic project

This chapter is an extended version of the work published in the proceedings of the International Conference Modern Developments in Linguistics and Language Teaching: the Problem of Method, Penza, 24–27 April 2019, vol. II: Principles and Methods in Language Teaching, edited by T.V. Dubrovskaya (referenced as Sinu 2019 in this article).

R. Sinu (✉)
Transilvania University of Braşov, Braşov, Romania
e-mail: raluca.sinu@unitbv.ro

8.1 Introduction

The starting point of this endeavour is the idea that

> lexicography as a disciplinary domain consists [...] of two interrelated fields, one theoretical, the other practical, each with its own research goals and practical pursuits. (Burada and Sinu 2016: 21)

From here it follows that teaching lexicography should serve both: students should have exposure to relevant topics in metalexicography as well as to the practical aspects of the process of dictionary-making. This point of view places us in the camp "that considers lexicography an independent scientific discipline", as formulated by Tarp (2010: 451), who underlines the fact that the status of lexicography remains highly debated even today.

This chapter intends to present the way in which two lexicographic projects—based on an already existing experimental online dictionary—were used to enable students to have a better grasp of the theoretical input they received in class, through discussions and practical involvement in one or several stages of dictionary-making, and their associated difficulties and challenges.

The paper will start with a short survey of the research in the area of teaching lexicography. Then it will focus on the development of two projects, namely LEXICA-Admin and English–Romanian Dictionary of Lexicography. These are presented as tools for teaching lexicography, as they allow the teacher to raise students' awareness of relevant decisions in compiling a dictionary and that the decisions have to be based on sound lexicographic theory.

8.2 Teaching Lexicography

This discussion about teaching lexicography in the academic context starts from the premise that there is a theory of lexicography, a "theoretical foundation in which the practice of dictionary-making is grounded" (Burada and Sinu 2016: 7); and that lexicography is more than the craft of dictionary-making, and as such it is not learnt only by practice. The changing status of lexicography, from a craft to an independent discipline over the past decades, has had deep implications for lexicographic pedagogy. Sinclair (1984) argued for establishing lexicography as an academic subject, stating that strong academic support would benefit lexicography and lexicographer training. The same year, Wiegand (1984: 13) discussed the general theory of lexicography, claiming that "lexicography is not a branch of the so-called applied linguistics". The debate concerning the nature and academic status of lexicography is still ongoing.

The dual nature of lexicography has been emphasised by many authors. Hartmann and James (1998: 85) provide the following definition of lexicography:

the professional activity and academic field concerned with dictionaries and other reference works. It has two basic divisions: lexicographic practice, or dictionary-making, and lexicographic theory, or dictionary research.

While there is general agreement concerning the practical side of lexicography, the existence of lexicographic theory has been refuted by some (e.g. Atkins and Rundell 2008), while others have supported it (e.g. Bergenholtz and Tarp 2003; Gouws 2011; Tarp 2012), even if they adopt different perspectives.

Gouws (2012: 222) brings into the discussion teaching and training in this field:

lexicography is taught as an academic subject in a number of university programmes. In the majority of cases it is done as part of a programme in language or linguistics; in only a few instances as part of a formal qualification in lexicography.

Other authors discuss curriculum issues in lexicography pedagogy (Hartmann 2001; Nkomo 2014; Martynova et al. 2015), including aspects such as dictionary structure, dictionary typology, user needs and consultation skills, dictionary functions, dictionary research, and dictionary criticism. However, we are only marginally interested in these, because the focus here will be on the interplay between theory and practice in teaching lexicography. The two facets of lexicography are interconnected: "teaching and researching lexicography constitutes the theoretical dimension of the field, while dictionary making and dictionary use are practical" (Nkomo 2014: 66).

Hartmann (2001: 4) believes that, when studying lexicography, one of the first things students have to do is to 'sort out' the relationship between theory and practice. The same author adds that "both practice (dictionary making) and theory (dictionary research) are necessary, particularly in an academic setting" (Ibid). Nkomo (2014) highlights the importance of exposing students to "the practical dictionary-making processes in a way that complements the theoretical sessions", because when students are taught about theoretical issues, like the ones mentioned above, "they acquire skills which improve their dictionary use", but "they do not acquire the practical skills of dictionary-making" (Nkomo 2014: 66). It could be added that the reverse is also true: learning on the job does not necessarily make one a better user, able to understand users' needs or equipped to handle the challenges of the process.

The importance of raising students' dictionary awareness has been highlighted repeatedly in the literature. Thus, Burada (2009: 71) states that, in addition to increasing their autonomy,

creating and refining our language students' dictionary awareness is one step further towards their becoming more sophisticated users with a sound sense of discrimination and, as the case may be, more responsible and competent lexicographers.

In the same vein, Nkomo (2014: 67–68) claims that:

Language students need to be trained to become competent dictionary users, skilled lexicographers and teachers who can effectively teach their own learners about effective dictionary use. Teaching lexicography becomes a form of dictionary research.

Although researching and improving dictionaries could benefit from lexicographic training, it has been noted that making dictionaries increasingly sophisticated is of little value unless the users have the reference skills needed to take advantage of such resources. It would appear that it is imperative to parallel lexicographers' efforts and users' dictionary skills.

It should be mentioned that this paper does not deal with pedagogical lexicography, defined by Hartmann and James (1998: 107) as "a complex of activities concerned with the design, compilation, use and evaluation of pedagogical dictionaries", described as reference works "specifically designed for the practical didactic needs of teachers and learners of a language".

Rather, it is interested in the way lexicography can be taught to students in the formal context of university training, and what role practical activities can play in teaching it. The intention is to highlight the benefits of coupling the theory with practical activities, such as compiling a corpus and preparing it for lexicographic use, in the lexicographic training of students, and also as a way to implement the students' formal instruction in dictionary-making.

We believe that teaching lexicography refers (or should refer) to more than dictionary training or teaching dictionary use (although we agree with their importance in advancing lexicography). It is extremely useful for students to be confronted with the theoretical complexity of this applied interdisciplinary field, in order to become aware of the challenges of dictionary-making, and better prepared to spot and assess the solutions implemented to deal with them in practice. Thus, it is important to design new activities for teaching lexicography while having in mind the two components of the lexicographic field.

8.3   The Lexica Project

Both projects discussed here are built on the infrastructure of *Lexica* (http://lexica. unitbv.ro/)—a bilingual pilot e-dictionary, available from 2008. *Lexica* was

> one of the outcomes of a lexicographic research project, *Competitiveness and Effectiveness in Intercultural Specialised Communication through the Optimization of Online Resources*, funded by the former National University Research Council (CNCSIS) and conducted in 2007 and 2008 by an interdisciplinary team of academics and research students from *Transilvania* University of Braşov. It was originally created as a pilot dictionary for the fields of politics, trade and law on the basis of a corpus made up of texts relating to the European Union. (Sinu and Micu 2013: 161)

The research project was aimed at improving the quality of online dictionaries in Romania, by revising the dictionary compilation process and paying more attention to its final outcome. In terms of dictionary-making, *Lexica* entailed undergoing all the stages in the compilation of a corpus-based dictionary for the online medium, presented in Fig. 8.1 below. It also brought an element of novelty consisting in the development of

> a text-parsing tool designed to process relevant linguistic data found in specialized texts pertaining to the European Community legislation. (Sângeorzan et al. 2008: 111)

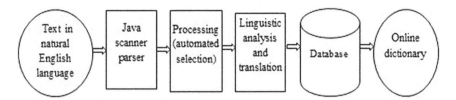

Fig. 8.1 The complete process from input to output in *Lexica* (Reproduced from Sângeorzan et al. 2008: 111)

As for the quality of the final product, the research team started by assessing seventy of the existing bilingual and multilingual public domain amateur dictionaries which included the combination of English and Romanian, available on the Internet. Before the evaluation, a set of qualitative criteria was designed,

> firstly, to identify, diagnose, and typify the problems commonly encountered when using such internet resources and secondly, to find solutions and design tools aimed at amending them. (Sângeorzan et al. 2008: 110)

Lexica was built based on the conclusions of this assessment as a specialised English–Romanian dictionary, which tries to eliminate the flaws identified in other online dictionaries: mactrostructural (in connection to the stock of words and the possible ways of accessing them), microstructural (referring to the types of information and their arrangement within the entries), and mediostructural (covering "the various means for achieving cross-reference in the dictionary" (Hartmann 2001: 64–65)).

Among the issues which *Lexica* addressed were:

- increased user-friendliness and readability by creating a dedicated site and by structuring the information clearly using boxes and colours;
- improved accessibility to the stock of lemmata by proposing a clear and easily manageable interface, but also interactivity by allowing the user to modify the search or to select the types of information to be displayed on the screen through a simple click on the relevant field;
- the elimination of the problem of reliability which stems from the lack of information about the authors of the project. *Lexica* solved the problem of reliability

> by providing data about the context in which the dictionary was compiled (in the section *Ce este Lexica—What is Lexica*)—part of a research programme developed at a university level—and about the people involved in building it (in the section *Echipa—The Team*), both lexicographers and IT experts, their institutional affiliations and their publications in the field (Sinu and Micu 2013: 162);

- a check of the quality of the metalanguage and of the translation;
- ensured consistency of the lexicographic input provided by the project team;
- reduced risk of misspellings and typographical errors, and the avoidance of ambiguous abbreviations, lack of diacritics, the unavailability of contexts and so forth, through attentive proofreading;

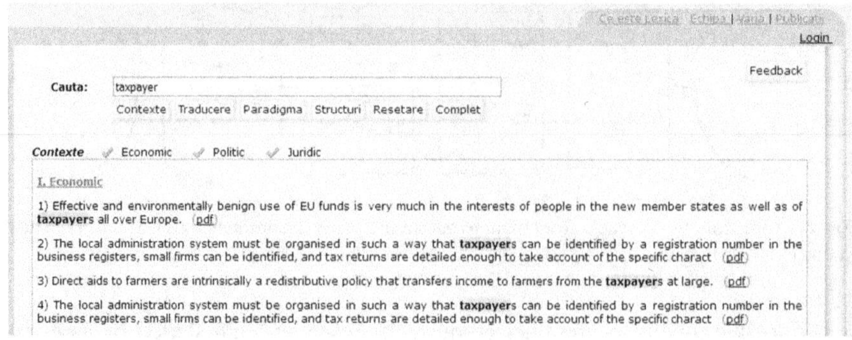

Fig. 8.2 Example of economic contexts for the headword 'taxpayer'

- access was provided to the original contexts of use and hyperlinks to the source documents used in the extraction of the terms (as illustrated in Fig. 8.2 below):

> The contexts are important because they allow the proficient user to check the behaviour of the word, its collocation patterns, as well as its translations. (Sinu and Micu 2013: 163)

The description provided on the dictionary site (http://lexica.unitbv.ro/), highlights the fact that

> the complex nature and flexible capabilities of the IT support have turned *Lexica* into a prolific metadictionary, capable of generating new corpus-based reference tools enabling meaning decoding/encoding processes in a variety of fields. (Sinu and Micu 2013: 161)

8.4 Teaching Lexicography Through Practical Lexicographic Projects

The two projects described in the next section were developed within the framework of the master programme (in English) *Language Studies for Intercultural Communication* (at the Faculty of Letters, Transilvania University of Brașov), with the help of the master's students enrolled in the programme, as part of their obligatory research activity. The second-year students of this programme undergo a module of theoretical lexicography (*Fundamentals of Bilingual Lexicography*) in the first semester, and continue in the second semester with an obligatory Scientific Research module, which in the past years has been dedicated to the compilation of various lexicographic tools. The lectures in *Fundamentals of Bilingual Lexicography* offer extensive coverage of metalexicography, dealing with both the dictionary as product (e.g. dictionary structure, classification, microstructural issues related to the definition, labels, and the assessment of dictionaries, etc.), and as process (e.g. stages in dictionary-compilation and its associated activities, electronic and online lexicography, etc.).

In what follows, the two projects, namely LEXICA-Admin and the English–Romanian Dictionary of Lexicography, will be presented with a focus on the workflow, the tasks performed by students and their contribution to the development of the projects.

8.4.1   LEXICA-Admin

The LEXICA-Admin glossary was built between 2011 and 2015 and became available on the intranet of Transilvania University of Braşov in November 2015. The master's students used the *Lexica* experimental dictionary as they fulfilled tasks related to the different compilation stages, confirming that

> *Lexica* is a valuable teaching tool as it enables the master's students taking the course in *Fundamentals of Bilingual Lexicography* to correlate the metalexicographic input with the lexicographic practice. (Sinu and Micu 2013: 163)

The interface of LEXICA-Admin (see Fig. 8.3) is a reduced version of the initial *Lexica* project, preserving only the translation option for the user, under the form of the button 'Traducere' (Engl. Translation), located below the search field, while in *Lexica* the user had access to contexts, paradigm, structures, and so forth. This entails the presence of only one microstructural element, namely the English equivalent or the translation of the Romanian term. The glossary was not designed as a static product, as evidenced by the presence of the button 'Propune un termen' (Engl. Propose a term) in the upper right-hand corner. On the contrary, it is meant to be a dynamic and interactive tool, easy to update and correct with the help of users, to better serve their needs.

In addition to its training purpose, the glossary was intended to serve

> our university staff involved in administrative work, especially those who write official documents in English and/or translate documents from Romanian into English, activity which has intensified as a result of the efforts towards internationalization made at university level in the context of globalization. (Sinu 2017: 377)

Working with LEXICA-Admin, students participated in different compilation stages, but all of them were exposed to the entire workflow, because their work plan comprised the previous and future stages of the project, which extended over several

Fig. 8.3 Interface of LEXICA-Admin

Fig. 8.4 Project stages and
associated activities
(Reproduced from Sinu
2017: 379)

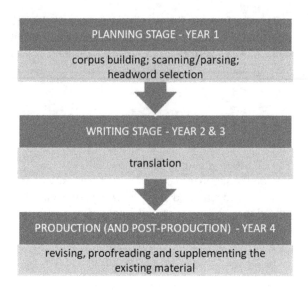

academic years, in order to give them a coherent picture. The tasks they were assigned were associated with the three major stages in dictionary-making: planning, writing, and production (Landau 2001: 343).

As represented in Fig. 8.4 below, year one was dedicated to the planning stage, including the activities of corpus building, scanning and parsing the texts in the corpus, and selecting the headwords. The writing stage covered the second and the third year of the project, including the translation of around 3,000 Romanian terms into English. The implementation of the glossary in the online medium was carried out by an IT expert, but students were involved in post-production activities in the fourth year, namely revising, proofreading, and supplementing the existing material.

In the planning stage, students were involved only in some of the decisions concerning the project, others had already been made, such as choosing the target audience, the languages involved, the covered field, and the types of information to supply for each headword. Their first task consisted in corpus building: they gathered around 150 texts belonging to the administrative field from the websites of different Romanian universities. Then, they had to format the texts (e.g. turn the files into .txt format, eliminate special symbols, tables, pictures, etc.) in order to be able to upload them into the text parsing programme developed for *Lexica* and extract words according to their frequency.

At the end of this stage, after perusing the lists automatically generated by the parser and discussing them, they put together a list of relevant terms. This proved to be one of the most difficult tasks because they had to decide which of the terms might be useful for the target audience (i.e. the university administrative staff), and this entailed becoming familiarized with types of administrative documents available on our university website and learning more about university procedures and regulations. (Sinu 2017: 379)

For example, keeping in mind the target audience and the aim of the project, students had to decide whether to include names of study programmes or course titles from the university curricula. As a result of the discussions on this topic, it was agreed that such items should not be part of the final list, because they were considered to be too specific and their translation was also a matter of the options expressed by each department or course convenor, and thus might be subject to variation. The specialised terms used in course descriptions were also eliminated from the glossary, including 'hepatită' (Engl. hepatitis), 'inspector de specialitate chimist' (Engl. chemical inspector), 'muzeograf' (Engl. museum curator), 'proză' (Engl. prose), 'paleografie' (Engl. paleography), 'studio (atelier)' (Engl. studio), 'solist instrumentist' (Engl. instrumental performer), and so forth (see Sinu 2017: 379).

The most time was devoted to the writing stage: students had to come up with the best English equivalents for the Romanian terms, a task which was often complicated because of the differences between the Romanian university system and higher education in English-speaking countries, such as the United Kingdom, the USA, Australia, and others. In many cases, the most helpful solution was to compare the definitions of the Romanian terms and their possible English counterparts. Also, they had to make sure to distinguish among various usages of the same term, for example, the Romanian form 'cod' may be translated in general as 'code', as well as in the contexts '**cod** (profesional) de etică' translated as 'code of academic ethics', and '**cod** de practică', rendered as 'code of practice', but also to '**cod** numeric', rendered as 'social security number' (important information on students' and employees' personal documents), or '**cod** poştal' conveyed as 'postal code'. As illustrated in Fig. 8.5 below, to differentiate among the possible meanings, short explanations were used, accompanying the headword. It should be mentioned that the documents issued at the level of the European Union (related to, for example, the Erasmus programme and European research programmes), which had already been translated into Romanian, represented an important source of equivalents.

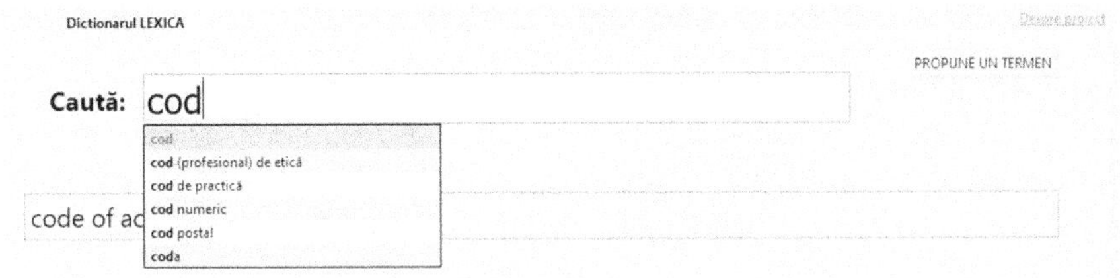

Fig. 8.5 The dropdown list for the lemma 'cod'

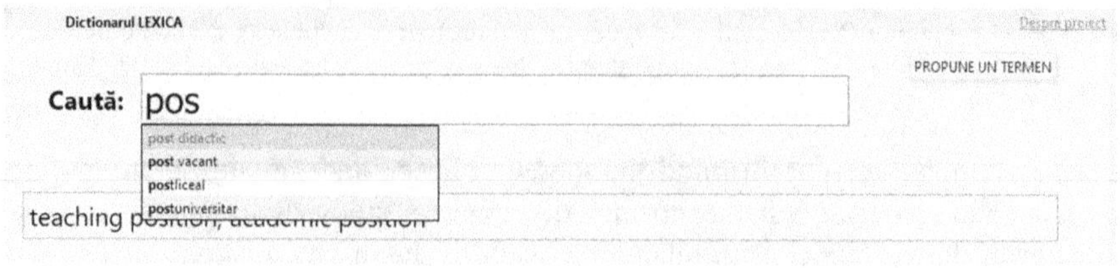

Fig. 8.6 The dropdown list for the lemma 'post'

Another example of a lemma more difficult to treat is the Romanian term 'bursă' whose English translation varies according to its type, for instance 'bursă contractuală' is 'contractual **sponsorhip**', 'bursă de doctorat' is 'doctoral **fellowship**', 'bursă de excelenţă' is 'excellence **grant**', 'bursă de studiu' is '**scholarship**' (also discussed in Sinu 2017: 379). Also, the form 'colocviu', which in Romanian covers two distinct meanings, signalled by short explanations accompanying the term, can be translated as 'colocviu (**conferinţă**)'—'colloquium', or as 'colocviu (**formă de examinare**)'—'oral examination'.

A similar example is represented by the form 'post' (see Fig. 8.6) which is treated as a noun in the contexts 'post didactic'—'teaching position, academic position', and 'post vacant'—'vacancy', but also a prefix, as in 'postliceal' translated as 'post-highschool' or 'postuniversitar', which in English is 'postgraduate'.

In the case of the lemma 'raport', we find the various translations of the noun in context, for instance '**raport** anual de evaluare a performantelor academice'— 'annual evaluation of academic performance'; '**raport** de audit'—'audit report'; **raport** de evaluare'—'evaluation report'; '**raport** de progres'—'progress report'; but we can also see the associated verb '**report**a'—'(to) report', as well as the derivative noun '**raport**are'—'reporting'.

At this stage, in many cases, students had to understand, first of all, the way the academic system worked in Romania in order to be able to find the suitable English equivalent for the Romanian term, and had to learn to avoid any possible translation 'traps', such as the issue of false friends, e.g. translating 'disciplină opţională' as 'optional course', instead of the correct equivalent 'elective course'; or 'student bugetat'—'budgeted student', instead of 'subsidised student'; or 'sesiune de examene' as 'exam session' instead of 'exam season/finals/examination period'. In the first example the translation is inaccurate, because it changes the meaning of the lemma, whereas in the second and the third the English equivalent is not a combination in use in the administrative language. Usage is an important factor in other cases as well, for example, in the translation of 'prorector', the identical English form is sometimes used as an equivalent in certain countries, but more frequently the title referred to is rendered as 'vice-rector'.

The project was implemented by colleagues from the Faculty of Mathematics and Computer Science, while our students dealt with revision, proofreading, and adding new terms. As previously mentioned, the project is still being enriched and occasionally corrected, with the help of master's students, in order to increase its usability.

8.4.2 English–Romanian Dictionary of Lexicography

The second project was initiated in 2015 and has not been completed yet. Its aim is to produce a bilingual (English–Romanian) glossary of lexicographic terms, which is currently missing from Romanian lexicography. As shown in Fig. 8.7, in a similar way to the workflow of the project previously described, in the planning stage students received a series of glossary parameters (audience, purpose, languages in contact, microstructure) and worked on (a) parsing a corpus of lexicographic texts, including dozens of articles from the *International Journal of Lexicography*, as well as other electronic lexicographic resources (textbooks, other research articles, etc.) available online; and (b) selecting the headwords based on the lists of terms obtained after the parsing. The lists obtained by each student after parsing were combined, then arranged alphabetically, and, after eliminating the less specific terms and the repeating ones, the results were divided into samples so each student had to handle approximately the same number of headwords.

In the writing stage, students were asked (a) to supply an explanation for each term, both in English and in Romanian, (b) to give the Romanian equivalent for the English terms, (c) to provide collocates for the English term, and (d) to indicate at least three sources from the specialised literature dealing with the English term which the interested reader could consult to find more information. For the English definitions, several well-known dictionaries of lexicography and/or dictionaries of linguistic terms were used, which proved quite comprehensive for the project's purposes. The situation was more complicated for the Romanian definitions, because in the absence of a dictionary or of dictionaries of lexicography, students resorted to other Romanian dictionaries available in the field of linguistics in general. However, in many cases, the Romanian definitions were not found in the existing resources and had to be composed by students based on the information which they had access to.

Fig. 8.7 Project stages and associated activities

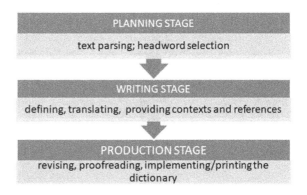

PLANNING STAGE

text parsing; headword selection

WRITING STAGE

defining, translating, providing contexts and references

PRODUCTION STAGE

revising, proofreading, implementing/printing the dictionary

As illustrated in Sinu (2019: 207), 'abridged dictionary' or 'concise dictionary' has no ready-made equivalent in Romanian, but 'the Romanian lexicographic tradition includes instances of 'mic dicţionar' (Engl. small dictionary), which could cover the two categories mentioned above'. Also, the designation 'unabridged dictionary' or 'comprehensive dictionary' in English can be rendered as 'dicţionar tezaur' in Romanian, but 'it should not be mistaken (as it often happens) with the English term 'thesaurus', which refers to another type of lexicographic work' (Sinu 2019: 207). In the case of newer lexicographic products, which are not present in the Romanian lexicographic landscape, for example, 'bilingualised dictionary' or 'bidirectional dictionary', the Romanian equivalents have not yet been created. But this decision presupposes a theoretical investigation into the evolution of international lexicography to identify the features and usage of the new products.

To be able to fulfil the tasks associated with the second stage, students have to demonstrate a good understanding of the meaning of the English lexicographic terms and to familiarise themselves with the situation of Romanian lexicography, being aware of the fact that it is based on the French lexicographic tradition, which might (at least partially) explain the terminological gap.

In order to ensure the coherence of the project in the writing stage, all students were asked to fill in a template form for each term they tackled. This entailed deciding on a uniform way of formulating the definition/explanation of each term: for example, the definition should start with the headword, it should be a genus-and-differentia type, or of presenting the references, observing the same sequence of information to ensure increased readability. The criteria for choosing the references to supply were also discussed and decided on. Among the factors we took into account were: access to the resource, for example articles in databases/journals available online, such as *Lexikos*, books/articles uploaded on specialised platforms such as the Proceedings of the *EURALEX International Congress*, the reputation of the author or of the specialised source, for instance the *International Journal of Lexicography*, the relevance of the resource in clarifying the meaning of the lemma to be explained, and the publishing date, favouring newer resources as well as classic articles/books. The information concerning phraseology includes combinations of the lemma, but also of derivatives of/compounds with the lemma in question, based on the treatment of the lemma in the resources consulted by each student, for example, *pictorial/ lexicographic* **illustration;** *to accompany/to include an* **illustration;** *academic* **lexicography**, *development of* **lexicography**, *meta***lexicography**, and others.

The discussions were also important in deciding on the equivalents for symmetrical concepts like *front matter*, *middle matter*, and *back matter*, *macrostructure*, *microstructure*, and *mediostructure*; or for related terms such as the types of information offered by labels, for instance *diafrequential information, diaintegrative information, diatechnical information, diatopic information, dianormative information,* and so on.

8.5   Project Outcomes and Conclusions

These projects allowed students to move from the theoretical aspects of lexicography to the practical side of compiling lexicographic tools, thus putting into practice their theoretical knowledge of lexicography—more precisely of bilingual lexicography, including, for instance, the features of electronic dictionaries, the principles and rules of definitions, the types of equivalents, the stages of the lexicographic process, and so on.

One of the major outcomes of involving students in these projects was that they were able to learn (by doing) about the various activities associated with the stages of the lexicographic process. The decisions taken in the planning stage influence the entire process and are ultimately determined by the aim of the product and the target audience which the lexicographers have in mind. Students were co-opted into projects which had already been designed, whose stages and activities were discussed in detail with them and adapted to their working pace and needs. In the planning stage, they extracted terms based on a corpus, applying rules of corpus linguistics to make the text corpus "reliable and relevant for the purpose" (Sinu 2017: 380), despite the fact that both projects were built on relatively small-sized corpora. The two projects fostered the idea that

> all serious future lexicography will be corpus-driven, no longer based merely on collections of citations and certainly not merely a matter of guesswork based on speculation. (Hanks 2012: 82)

After the selection of pertinent texts to include in the corpus, a list of recommendations was drafted for the parsing activity, also based on the parsing experience of the initial *Lexica* project. Although we cannot talk about a proper Style Guide, the list mentioned above can be assimilated to the one drafted initially. When deciding on which terms to include in the final list some criteria were devised, like the frequency of the term, its relevance for the field, and so on, however, some of the terms still attracted discussions before choosing whether to include them or not. In some cases, further research was needed, especially when students identified related terms which were not in the list.

The writing stage of LEXICA-Admin consisted exclusively of translation work, which entailed finding out more about the field, namely university administration work, but also about the differences between the Romanian education system and those of various English-speaking countries. Students became aware that a literal translation of the Romanian terms was unclear or insufficient at times, or simply incorrect, and that a comparison of the concepts was needed before finding an appropriate equivalent. In the writing stage of the English–Romanian Dictionary of Lexicography, in addition to the Romanian equivalent, the microstructure also provided the explanation of the term in English and Romanian, the contextualisation of the English term, and references to supplementary material that the user could consult to learn more about the term. In filling in all the microstructural fields, students resorted to the (meta)lexicographic literature and learnt more about the field and the existing resources whose usefulness they assessed based on their own needs in the specific work context. They also became increasingly aware of the differences between the Romanian lexicographic tradition and the English one, which sometimes created gaps to be filled in carefully with the help of paraphrase or borrowing. Students were not involved in the production stage of LEXICA-Admin, but their input was used in post-production, correcting the mistakes they identified and suggesting possible missing terms.

In accordance with the starting point of this chapter, we are of the opinion that combining theory and practice supports our students in understanding lexicography correctly as a field of research and practice and also develops their lexicographic skills, turning them into more competent dictionary users.

Another outcome resulting from these projects is the students' exposure to the lexicographical function theory (see Bergenholtz and Tarp 2003). From this perspective,

> the most fundamental aspects characterising all types of lexicographical works is that they are utility tools which implies that they have been produced in order to meet certain types of human needs detected in society. (Tarp 2010: 458)

The students' contribution was aimed at a well-defined audience and served a clear purpose, both of which were introduced from the very beginning of their work. By reinforcing the idea that

> lexicography deals with utility tools designed to be consulted in order to satisfy punctual information needs related to specific types of users and specific types of social situations and varying from culture to culture, from epoch to epoch (Tarp 2010: 459),

the projects showed students the needs that lexicographic products can (attempt to) satisfy in different contexts, for the administrative staff working in universities, or for students and teachers of lexicography who are not familiar with the English terminology in this field. We believe that knowing that their work will lead to a concrete product meant for specific users has also helped to increase the students' level of motivation.

Moreover, LEXICA-Admin showed the role that the online medium can play in the lexicographic process and in popularising its results: the texts to be parsed were collected from the websites of various universities; the research concerning the most appropriate equivalent often involved accessing the websites of universities in English-speaking countries for a better understanding of the concepts associated with the Romanian terms; the final product was uploaded on our university's intranet where it can be accessed by administrative and teaching staff.

While being aware of the fact that the two projects are very small and as such their impact on the audience is limited, it should be stressed that the compilers underwent all the stages of the lexicographic process to complete these tools which fulfil (or will fulfil when completed) the specific needs of a particular group of target users. It should also be acknowledged that the lexicographic value of the contributions brought by students in these projects is not comparable to the input of professional lexicographers. Nevertheless, these are the students' original contributions, reflecting their understanding of a certain field with which they are more or less familiar.

Maintaining the coherence of the projects has proved difficult on occasions because successive classes of students are involved, sometimes continuing an activity started by the previous class.

To conclude, despite the difficulties and the drawbacks of these hands-on projects, it can be argued that teaching lexicography might strengthen dictionary research and improve lexicographic practice, and that, ultimately

> teaching lexicography can play a complementary role with dictionary research in order to improve lexicographic practice and dictionary culture. (Nkomo 2014: 55)

References

Atkins, Sue, and Michael Rundell. 2008. *The Oxford Guide to Practical Lexicography*. Oxford: Oxford University Press.

Bergenholtz, Henning, and Sven Tarp. 2003. Two Opposing Theories: On H.E. Wiegand's Recent Discovery of Lexicographic Functions. *Hermes, Journal of Linguistics* 31: 171–196.

Burada, Marinela. 2009. Blueprinting Online Dictionaries: The Making of Lexica. In *Conference on American and British Studies*, ed. M. Burada, 65–71. Braşov: Transilvania University Press.

Burada, Marinela, and Raluca Sinu. 2016. *Research and Practice in Lexicography*. Braşov: Transilvania University Press.

Gouws, Rufus H. 2011. Learning, Unlearning and Innovation in the Planning of Electronic Dictionaries. In *E-Lexicography: The Internet, Digital Initiatives and Lexicography*, ed. P.A. Fuertes-Olivera and H. Bergenholtz, 17–29. London/New York: Continuum.

Gouws, Rufus H. 2012. Who Can Really be Called a Lexicographer? *Lexikos* 22: 217–225.

Hanks, Patrick. 2012. Corpus Evidence and Electronic Lexicography. In *Electronic Lexicography*, ed. S. Granger and M. Paquot, 57–82. Oxford: Oxford University Press.

Hartmann, Reinhard R.K. 2001. *Teaching and Researching Lexicography*. Harlow: Longman-Pearson Education.

Hartmann, Reinhard R.K.., and James Gregory. 1998. *Dictionary of Lexicography*. London and New York: Routledge.

Landau, Sidney. 2001. *Dictionaries: The Art and Craft of Lexicography*. Cambridge: Cambridge University Press.

Martynova, Irina N., Natalya Y. Shugayeva, Natalia V. Kormilina, Larisa V. Nikitinskaya, Yelena N. Gromova, and Yelena N. Vassilyeva. 2015. Modern Approaches to Teaching English Lexicography at the University of Freiburg Germany. *Journal of Sustainable Development* 8 (3): 220–226.

Nkomo, Dion. 2014. Teaching Lexicography at a South African University. *Per Linguam* 30 (1): 55–70. https://doi.org/10.5785/30-1-558.

Sângeorzan, Livia, Marinela Burada, and Kinga Kiss Iakab. 2008. Designing a Text Parsing Programme for a Specialized Bilingual Online Dictionary. In *New Aspects of Applied Informatics and Communications. Proceedings of the 8th WSEAS International Conference on Applied Informatics and Communications*, 110–114. Greece: WSEAS Press.

Sinclair, John M. 1984. Lexicography as an Academic Subject. In *LEX'eter '83 Proceedings. Papers from the International Conference on Lexicography at Exeter, 9–12 September 1983*, ed. R.R.K. Hartmann, 3–12. Tübingen: Max Niemeyer.

Sinu, Raluca. 2017. Involving Students in the Creation of an Intranet Glossary: Outcomes and Challenges. In *The 12th International Conference on Virtual Learning ICVL 2017*, ed. M. Vlada, G. Albeanu, A. Adăscălitei, and M.D. Popovici, 376–380. Bucharest: Bucharest University Press.

Sinu, Raluca. 2019. Teaching Lexicography: From Theory to Practice. In *Modern Developments in Linguistics and Language Teachings: The Problem of Method* [Soveremennyje Napravlenija v Lingvistike i Prepodavanii Jazykov: Problema Metoda.] *III International Conference Proceedings, Penza, 24–27 April 2019, Vol. II Principles and Methods in Language Teaching*, ed. T.V. Dubrovskaya, 204–208. Penza: Penza State University Publishing House.

Sinu, Raluca, and Corina Silvia Micu. 2013. Using a Pilot E-dictionary to Teach Lexicography and Raise Dictionary Awareness. In *Proceedings of the 8th International Conference on Virtual Learning ICVL 2013*, eds. M. Vlada, G. Albeanu, A. Adăscăliței, M.D. Popovici, R. Jugureanu, and O. Istrate, 160–165. Bucharest: Bucharest University Press.

Tarp, Sven. 2010. Reflections of the Academic Status of Lexicography. *Lexikos* 20: 450–465.

Tarp, Sven. 2012. Do we Need a (New) Theory of Lexicography? *Lexikos* 22: 321–332.

Wiegand, Herbert Ernst. 1984. On the Structure and Contents of a General Theory of Lexicography. In *LEX'eter '83 Proceedings. Papers from the International Conference on Lexicography at Exeter, 9–12 September 1983*, ed. R.R.K. Hartmann, 13–30. Tübingen: Max Niemeyer.

Part III
Cognitive Approaches to Language and Pedagogical Design

Chapter 9
Writing, Imitation, and the Brain: Insights from Neuroscience Research

Irene Clark

Abstract Referencing recent research in neuroscience, this chapter argues that Writing Studies teachers and scholars should reconsider imitation as a valid pedagogical and theoretical approach, because it can enable students to fulfil the requirements of academic writing tasks more successfully. It maintains that imitation can be used not only to help students perform the act of writing with greater insight, but also that if imitation is conceptualized as a type of performance, it can enable students to develop a sense of *writerly identity* that will contribute to their continued improvement. This interconnection between performance and identity is supported by current research in neuroplasticity that discusses the interaction between what one 'does' or performs and the neuronal brain activity that occurs as a result of that performance. This chapter consists of four sections. The first presents an overview of how the discipline of writing studies developed in terms of classroom pedagogy and the extent to which imitation corresponded to these perspectives. The second discusses recent ideas in neuroscience that support the conception of writing as performance. The third reports on a study that evaluated the use of imitation in several first-year writing classes, and the fourth suggests strategies for classroom use.

Keywords Imitation · Writing · Neuroscience · Performance · Identity

9.1 Introduction

Imitation has not recently received a great deal of attention in the field of Writing Studies in either the scholarship or recommended classroom practice—in fact, it has been not only neglected, but also strongly disdained. As noted by Paul Butler (2001: 108), using imitation in the writing class has drawn criticism from "two sites of composition theory: the process movement and the expressivist idea of individual genius". Process-oriented views maintain that imitation privileges the analysis of 'products' (exemplary essays, often focused on literary analysis) without

I. Clark (✉)
California State University, Northridge, CA, USA
e-mail: irene.clark@csun.edu

© The Author(s), under exclusive license to Springer Nature Switzerland AG 2021
N. V. Sukhova et al. (eds.), *Multimodality, Digitalization and Cognitivity in Communication and Pedagogy*, Numanities - Arts and Humanities in Progress 20, https://doi.org/10.1007/978-3-030-84071-6_9

enabling students to develop a writing 'process' that they can apply to other writing tasks. Expressivist views, which privilege individual self-expression in order to help students find their own personal voice, view that goal as incompatible with imitation. Additional objections are that a pedagogy which includes imitation is inconsistent with rhetorical invention, squelches possibilities for creativity and discovery and encourages plagiarism.

These concerns, of course, warrant continued discussion. Nevertheless, this chapter will argue for reconsidering imitation as a valid approach in Writing Studies, both theoretically and pedagogically, because it can enable many students—but particularly those who are educationally disadvantaged—to fulfil the requirements of academic writing tasks more successfully. It will maintain that imitation can be used not only to help students perform the act of writing with greater insight, but also that if imitation is conceptualized as a type of performance, it can enable students to develop a sense of *writerly identity* that will contribute to their continued improvement. This idea, that performance and identity are linked, is in accord with a statement attributed to Aristotle that "We are what we repeatedly do. Excellence, then, is not an act but a habit" (quoted in Cozolino 2013: 143). It is an idea that is also supported by current research in neuroplasticity—the ability of the brain to change in response to performance—which discusses the interaction between what one 'does' or performs and the neuronal brain activity that occurs as a result of that performance. 'Imitation' in this chapter will be conceptualized as

> the approximation, whether conscious or unconscious, of exemplary models whether textual, behavioral or human, for the express goal of improved student writing. (Farmer and Arrington 1993: 13)

The chapter will maintain that the term 'imitation' need not be preceded by negative adjectives, such as 'slavish' or 'mere', but rather that it can be both creative and generative. It can be used to reveal what *might* be done, not what *must* be done on particular assignments, and it can generate mindful reflection that can lead to deeper understanding. A perspective informing this concept of imitation is that mimicking surface features can lead to rhetorical insight, because even a surface awareness can contribute to a deeper understanding of relational properties. As Gerald Nelms (2015) maintained:

> it is difficult to imagine many circumstances where any writer (even experienced writers, successful in other communities) doesn't, at least to some degree, fall into mimicking the language of the target audience's community.

Imitation can thus be used to foster understanding and need not be done mindlessly. It is likely that many, if not all, readers of this essay have imitated writers whose work they admire—ideas, approaches, structures, patterns and styles.

The interconnection between writing, performance, identity and the brain will be addressed in this chapter in four sections: Sect. 9.2 will provide a brief overview of how the discipline of Writing Studies evolved in terms of classroom pedagogy and the extent to which imitation corresponded to these perspectives. Section 9.3 will discuss recent ideas in the field of neuroscience that support the underlying thesis of this chapter—that writing is a form of performance and that the repeated performance of an act is manifested in the brain and can have an impact on one's identity. Section 9.4 will report on the results of a study that evaluated the use of imitation in several first-year writing classes, and Sect. 9.5 will suggest several strategies using imitation that teachers can use in their writing courses.

9.2 Perspectives on Imitation and Writing

9.2.1 The Process Movement and Imitation

Early scholarship concerned with the teaching of writing is characterized by the movement from a product- to a process-oriented approach (see Clark 2019; Elbow 1986; Macrorie 1970; Murray 2001; Perl 1994; Sommers 1980, among many others). The accepted account of how the field developed is that, in the early part of the twentieth century, assignments in first-year writing classes privileged grammatically correct, coherently constructed essays focused on analysing literary works, although sometimes lengthy 'research papers' were also assigned. Writing prompts were given, and essays were assigned a grade. However, the *process* by which students were expected to write their essays was rarely, if ever, explained in detail. The idea was that if students read and discussed literature, they would somehow be able to write their essays, sometimes in a timed writing setting. As Richard Fulkerson observed in a review essay titled 'Of Pre- and Post-Process: Reviews and Ruminations' (2001), the situation of teaching first-year writing at that time was viewed as similar to "riding a bicycle. If you knew how to do it, then you could demonstrate your ability on demand" (Fulkerson 2001: 96).

This pedagogical approach, which is often referred to as Current Traditional (Berlin 1987; Stewart 1972) emphasized the importance of creating an acceptable *product*, but teachers rarely taught students anything about the writing *process*. In terms of imitation, writing pedagogy involved assigning readings, distributing a prompt and expecting students to produce the desired text on their own.

This product-oriented view characterized the teaching of writing through the 1950s and 1960s. Then, in 1963, at the Conference of College Composition and Communication, it became apparent that the field was undergoing a change. Recognizing the need to help students develop as writers, writing pedagogy began to emphasize *process*, a perspective that led to a flurry of research and scholarship concerned with a student-centred approach. The saying 'writing is a process' became a slogan for the enlightened, resulting in a new emphasis on enabling students to discover their own writing processes. Instead of assigning exemplary texts and expecting students to figure out how to produce them, teachers incorporated a number of process-oriented methods and techniques: scaffolded writing, conferencing, strategies of invention, multiple drafts, collaborative groups, student–teacher conferences and revision; these activities are now considered essential components of all writing classes. The process approach also focused on developing a facilitative learning environment so that students could become active participants in their own learning. As the learning theorist Jerome Bruner (1966: 72) maintained:

> to instruct someone in [a] discipline is not a matter of getting him to commit results to mind. Rather, it is to teach him to participate in the process that makes possible the establishment of knowledge… Knowledge is a process, not a product.

Another aspect of the 'process' movement during these early days was an emphasis on personal writing, often referred to as 'expressivism', an approach that encouraged students to express their thoughts and feelings and discover their own voice. Theorists such as Ken Macrorie (1970: vii–viii) defined the teaching of writing in the following terms:

> enabling students to use their own powers, to make discoveries, to take alternative paths. It does not suggest that the world can best be examined by a set of rules… The program gives the student first, freedom to find his voice and let his subjects find him… for both teacher and student, a constant reading for truth, in writing and commenting on that writing.

Process pedagogy is now a well-established approach in most writing classes. Nevertheless, many students continue to struggle to meet the expectations of the writing genres assigned at the university level. Many students are unfamiliar with the writing genres assigned in their classes, especially those who attend large public high schools, where teachers may be responsible for at least 100 students per week.

For these students—in fact, for most students—the use of imitation in first year university writing classes can be very helpful. If used mindfully in the classroom, imitation can help students understand what they are expected to produce in terms of the rhetorical, structural and stylistic choices that effective writers make. Moreover, imitating the authorial persona deemed appropriate for these essays can influence students' conception of themselves as writers. As Fecho and Clifton (2017: 26) argued, "when a person acts and interacts in a particular context, that person is recognized by the self and by others—as acting and interacting as a certain 'kind of person'". Similarly, as James Paul Gee (2001: 204) emphasized, any time someone uses reading or writing, they're reinventing and performing a social identity.

> Discourses are ways of being in the world, or forms of life which integrate words, acts, values, beliefs, attitudes and social identities as well as gestures, glances, body positions and clothes. (Gee 2001: 127)

In other words, practising writing in an academic context can have an impact on one's identity, because, as Cozolino (2013) maintains, when we observe what others do, our brains practise doing the same, so we are stimulated to imitate those actions in order to reap rewards as the brains connect those behaviours with goal achievement. This process is done through mirror neurons, which "link visual and motor programs, turning observation into rehearsal" (Cozolino 2013: 141).

9.2.2 Ancient Rhetoricians and Imitation

Ancient rhetoricians, of course, recognized the value of imitation in enabling young men to function successfully—politically, socially and artistically. Aristotle maintained that imitation does not involve the slavish copy of appearances or images but rather that it enables learning. He argued in the *Poetics* that imitation is not only natural to human nature, but is also a source of delight. Imitation, he explained, is natural to man from childhood: he is the most imitative creature in the world and learns at first by imitation. It is also natural for all to delight in works of imitation (Aristotle 2006: 53).

In his *Institutio Oratorio*, Quintilian similarly maintained

> that a great portion of art consists in imitation—for even though to invent was first in order of time and holds the first place in merit, it is nevertheless advantageous to copy what has been invented with success. (Quintilian 1987: 132)

Even Longinus, who is often associated with the Romantic concept of individual genius, argued in his rhetorical treatise *On the Sublime* that

> by reading other authors we may have borne in upon us divine impulses, effluences from their spirits, like that which inspires the Pythian priestess… and that the best way to obtain sublimity of style, the best way to imitate yet be original, is to ask ourselves how the great writers who have preceded us would have written on this very subject. (Nitchie 1935: 588)

9.2.3 Modern and Post-modern Perspectives on Imitation

Although composition pedagogy during the height of the 'process' movement did not privilege imitation, a few scholars during that period did endorse imitation as a useful approach. Edward Corbett (1971: 190), for example, maintained that it is

> the internalization of structures that unlocks our powers and sets us free to be creative, original, and ultimately effective. Imitate that you may be different,

and David Bartholomae (1986: 11) argued that mastering academic discourse is "more a matter of imitation or parody than a matter of invention or discovery". Donna Gorrell (1987: 53) argued that

> imitation is an effective approach to teaching form and sense of language while encouraging rather than stifling creativity,

and Frank d'Angelo (1973: 283) argued:

> Imitation exists for the sake of variation. The student writer will become more original as he engages in creative imitation.

Post-modern perspectives on language also support a reconsideration of imitation, because they problematize modernist assumptions about originality. Bakhtin, for example, maintained that all language is situated in dialogue, which enters our speech through unconscious imitation. As he argued in *The Problem of Speech Genres*,

> the unique speech experience of each individual is shaped and developed in continuous and constant interaction with others; individual utterances (Bakhtin 1986: 89),

an occurrence that Minock (1995: 495) stated is the same when we write. Going beyond Bakhtin's perspective, Derrida maintained that mimicry is theoretically impossible because all linguistic elements or 'marks' have the capacity to be repeated in a new context in order to forge new meaning, a quality that Derrida (1982) referred to as 'iterability'. Derrida explained that, because words cannot be controlled by conscious intentions of authors, language in its ability to be reproduced cannot be owned by anyone (Derrida 1982: 317). Moreover, Lacan's psychoanalytic perspective (Lacan 1968) emphasized the role of language in the formation of a self. As Minock (1995: 498) explained,

> Because we appropriate the language of others to grow and define ourselves in new ways, Lacan's concepts of transference and resistance allow us to discuss the ways in which unconscious desires are played out in relationship to the language of others.

Lacan viewed the self as continuously developing in interactions with others who initially provide the impetus for the development of the unconscious (Lacan 1968). In essence, then, post-modern perspectives on the possibility of owning language and on the existence of an original, absolute self counter objections to imitation.

9.2.4   Imitation and Academic Genres

The use of imitation in university writing classes can also be justified because many students, both graduate and undergraduate, may never have read the types of essays they are being asked to write—thesis-driven arguments, literary or rhetorical analyses, lab reports, grant proposals or research studies. To help students understand the type of writing they are expected to produce, providing them with examples they can imitate can be enlightening, especially when these examples are accompanied by rhetorical and stylistic analyses.

When students begin to write in unfamiliar genres and interact with people who engage habitually with these genres, their self-concept or identity is likely to be affected. A perspective pertaining to this phenomenon was offered by Robert Brooke (1988) in an article titled 'Modeling a Writer's Identity: Reading and Imitation in the Writing Classroom', in which Brooke argued that students learn to view themselves as writers not only by imitating a text or a process, but by imitating 'another person'. Brooke maintained:

> Writers learn to write by imitating other writers, by trying to act like writers they respect... Imitation, so the saying goes, is a form of flattery: we imitate because we respect the people we imitate, and because we want to be like them. (Brooke 1988: 23)

Brooke's perspective is that students learn by imitating identities. When they imitate an identity—perhaps someone like a teacher, or someone who is member of a community that a student wants to join, students gain motivating energy and incentive—they perceive a model of someone they'd 'like to be like' and try to copy it (Brooke 1988: 23). By imitating people one respects, Brooke explained, "one forms aspects of one's 'identity,' one's public and acknowledged 'sense of 'self'"" (Brooke 1988: 24). It is likely that many of us decided to enter the academy because we admired a particular teacher and/or wanted to be part of their world, a desire that motivated us to imitate their literacy activities, either deliberately or unconsciously.

9.3 Imitation and Neuroplasticity

9.3.1 Performance and the Brain

Recent research in neuroplasticity—that is, how the brain changes as a result of experience—indicates that the brain can change frequently in response to various environmental factors and that certain skills and experiences that contribute to identity formation can now be discerned in the brain using modern imaging techniques. Current work in neuroplasticity demonstrating that the brain can change and respond to many types of experiences thus suggests that identity is not static, fixed or stable. Rather, it consists of a dynamic set of expanding and constantly reorganizing resources that can be evoked and reassembled in response to situation and context. It is now recognized that everything the brain enables us to do—feel, think, perceive and act—is linked or correlated with changes in oxygen consumption and regional blood flow in the brain. When a person responds to a task, such as looking at photos or solving a math problem, specific regions of the brain are typically engaged and receive more oxygen-laden or oxygenized blood. The increased blood flow and the boost in oxygen associated with it are proxies for increased neuron activation (Satel and Lilienfeld 2013: 5).

Understanding that the brain can change has significant implications for how we define 'learning', because change, characterized by the generation of new neurons, occurs through experience, and learning is a form of experience. As Begley (2007: 8–9) notes,

> the actions we take can literally expand or contract different regions of the brain… The brain devotes more cortical real estate to functions that its owner uses more frequently and shrinks the space devoted to activities rarely performed… The brain forges stronger connections in circuits that underlie one behavior or thought and weakens the connections in others… Merely thinking about playing the piano leads to measurable, physical change in the brain's motor cortex and thinking about thoughts in certain ways can restore mental health.

Learning and various kinds of experiences, then, are inscribed in the brain in a physical, discernible way.

The idea that the brain can change in response to what we do or perform is an insight with potential implications for educators. As Berninger and Richards maintain in *Brain Literacy for Educators and Psychologists* (2002: 4), cognitive neuroscience now provides a "conceptual foundation for educational practice" because it demonstrates the importance of environmental and instructional influences on brain and behaviour interactions. Several examples include the Juggling Study, the Taxi Drivers study, a study examining the effect on the brain of musical training and a study concerned with helping students diagnosed with dyslexia improve in oral language and reading performance. In the Jugglers' study, published in the journal *Nature*, Draganski and colleagues reported that when subjects were taught to juggle, brain scans were able to detect changes in the brain associated with vision and movement, and in the Taxi Drivers Study, taxi drivers in London were given brain scans before and after they had memorized the names of London streets (Draganski et al. 2004). The post-scans revealed that the hippocampus, which is the part of the brain concerned with navigation had enlarged significantly. The study concerned with dyslexia (Temple et al. 2003) indicated that children who had previously been diagnosed with dyslexia but had improved in their reading abilities showed increased activity in the left temporo-parietal cortex, activity that approached the level associated with children who are not dyslexic. Significant neuroscience scholarship has already enhanced understanding of long- and short-term memory, handwriting, information flow across text types and modalities and metalinguistic development (see Berninger and Richards 2002), indicating changes in neuron and synapse production that can be discerned through advanced scanning techniques.

9.3.2   Neuroplasticity and Identity

Neuroscientists can now discern changes in the brain as a result of learning and experience. But if the brain changes, does that mean identity changes correspondingly? According to Sebastian Seung, professor of computational neuroscience at MIT and author of *Connectome: How the Brain's Wiring Makes Us Who We Are* (2012), identity is strongly linked to what he referred to as a 'connectome', which he defined as "the totality of connections between the neurons in a nervous system". Seung maintained that "minds differ because connectomes differ" (Seung 2012: xiv) and that a person's "connectome changes throughout life" (Seung 2012: xv), reconnecting, rewriting, retracting and regenerating. He explains that although we don't know exactly how life events change a connectome,

> there is good evidence that all four R's—reweighting, reconnection, rewiring, and regeneration—are affected by one's experience (Seung 2012: xv),

and that these neuronal activities constitute the basis of identity.

Neuroscientists thus view identity as strongly associated with the brain's chemical and electrical impulses, which are affected by experiences, a perspective that is similar to Dr Susan Greenfield's comparison of experience to a type of narrative or story. Greenfield, who is a prominent British neuroscientist, maintained that these 'stories' are registered directly in the brain and the differing roles we play as part of those stories are manifested as "differing cerebral blood flow with different personality states" (Greenfield 2011: 34). Greenfield cited examples of patients with a history of exposure to traumatic stress whose brains showed smaller volumes of blood in the brain area related to memory (the hippocampus). Other examples concerned patients with multiple personality disorder, whose brainwaves registered differently according to the particular state they were in. In the context of how imitation can be used in helping students write more effectively and learn to view themselves as writers, Greenfield's neurobiological research indicates that as the brain adapts to an environment, it has a transformational impact on the roles we are able to play. This perspective suggests that when students engage in writing, they are, in essence, performing an authorial role, a performance that will be manifested in the brain, impacting, at least to some extent, their sense of self. This is an idea that James Paul Gee (2001) has argued in the context of how students acquire literacy. Gee (2001: 525) maintained that any time someone uses reading or writing, they're inventing and performing a social identity because

> Discourses are ways of being in the world, or forms of life which integrate words, acts, values, beliefs, attitudes and social identities as well as gestures, glances, body positions and clothes.

Gee's perspective corresponds to Bazerman's discussion of how a genre can have an influence on a student's identity. Bazerman (2002: 14) explained that when people begin writing or speaking in a particular genre, they begin

> thinking in actively productive ways that result in the utterances that belong in that form of life', taking on 'all the feelings, hopes, uncertainties, and anxieties… associated with that identity.

From this perspective, it is presumed that familiarity with and habitual involvement in a genre can have a substantial impact on the identity of the participant, and that when students repeatedly perform the role of author in an academic text or professional context, their sense of their own academic or professional self is impacted. This is a phenomenon that many of us have encountered when a person we know personally enters a particular profession—such as law or medicine. They begin to speak differently, and perhaps think differently—we say that they now 'seem' like lawyers or doctors. This is also a phenomenon that some students from educationally disadvantaged backgrounds have experienced. In fact, recently, in a workshop concerned with how immersion in academic or professional genres can impact identity, a colleague said that when she left for college, her father, who was from a working class background, said, 'I know that I am going to lose you'. Moreover, she acknowledged, 'to some extent, he was right'—not that she no longer loved her father; rather that she now had a perspective on the world, and on herself, that was different from how it had been in the past. I have heard similar stories from students in my classes.

9.4   The Imitation Project

In the Fall of 2015, I conducted a study titled "The Imitation and Modelling Study," which was concerned with the pedagogical application of imitation in first-year writing classes. The study involved the distribution of surveys to 220 students and 10 experienced writing instructors at the beginning and end of the semester. The instructors developed curricular materials concerned with imitation which they then incorporated into first-year writing classes and a few classes focusing on business writing. Some of the materials they developed were derived from composition text-books, most of which focused primarily on sentence structure or use of adjectives or active verbs to develop style; some were created directly by the instructors. In fact, several instructors 'confessed' that they had been using imitation and modelling already in their classes and were pleased to have been given 'permission' to do so. The materials derived from the project also included reflections by both instructors and students about how well imitation worked for them and responses from surveys in which students evaluated its usefulness in helping them write more successfully.

Goals of the Project

The primary goals of the Imitation Project were as follows:

- to compare students' use of imitation at the beginning of their first university semester with their use of imitation at the end of that semester;
- to determine the extent to which the use of imitation helped to alleviate students' self-reported writing anxiety; and
- to determine the extent to which instructors using imitation in their writing classes thought it had been helpful in assisting their students.

The Surveys

Surveys distributed at the beginning of the semester asked students whether they habitually used imitation when assigned to write in an unfamiliar genre. They were also asked how they rated their own writing ability and about their degree of writing anxiety. The surveys distributed at the end of the semester asked students how useful they had found the use of imitation and also about their degree of anxiety.

9.4.1   Reflections and Results

Instructors wrote reflections discussing how their courses incorporated imitation and indicated how useful they felt it had been in their teaching. Students also wrote reflections about how useful imitation had been for them in enabling them to write more successfully. They were also asked to address the following question: if you were given the task of helping an entering university student learn to write in an unfamiliar genre, would you recommend imitation?

The Instructors' Reflections

Instructors in the project indicated that they were pleased that they had incorporated imitation into their curriculum. Many of them reported that their students' papers were 'discernibly better once they had seen and analysed examples, particularly in organization, scope, in-text citations, and the Works Cited page'. They all felt that imitation was not only helpful, but necessary if the student had not written that type of essay before.

Below are a few comments from some of the instructors in the project:

I teach 4 sections of business / professional writing and one graduate music business section, and I find it critical and mandatory to use templates for these classes. As someone with nearly twenty years in the business world, I learned professionally to design powerpoints, proposals and bids/offers by reading and modeling those above me. Early on, my boss would review my work and make any needed adjustments. I would revise the work for final output to clients, the company, or the media, and eventually, my work was fine to submit without review. This is much like what happens in my classes here at the university.

Another instructor wrote:

My students were given the opportunity to write about any topic they chose, but were required to research what genre of writing would be appropriate for the categories they had selected. Students who wanted to write about political issues, for example, were required to analyze articles from political blogs and newspaper articles. Students interested in sports or athletics located academic sources for studies in the field of Kinesiology, as well as looking into the style and writerly voice of sports medicine magazines. They also identified vocabulary that they thought was interesting or that they would like to incorporate into their own modes of speech.

Another instructor wrote:

I am very pleased with the 'freedom' to openly discuss modeling. In my years of teaching, students have always asked to see an assignment that got an 'A', so that they could follow the path to an 'A' for themselves. I was reluctant for three reasons:

1. I assumed the better students would be able to produce their own version of an 'A' from the instructions, prompt, and questions they asked and the struggling students needed to wrestle with the challenge on their own.
2. I had some fear that students would just 'ape' the model and not be original in their response.
3. Somehow, I had the idea that it was considered 'cheating' to show a model.

Nevertheless, one instructor indicated that some of the less able students did rely too heavily on the examples provided, mimicking not only the formal and overall structure of the models but also the sentence and paragraph structure.

Students' Responses and Comments

Students' responses and comments were, without exception, enthusiastic, indicating that they had increased the frequency with which they used imitation in approaching a writing task and had found imitation to be a helpful strategy. When asked about how often they used a model of a genre in their writing, the response from 202 students at the beginning of the semester was 77.3% of the time compared to 80.8% of 209 students at the end. Correspondingly, at the end of the semester, 159 out of 209 students indicated that they had found the use of imitation either useful or very useful (76.1%). When asked to reflect on the extent to which the focus on imitation had contributed to their improvement in writing, students wrote:

1.   I feel as if looking at sample essays helped me become a better writer because in my previous English classes my teachers were always afraid of showing sample essays because they believed students would plagiarize but I thought otherwise. Looking at sample essays helped me get better at organizing my information which is something I had trouble with when I began the course. Therefore, I believe looking through several sample essays before beginning my essay was helpful.
2.   It really did contribute to my improvement as a writer. I learned ways to organize information that I never used before. It also helped me with my conclusions since I always had trouble ending my essays.
3.   Peer reviews were really helpful because I could see how other students write and how it compares to my own style of writing.
4.   If I had to help other students, I would tell them to look at samples of writing if they wanted to improve, because that helped me a lot.

Perspectives on Imitation from the Project

The most valuable conclusion resulting from the project was that imitation had been useful in helping students fulfil the expectations of unfamiliar writing genres, with both instructors and students expressing enthusiasm in their reflections. Moreover, information obtained from pre- and post-semester surveys indicated that student anxiety about their writing ability had decreased from 45.6% at the beginning of the semester to 41.1% at the end, and that their view of themselves as Good or Excellent writers had increased from 58.1% at the beginning of the semester to 68.1% at the end. Of course, it must be acknowledged that other approaches used in these classes may also have contributed to the decrease in writing anxiety and increase in self-rating. However, the reflective pieces indicated that imitation was at least partially a contributing factor.

Moreover, even in cases in which some students adhered too closely to a model, participants felt that these instances could serve as 'teachable' moments in which teachers would show students how exact their imitation had been and then have them alter and change what they had produced. Questions to discuss would include how much change would be appropriate or how much change would require other changes. Imitation, in this case, would thus generate discussion and awareness— certainly useful for helping students practise the analysis that could ultimately enable them to view themselves as writers.

9.5   Using Imitation in the Classroom

What sort of imitation would be most useful for students in the classroom? The section below offers several possibilities. These include modelling process behaviour, focusing students' attention on structure, copying and transcription, and reading aloud.

Modelling Process Behaviour

An approach that is likely to influence how students perform as writers is to model process *behaviours* that students can imitate, an approach suggested by Muriel Harris as a way to focus students' attention on how different writers revise. Harris's article, entitled 'Composing Behaviors of One-and-Multi-Draft Writers' (1989), emphasized that writers use different processes to revise their work, some developing ideas in their minds before beginning to write, others generating multiple drafts and discovering ideas through the act of writing. In my own classes, I frequently discuss my own process to show students an approach that they might imitate.

Recently, in a graduate seminar aimed at helping students revise their work for publication, I demonstrated how I wrote an abstract in response to a call for papers for the Writing Program Administration (WPA) conference. The theme of the conference, stated as 'What if We Tried This', invited innovative approaches and suggested that abstracts should be framed 'in the form of problem statements: We face X which interferes with a core element of teaching writing in current times. So what if we tried Y instead'?

In showing my graduate students how I wrote my abstract, I began by choosing a primary term in the call for proposals,—in this case, the word 'problem', because most, if not all, academic scholarship tends to address some form of a problem or exigency. I then asked students what they thought a conference concerned with Writing Program Administration would consider a *problem* or at least an issue worth addressing, and it was easy for everyone to identity it as the need to help students become better writers, particularly those whose educational backgrounds and prior knowledge did not place them at an advantage.

I then had students examine the title I had tentatively chosen 'Reconsidering Imitation and Modelling in a Rhetorical Context', and had them consider the choices I had made. Why had I used the term 'reconsidering' rather 'using'? Why did I link the terms imitation and modelling, with the phrase 'rhetorical context'? These questions enabled students to understand that the term 'reconsidering' implies the idea of changing one's mind, and that I had chosen it to show that I was aware that Writing Studies scholarship has not tended to endorse imitation and modelling and thus that this approach needs to be reconsidered. They were also able to understand that the term 'rhetorical context' is one that is used frequently in Writing Studies scholarship, so a connection between that term and the terms imitation and modelling served to establish my identity as someone who is familiar with issues in the field.

After analysing the title, I then moved to the first sentence of the abstract I had written, explaining that I had used the word 'suggest'—a term often used in academic writing—because it indicates thoughtfulness, or a subtlety of perspective. I also directed their attention to the phrase 'educationally disadvantaged students', because these are the students who are most in need of additional assistance, and to my use of the terms 'thoughtfully, mindfully, and reflectively'—terms that are regarded as desirable in academic writing.

For practice, I had students fill in the blanks for my first sentence, as in:

In this presentation, I will suggest that _____ in conjunction with _____ will contribute significantly to _____ particularly benefitting _____ who often struggle to _____. It will emphasize that a _____approach to _____ is in accord with _____ perspectives in _____ and that if this approach is integrated thoughtfully, mindfully, and reflectively.

The value of demonstrating a process is in accord with what is understood about 'mirror neurons'—the idea that our brains actually practise doing what we observe another person doing, particularly if we wish to achieve the goal toward which the behaviour is oriented. As Cozolino (2013) explained in his discussion of mirror neurons, when we observe another person doing something, we are stimulated to imitate those actions to achieve a similar goal or reward.

Focusing Students' Attention on Structure

Although many textbooks that include imitation often focus on sentences or word choices, an annotated example in which structural and functional elements are identified can help students gain insight into the author's choices about where various components of the essay were placed. Students could then imitate that structure in their own essays and experiment with creative variation. The use of peer review could focus students' attention on how other students structured their texts and developed their ideas.

Copying and Transcription

One of the participants in the imitation study had students engage in transcription, wherein they selected a particular text to transcribe over the course of a number of days, identifying vocabulary that they thought was interesting or that they would like to incorporate into their own writing. Students selected a text to read, then read aloud, record and rewrite. They then recorded themselves reading selections from different texts, paying attention to patterns of speech. They also identified vocabulary that they thought was interesting or that they would like to incorporate into their own modes of speech.

Reading Aloud

Sharon Crowley in her textbook *Ancient Rhetoric for Contemporary Students* (1994) suggested that reading aloud can help students develop an ear for sentence rhythms and become aware of stylistic variations. Reading aloud is a technique that also fosters the ability to 'listen' to text, another strategy that was advocated by Quintilian, and it is likely that many readers of this chapter use this technique to 'listen' to their own writing.

9.6 Conclusion

When students imitate the approaches and strategies used by other writers, they will not only gain knowledge about writing, but will, in essence begin to assume a writerly role, which, if performed with sufficient frequency, can become habitual. This is an experience recounted in Victor Villanueva's well-known literacy autobiography, *Bootstraps* (1993). Growing up Puerto Rican in New York City, Villanueva enrolled in a community college, where he received high grades on his essays. However, when he enrolled in a four-year college, he was mortified to receive a score of 36 out of 100 on his first essay. 'Devastated and determined', Victor went to the library 'to look up what the Professor himself had published' and was able to see the pattern:

> an introduction that said something about what others had said, what he was going to be writing about, in what order, and what all this would prove, details about what he said he was going to be writing about, complete with quotes, mainly from the poetry… It wasn't the five-paragraph paper Mr. Lukens had insisted on, not just three points, not just repetition of the opening in the close, but the pattern was essentially the same. (Villanueva 1993: 70)

As a result of his efforts, Villanueva's grades improved, and 'professorial analysis' becomes "a standard practice: go to the library; see what the course's professor had published; try to discern a pattern in her writing; try to mimic the pattern" (Villanueva 1993: 71). Soon, writing came as easily to him at a four-year college as it had when he was at community college. Villanueva's experience illustrates how imitation, if practised frequently and insightfully, can enable students to perform as writers—potentially to assume a writerly identity, which was certainly the case with Villanueva. This outcome, was, of course, not surprising. As Donna Gorrell pointed out

> writers imitate other writers, just as surely as painters imitate other painters, violinists imitate other violinists, golfers imitate other golfers. It's one of the ways beginners learn how it's done. (Gorrell 1987: 53)

Although imitation has not received a great deal of attention in the field of Writing Studies, there appears to be renewed interest in the topic. At the 2019 Conference on College Composition (CCC), for which I organized a panel and presented a paper concerned with imitation, many conference participants over the course of several days expressed enthusiastic support for this topic, revealed that they, themselves, often used imitation in their writing classes (sometimes secretly) and indicated their desire to learn more about its correlation with identity, performance and current neuroscience research. Perhaps exploration of this intriguing interrelationship will soon lead to increased Writing Studies scholarship and classroom application.

References

Aristotle. 2006. Poetics. In *Critical Theory Since Plato,* eds. A. Hazard and S. Leroy, 52–69. Peking: Peking University Press.

Bakhtin, Mikhail M. 1986. *Speech Genres and Other Late Essays,* trans. Caryl Emerson, Michael Holquist. Austin, TX: University of Texas Press.

Bartholomae, David. 1986. Inventing the University. *Journal of Basic Writing* 5 (1): 4–23.

Bazerman, Charles. 2002. Genre and Identity: Citizenship in the Age of the Internet and the Age of Global Capitalism. In *The rhetoric and Ideology of Genre: Strategies for Stability and Change,* ed. R. Coe, L. Lingard, and T. Teslenko, 13–38. Creskill, NJ: Hampton Press.

Begley, Sharon. 2007. *Train your Mind, Change your Brain. How a New Science Reveals our Extraordinary Potential to Transform Ourselves.* New York: Ballantine Books.

Berninger, Virginia W., and Todd L. Richards. 2002. *Brain Literacy for Educators and Psychologists.* Amsterdam: Academic Press.

Berlin, James A. 1987. *Rhetoric and Reality: Writing Instruction in American Colleges 1900–1985.* Carbondale, IL: Southern Illinois University Press.

Brooke, Robert. 1988. Modeling a Writer's Identity: Reading and Imitation in the Writing Classroom. *College Composition and Communication* 38 (1): 23–41.

Bruner, Jerome. 1966. *Toward a Theory of Instruction.* Cambridge, MA: Belknap Press.

Butler, Paul. 2001. Toward a Pedagogy of Writing Immersion. *Journal of College Writing* 4: 107–114.

Clark, Irene L. 2019. Processes: Approaches and Issues. In *Concepts in Composition: Theory and Practices in the Teaching of Writing,* 3rd ed., ed. I.L. Clark, 1–51. New York, NY: Routledge.

Corbett, Edward P. J. 1971. The Theory and Practice of Imitation in Classical Rhetoric. *College Composition and Communication* 22 (3): 243–250.

Cozolino, Louis. 2013. *The Social Neuroscience of Education: Optimizing Attachment and Learning in the Classroom.* New York, NY: Norton.

Draganski, Bogdan, Christian Gase, Volker Busch, Gerhard Schuierer, Ulrich Bogdahn, and Arne May. 2004. Changes in Grey Matter Induced by Training. *Nature* 6972: 311–312.

Crowley, Sharon. 1994. *Ancient Rhetorics for Contemporary Students.* New York, NY: Macmillan.

D'Angelo, Frank J. 1973. Imitation and Style. *College Composition and Communication* 24: 283–290.

Derrida, Jacques, 1982. *Margins of Philosophy.* Trans. Alan Bass. Chicago: University of Chicago Press.

Elbow, Peter. 1986. *Embracing Contraries: Explorations in Learning and Teaching.* New York, NY: Oxford University Press.

Farmer, Frank M., and Phillip K. Arrington. 1993. Apologies and Accommodations: Imitation and the Writing Process. *Rhetoric Society Quarterly* 23: 12–34.

Fecho, Bob, and Lucille Clifton. 2017. *Dialoguing Across Cultures, Identities, and Learning.* New York, NY: Routledge.

Fulkerson, Richard. 2001. Of Pre-and-post Process: Review and Ruminations. *Composition Studies* 29 (2): 93–119.

Gee, James Paul. 2001. Literacy. In *Discourse, and Linguistics: Introduction and What is Literacy? In Literacy: A Critical Sourcebook,* ed. E. Cushman, E.R. Kintgen, B.M. Kroll, and M. Rose, 525–544. Boston, MA: Bedford St. Martins.

Gorrell, Donna. 1987. Freedom to Write—Through Imitation. *Journal of Basic Writing* 6 (2): 53–59.

Greenfield, Susan. 2011. *You and Me: The Neuroscience of Identity.* London: Notting Hill.

Harris, Muriel. 1989. Composing Behaviors of One- and Multi-Draft Writers. *College English* 51 (2): 174–191.

Lacan, Jacques. 1968. *The Language of the Self: The Function of Language in Psychoanalysis.* Trans. Anthony Wilden. New York, NY: Dell.

Minock, Mary. 1995. Toward a Postmodern Pedagogy of Imitation. *JAC* 15 (3): 489–709.

Macrorie, Donald K. 1970. *Telling Writing.* Rochelle Park, NJ: Hayden.

Murray, Donald. 2001. *Write to Learn*. Boston, MA: Heinle & Heinle.

Nelms, Gerald. 2015. Why Plagiarism doesn't Bother Me at All: A Research-based Overview of Plagiarism as Educational Opportunity. https://teachingandlearninginhighered.org/2015/07/20/plagiarism-doesnt-bother-me-at-all-research/. Accessed 8 Sep 2017.

Nitchie, Elizabeth. 1935. Longinus and the Theory of Poetic Imitation in Seventeenth and Eighteenth Century England. *Studies in Philology* 32 (4): 580–587.

Perl, Sondra. 1994. Writing Process: A Shining Moment. In *Landmark essays on writing process*, ed. S. Perl, xi–xx. Davis, CA: Hermagoras Press.

Quintilian. 1987. *Quintilian on the Teaching of Speaking and Writing: Translations from Books One, Two and Ten of the* Institutio Oratoria, ed. J.J. Murphy. Carbondale: Southern University Press.

Satel, Sally, and Scott O. Lilienfeld. 2013. *Brainwashed: The Seductive Appeal of Mindless Neuroscience*. New York, NY: Basic Books.

Seung, Sebastian. 2012. *Connectome: How the Brain's Wiring Makes Us Who We are*. Boston, MA: Houghton Mifflin.

Sommers, Nancy. 1980. Revision Strategies of Student Writers and Experienced Adult Writers. *College Composition and Communication* 31 (4): 378–388.

Stewart, Donald C. 1972. *The Authentic Voice: A Prewriting Approach to Student Writing*. Dubuque, IA: William C. Brown.

Temple, Elise, Gayle K. Deutsch, Russell A. Poldrack, Steven L. Miller, Paula Tallal, Michael M. Merzenich, and John D. E. Gabriell. 2003. Neural Deficits in Children With Dyslexia Ameliorated by Behavioral Remediation: Evidence from Functional MRI. *Proceedings of the National Academy of Sciences* 97 (25): 13907–13912.

Villanueva, Victor. 1993. *Bootstraps: From an American Academic of Color*. Urbana, IL: NCTE.

Chapter 10
Modelling Spoken Genres for Foreign Language Learners

Yulia A. Lobina

Abstract Genre teaching is considered vital for language and literacy pedagogies. Several genre models have been suggested based on various approaches and fitting various goals of teaching genres. In the present chapter I propose a technique of modelling spoken genres for cognitive development of EFL students. It consists of three stages, starting with modelling the native interlocutor's view of genre, proceeding with building the language teacher's model, and finally coming to the student's model created for each specific target learner audience. The resulting model explicitly outlines the essential features of genre to be emulated by the learners, expounds discrepancies between analogous genres in L1 and L2 cultures, and reveals gaps in learners' prior genre knowledge. The technique draws on the theory of zones of proximal development, identifying the skills to be acquired while learning genres in the EFL classroom. The technique was used in building a model of the genre of storytelling for education students in a Russian university. Implementation of the model in a communication course enabled the students to acquire new interaction techniques and communicative skills.

Keywords Genre-based pedagogies · Cognitive development · Modelling genres · Teaching English as a foreign language · Spoken genre

10.1 Introduction

Recent decades have seen the notion of genre become crucial for research in various spheres of c ommunication (Swales 2019: 75), as well as for practice of language and literacy instruction (Hyland 2007: 148). Changes in the target learning audiences have emphasised "an urgent need for more theoretically robust, linguistically informed, and research-grounded text descriptions" (Hyland 2007: 149). The existing models for genre description, however, some of them quite universal, some encompassing genres of a particular set (such as the highly popular Swalesian CARS model (Swales

Y. A. Lobina (✉)
Ulyanovsk State University of Education, Ulyanovsk, Russia

N. V. Sukhova et al. (eds.), *Multimodality, Digitalization and Cognitivity in Communication and Pedagogy*, Numanities - Arts and Humanities in Progress 20, https://doi.org/10.1007/978-3-030-84071-6_10

1990)), proved to be scarcely suitable, unmodified, for teaching spoken genres in the L2 classroom. One of the core problems appears to be the tendency to overlook the dynamic cognitive nature of genre and disregard the opportunities genre pedagogies present for students' social and personal development.

In this chapter I present my experience of building a model of a spoken genre informed by structural, functional, and cognitive approaches to genre. Firstly, genre is viewed as a complex sign of communicative context, which cannot be interpreted regardless of other signs in the genre system. Secondly, the principle of modelling is based on describing the functions of formal features in accomplishing rhetorical purposes. Finally, individual perception of the interaction and its social context is included in the model, which is, however, typical in its essential characteristics of a certain discourse community.

In what follows I briefly discuss current conceptions of genre and genre peda-gogies, followed by an overview of explicit and implicit approaches to modelling genres for pedagogical purposes. I go on to describe my experience of modelling the genre of storytelling for EFL students. I discuss problems I faced at each of the three modelling stages and choices I made in solving them. In the conclusion I suggest some ways of checking the validity of the model.

10.2   Approaches to Genre and Genre-Based Pedagogies

Although relevance of the concept of genre for understanding human communica-tion has long become obvious, approaches to its meaning and application to devel-oping communicative competence vary considerably. More often than not a genre researcher follows one of the three distinct traditions of investigating genre iden-tified by Hyon (1996) and currently considered to be the most influential in the field. Genres are viewed as 'social processes' in the Sydney school of genre analysis (Martin 1997). Following the principles of systemic functional linguistics Australian genre researchers explore typified ways of linguistically interacting in recurrent situ-ation types. In genre studies within the English for Special Purposes (ESP) context, the emphasis is on the discourse community which possesses genres, using them as "mechanisms of intercommunication among its members" (Swales 1990: 25). Swale-sian genre theory views genres as tools enabling a discourse community to achieve its goals and initiate new members. For New Rhetoricians, genres are forms of social interpretation, establishing a link between certain situations recognised as recurrent and typified strategies used to act within them (Miller 1994). New Rhetoric focusses on the genre users' intentions and motives, ways of negotiating their identity, estab-lishing their affiliations, and cooperating with others in the social construction of reality.

Some areas of analysis, however, seem to be of equal interest to genre researchers regardless of tradition. According to Swales (2009), common trends in genre analysis shared by the three schools include examining constraints imposed by a genre on its users and choices available to them within a genre, addressing the impact of local context on generic features, focussing on genre evolution, and determining implications of genre studies for genre-based pedagogies.

This last trend has arguably been characteristic of genre studies since their beginning, or at least since linguistic and socio-rhetorical approaches to genre emerged. In fact, Hyon (1996) in her widely cited paper suggests targeting various learning audiences as a plausible explanation for theoretical differences between the three traditions in genre studies. Approaches to genre pedagogy, though, tend to vary to no lesser degree than perspectives on the definition of genre, its structure, or essential features.

A range of goals is distinguished in genre pedagogy depending on the needs of the target audience (see, for instance, Russell and Fisher 2009). The first goal, genre acquisition, is typically realised in courses for linguistically and culturally disadvantaged students, including school-age children. The genres produced by the students, their range inevitably limited, are considered to be basic for the culture the learners are striving to enter. The aim of such courses is to enable a student to reproduce a text type using a template provided. Although criticised for perpetuating social inequality (Cope and Kalantzis 1993: 6), this approach proved to be fairly effective when used in Australian schools.

The goal of genre acquisition is viewed more broadly in the ESP approach, which requires not only knowledge of the formal features of texts but also awareness of the values and rhetorical purposes of a discourse community—often a professional one—which produces the texts. An ESP typical target audience consists of international students in British and US universities, who seek proficiency in disciplinary or professional genres. The pedagogical purpose of the ESP genre approach is to help advanced non-native English-speaking students to act effectively in new cultural contexts. However, the students are not expected or prepared to question shared communicative goals.

A different goal is raising genre awareness, mostly in native English speakers taking a course in composition and rhetoric which enables them to perform the roles of actors in the social construction of the world. The courses are designed to assist students in developing "a critical consciousness of both rhetorical purposes and ideological effects of generic forms" (Devitt 2008: 192). Their rhetorical competence should be flexible enough to allow transferring genre knowledge to ever-evolving contexts. Mastering genres provides students with the means of making their voice heard in public discourse, as well as negotiating their identities, stances, and values.

For Second Language Acquisition (SLA) theory and practice, however, the goal of cognitive development through teaching genres seems to be more relevant, especially for EFL teachers of the expanding circle (Kachru 1992) teaching general English as part of comprehensive secondary education. Cognition-oriented genre pedagogies shift the focus from the individual's role in the community, whether more or less active, to their own cognitive refiguration occurring while mastering a genre (Bazerman 2009).

The impact of learning a new language on personality development has long been discussed in bilingualism studies. Reviewing the problem as seen by theoreticians and bilinguals themselves since the first half of the twentieth century, Pavlenko (2006) notes similarities between acquisition of new registers in the native language and learning a new language. She argues, however, that "acquisition and use of a new language, in particular one that is typologically different from one's native language, is a much more challenging enterprise", with a considerably deeper impact on the speaker's identity and self-perception (Pavlenko 2006: 2). This view is consistent with Koven's (2007) findings concerning Portuguese–French bilinguals and the way they perceive their own experience of communicating in L1 and L2. Koven's data appear to prove that the use of two languages may result in the emergence of different selves.

There is considerable controversy over the benefits of bilingualism and the resulting possession of multiple identities, with recently prevailing tendency to see them as a source of creative enrichment (Pavlenko 2006: 2–5). Some SLA theories actually maintain that the emergence of a new language personality with a worldview peculiar to a different culture is a natural consequence of, and a necessary condition for, acquiring communicative competence in a foreign language. For instance, shaping a secondary language personality in non-native English learners, as well as non-native English teachers, is considered a strategic aim by language educators in Russia (Gumovskaya 2017). However, there has been little discussion on the role of teaching genres of a new culture in developing a secondary language personality.

In cognitive-oriented genre pedagogies genres are viewed as 'socio-cognitive schemas' (Jones 2008: 239) representing typical situations of social interaction and, consequently, 'tools of cognition' (Bazerman 2009: 283). Citing Vygotsky (1986) and Luria (1970), Bazerman (2009) considers learning to be the basis of development. Learning the conventions of a new genre, in particular, is argued to be a cognitive practice of internalising social interaction experience which leads to emergence of new cognitive tools, effective in further engagements with the social world.

According to Vygotsky (1986), entering new domains of practice stimulates personal development by offering opportunities for restructuring thought. Bazerman sees genre as such a domain, presented metaphorically in his earlier work as "a kind of habitat for the writer to inhabit both psychologically and socially" (Bazerman 1994: 19). Writing courses, seen from this perspective, are likely to provide students with an opportunity of entering a series of such 'habitats' to improve their writing skills and, more significantly, to develop their ability to step into new social roles and produce appropriate social forms of response.

The crucial part of Vygotsky's theory, however, is the concept of the zone of proximal development (Vygotsky 1986). According to the scholar, personal development takes place in the area between what a student can do with and without the help of a more knowledgeable other (the educator). The teacher's task, then, is to identify the zone their students can cover in learning a particular genre and to scaffold the experience which leads to acquiring new skills and strategies.

On the one hand, learners of the Expanding circle endeavouring to acquire genres of English-speaking cultures are obviously disadvantaged in getting this kind of experience. Lack of immersion in the simulated context appears to result in the genre being severed from its semiotic environment. Even when both teachers and students are native speakers this causes difficulties in teaching genres (Freadman

1994: 48). Evidently, providing the appropriate uptake of the genres for students in non-native environments is yet more problematic. On the other hand, the connection between formal features of genre and its social purposes may enable students to gain access to knowledge of typified social interactions in a new culture. As Williams and Colomb put it,

> [w]hen we learn social context, we are also learning its forms; but when we learn forms, we may also be learning their social contexts. (Williams and Colomb 1993: 262)

In the present chapter I propose that a course of cognitive spoken genre teaching might be most effective if based on a genre model which should:

- have the adequate degree of conciseness;
- specify divergence in the structural and contextual features of the genre in the native and target cultures;
- be modified for each learning audience with its specific generic knowledge and cognitive development.

10.3   Explicit and Implicit Approaches to Genre Modelling

A major issue in building such a model is who might be responsible for its creation. The issue is closely connected with the question of which features of the genres should be explicitly described in the model.

The debate over efficacy of explicit instruction and tacit acquisition of genres is central to the current genre teaching discourse. Implicit genre pedagogies shift the responsibility for building the model of the genre under study onto students, relying on their prior generic knowledge and transferability skills. As most of the research following this approach was carried out in university contexts the knowledge is likely to be drawn from students' previous school writing experience. The efficacy of implicit learning models depends largely on students' ability to modify the map of the genre according to the new context through studying the assignment, participating in class discussions, and making use of the teacher's feedback on the texts produced by the students (Freedman 1987).

An educator adopting the explicit approach to genre pedagogy assumes a greater responsibility for production of the genre. Instructors play the leading role in two of the three stages of the teaching–learning cycle proposed by the Sydney school (Martin and Rose 2008). During the first stage the teacher provides students with a genre model, during the second one they produce a new text jointly. It is only during the third stage that learners start working independently. Non-native students definitely need quite a lot of explicit instruction on linguistic and rhetorical patterns of genres, as well as conventions of the community which uses them. From the cognitive perspective, however, there is the disadvantage of receiving and trying to implement a model built externally, not related to the students' own genre schemas, and probably having more to do with learning than development.

As Hyon (2002) found in a study of a role of genre in an SLA course, the degree to which non-native students can profit from totally implicit pedagogical models is rather limited (Hyon 2002). While immersion in the process of text production appears to be crucial for internalisation of the skills and strategies involved, non-native speakers/writers are likely to lack linguistic resources necessary for the modification of prior generic knowledge. Still more importantly, the knowledge of genre conventions which students have when they enter the course must necessarily be culture specific, drawn from their exposure to L1 genres. Transfer of L1 generic skills to a new cultural context is as likely to help building an authentic model of the genre as to hinder it.

To ensure students' involvement in genre creation, encouraging their active participation in investigating the genre has been suggested (Motta-Roth 2009). Learning to investigate genre systems and their components, both on a rhetorical and lexico-grammatical level, is supposed, according to Motta-Roth, to teach students how to become genre analysts.

Performing rhetoric analysis, however, calls for appropriate qualification. The relationship of formal features of the text to contextual variables has been researched extensively in various branches of the humanities. Scholars have focussed on such features of context as the register of the situation, the mode of communication, the social position of the speakers, their gender, age, and ethnicity, to name but a few. Much work on the role of phonetic, lexico-grammatical, stylistic elements of the text in making the recipient aware of the context has been carried out in stylistics, pragmatics, sociolinguistics and, more recently, discourse analysis, yet a great deal of results are still intuitive and interpretative. The search for reliable methods of identifying functions of formal elements in a pragmatic context is still going on. Formal and contextual analysis of a genre may, therefore, prove quite a demanding task for a student, especially one majoring in fields other than humanities, let alone high school or even secondary and primary school students taking a composition course.

Another objection to basing a genre course on the students' involvement in genre analysis is that whatever the analyst's qualification, the procedure is highly time-consuming. While cognitive development of students can, indeed, be enhanced by their acquiring analytical skills through genre research, the number of genres to be learnt in a course will necessarily be quite limited. If the cognitive development is supposed to be fostered through 'inhabiting' genres, and not doing pure research, the curriculum should cover most of the new culture's basic genres.

To overcome the problem, interactive models aimed at synthesising implicit and explicit approaches suggest that students produce an initial text in the genre being studied using their prior genre experience. Further steps include discussing genre samples, identifying their characteristics compared to similar genres, developing an outline of the text, producing the text, and getting feedback (Guimarães 2009). This sequence is supposed to ensure learners' involvement in the writing process, at the same time providing them with necessary support.

Thus, I suggest that a practical solution to the problem of dividing responsibility for creating a genre model is building a major part of it out of the classroom, by researchers and educators. To ensure internalisation of the model by the learners, though, it is paramount that they should join the process at some later point. Building such a model is difficult to conceive as a one-stage process involving a single actor. Responsibility for creating a genre model should be distributed among genre researchers, genre teachers, and genre learners, spreading the process over several stages.

10.4 Modelling the Genre of Storytelling

In my study I investigated the possibilities of building a model of a genre for future English teachers in Russia. The study involved modelling a spoken genre, firstly, because the area is definitely under-researched, specifically that of genre pedagogy concentrating mostly on teaching writing (Millar 2011: 3); secondly, because involvement in on-the-spot real-time spoken communication arguably contributes to acquiring the 'felt sense' of the genre (Freedman 1987: 101) to a greater degree.

I recount my experience of modelling genres for education undergraduates in an EFL course aimed at acquiring the communicative norms of spoken and written English. As a result of the course, the students role-played a dinner table conversation. To identify components of this communicative form I turned to Tannen's widely cited book *Conversational Style* (Tannen 2005). In her study, Tannen addresses the question of how language is used to signal the speaker's intentions and create social worlds. While analysing an audiotaped dinner table conversation she mentions the genres used by the participants, which include the telling of stories, jokes, and discussions. In the course of preparation of the role-play models three genres were built, and in the present chapter I focus on the genre of storytelling.

Echoing Bazerman's (1994) description of writing process, the cognitive model of storytelling was built in three stages. Bazerman outlines the struggles of a writing situation from the point of view of the writers themselves, intimate observers, in particular teachers or coaches ready to offer guidance in understanding the social environment, and middle-range observers, providing social interpretation of the texts produced (Bazerman 1994: 10–36). Similarly, but in the reverse order, I started with modelling the genre from the potential native interlocutor's perspective, proceeded with the non-native teacher's adaptation for a particular L1 culture and, finally, came to the perspective of the student, the actual non-native producer of the genre.

10.4.1 Building the Native Speaker's Model

The first stage involved designing a model of genre as used by a native speaker—the ultimate recipient of the genre. The model reflects how the discourse community perceives the situational context of the genre, its structural elements, and language features. The responsibility for creating the native speaker's model of genre lies with professional researchers, although there seems to exist no reason why a genre teacher cannot assume the role, given gaps in the data of the genre being studied.

If the goal of the course is to provide students with an opportunity to 'inhabit' the social situation, performing the roles of the participants and employing communicative strategies recurrently used by native speakers, the genre model should highlight the correlation of lexico-grammatical and pragmatic generic features. Some thorough research has been done into narrative genres in this respect. In fact, there is quite a comprehensive model of the genre of storytelling. In building the native speaker's model I drew heavily on Rühlemann's description of English conversational narrative, a corpus-based research (Rühlemann 2014).

Rühlemann demonstrates how reaching the general purpose of the genre—sense-making—is connected with the type of participants involved and the typical structure of the genre. He treats storytelling as a dialogical genre, with two broad categories of participants: 'narrator' and 'recipient', further subdividing them into six narrower types (Rühlemann 2014: 9). Storytelling is also shown as a variable genre, with the participants negotiating the size of their contribution to sense-making through turntaking techniques (Rühlemann 2014: 76–109).

As for the structure of the genre, according to Rühlemann (2014), the process of making a point is completed through following several stages. It starts with a pre-narrative stretch leading to the topic discussed being followed by an introduction signalling the beginning of the narration proper. The background describes the told situation, while the problem reveals the difficulty its participants encountered. The tension of the story is at its highest at the stage of the resolution, falling towards the comment, which merges with the post-narrative stretch (Rühlemann 2014: 24–29).

The principal persuasive technique enabling the participants to make their point in the collaborative process of making sense is dramatisation. It turns the listener into a 'witness' of the events and so adds credibility to the narrator's position and point (Rühlemann 2014: 155). Rühlemann dwells on involvement strategies recurrently realised in storytelling: resorting to quotation, changes in intonation, and mimetic devices.

> As a result, recipients are no longer only participants in the telling situation, they also become participants in the told situation. (Rühlemann 2014:155)

Rühlemann's model is complex, allowing for the variability of the genre. He discusses in great detail two principal devices for marking quotation: interjections and pauses, both silent and filled (Rühlemann 2014: 123–154) and their role in involving the listener in the situation of narration. In his analysis of a corpus of narratives, Rühlemann investigates the structure sequences of using dramatisation devices, such as intonational means and mimetic devices, which culminate in the crucial structural points of the story (Rühlemann 2014: 155–172).

Using elaborate corpora techniques enabled Rühlemann to create a detailed description of a narration employed within a dialogue. This very detailed character, however, prevents it from being immediately implemented in a genre teaching class.

It is evident that genre competence of native speakers varies. Good storytellers, with their deep understanding of the nuances of the process, have always been valued in a community. Acquiring such competence might take years of practice and prove to be quite out of the students' zone of proximal development for the moment.

To be effectively used in the classroom, the native speaker's model should be modified to be as concise as possible. At the same time, 'inhabiting' the genre should be realistic, the learner's performance should be recognisable as storytelling, and the learner as a storyteller. If the student's product includes all the essential generic traits it will stimulate the appropriate uptake.

The notion of uptake was introduced by Freadman (2002), who proposes that the text standing in syntagmatic relationship with the text under study can confirm or deny the latter's generic status.

> The text is contrived to secure a certain class of uptakes, and the interpretant, or the uptake text, confirms its generic status by conforming itself to this contrivance. It does so, by – say – 'taking it as' an invitation or request. (Freadman 2002: 40)

Making the model concise, yet realistic, and retaining the social functions of the genre is the task for the second stage.

10.4.2 Building the Teacher's Model

The responsibility for modifying the model at this stage, namely adapting it for classroom use, lies with the educators. The description of the genre for a foreign language student should necessarily be limited to the key contextual features. Emulating the lexico-grammatical, phonetic, and stylistic features related to the key contextual traits appears to be indispensable for the student to 'inhabit' the genre, developing a storyteller's identity. In search of the principles of determining the basic features, and building the teacher's model was informed by Dolinin's theory of genre as a means of organising social interaction (Dolinin 1999).

Dolinin distinguishes three principal functions of genre: modelling the context of interaction, projecting the author's identity, and conveying the communicative norms of the discourse community (Dolinin 1999: 10–13). Dolinin (1999) regards genre as a function of recurrent social situations with its reflection of the discourse community ideology. The speaker perceives the interaction episode as a certain frame and sends out signals of this perception. Structural and linguistic features of a genre function as such signals. Accepting the speaker's perspective on the situation results in the recipient's providing the appropriate uptake.

To reproduce the frame, the participants take on certain social roles. Their identities, while subject to negotiation in the course of the communicative episode, should meet the interlocutors' general expectations of a competent genre performer.

Finally, every genre emerges and functions within a certain discourse community (Swales 1990). Being initiated into the genre system of the community means functioning as its recognised member. The teacher's model of genre should include the features identifying their user as belonging to a discourse community, sharing its ideology.

The minimal set of features characterising storytelling is identified by analysing the syntagmatic and paradigmatic relationships of the genre. In the teacher's model of storytelling the types of participants are restricted to the type of unsupported narrator, performing without any back channelling or contributions from the audience (Rühlemann 2014: 9). As long as the storyteller includes asides to the listener in his text, he or she still retains the dialogicity inherent in the genre and can be sure of the audience's participation in the sense-making. The listeners provide the appropriate uptake: they discuss the point of the story or start a story which supports or contradicts the point (Tannen 2005: 126).

From a structural point of view, the story is recognisable as such and may be included in a friendly conversation without adding a pre-narrative stretch, turn-by-turn talk discussing the problem. Presenting an introduction is a sufficient signal of the communicative episode which follows as storytelling. Thus, the teacher's model of storytelling structure included the introduction, background, problem, resolution, and coda, commenting on the told story. I used the sample story of a vanishing hitchhiker from the textbook *New Inside Out: Advanced Student's Book* (Jones et al. 2010). In it, the narrator starts with an introduction, presenting the events to be recounted as part of her personal experience, goes on to describe the background of driving down a lonely road late one inclement evening. She goes on to pose a problem of the inexplicable disappearance of a girl to whom she had given a lift, and suggests a resolution implying that the passenger was a ghost, finishing the story by admitting the incredible nature of the whole thing but still insists on having experienced it.

These parts are essential for recognising the communicative episode as story-telling. The structure of the story cannot be made more concise, if the appropriate uptake is expected. Further reduction of the parts of the story interferes with it carrying out the genre's function. A narration which stops at expounding the problem, and which is missing the resolution and comment, can be recognised by the interlocutor as a different genre, namely an everyday complaint (see a description in Werzbicka 1983). A complaint presupposes the interlocutor's immediate reaction after the stage of revealing the problem, with another speaker getting the turn—with the uptake quite different from that expected in storytelling.

Introduction of a complaint into a friendly conversation, which the students were trying to emulate, appears to be risky. Laforest categorises complaints as face-threatening acts, which can be safely realised providing that the relationship between the interactants is highly intimate, for instance in family conversations (Laforest 2002). The intention of a person who complains is to seek compassion or help while the purpose of storytelling is to get the point of the story across to the listener and trying to engage them in building a shared world. In cultures with smaller horizontal distance, pleading for compassion with dinner table interlocutors might be considered an appropriate way to establish rapport. Given the comparatively great horizontal distance in anglophone cultures, introducing the genre of complaint in the context of dinner table conversation in English might constitute a breach of communicative norms, confusing the interlocutors as to the speaker's perspective on the context of interaction.

As Rühlemann's corpora analysis shows (Rühlemann 2014), experienced story-tellers build up their dramatisation devices in sequences culminating in the crucial points of the story. In such a way they get their point across to listeners with marked effect. Their skills allow them to become leading actors in the shared world they are constructing without being presumptuous. They manage to retain the role of a peer in a friendly conversation. Developing a sufficient level of expertise to take up this position in a discourse community requires considerable time, effort, and prob-ably, real talent. It might not be achieved by every native speaker and setting it as a classroom goal for L2 learners would be unrealistic.

Nevertheless, excluding dramatisation devices from the teacher's model of story-telling altogether would prevent the students from 'inhabiting' the genre in the role of storyteller. Avoiding dramatisation devices in the narration results in the speaker's resorting to more direct persuasive techniques, changing the generic type of the narra-tion into a closely related genre of parable, diverging from storytelling in the degree of directness of employed strategies, but similar in terms of intention and structure.

A parable is "an expanded analogy used to convince and persuade" (Snodgrass 2008: 9). Parables, according to Snodgrass, "by their very nature seek to make a rhetorical point" (Snodgrass 2008: 2) which makes the stages of resolution and comment as indispensable for them as they are for stories. Yet, telling a parable in a dinner table conversation threatens the interlocutors' perception of the narrator's identity and communicative role. Strategies used in a parable tend to be more direct than those employed in storytelling. A parable emphasises 'simplicity' and clarity of the message. The main force behind the impact a parable has on the listener is the inherent authority rather than artfulness of the speaker (Snodgrass 2008: 2–3). This asymmetry of the participants' roles marks the religious context, rather than everyday setting. The interlocutors are likely to be confused by the controversial signals the speaker is sending, interpreting their behaviour as domineering.

To avoid this undesirable result, the teacher's model includes major means of dramatising the point of a story such as giving additional details, repetition, using direct ways of introducing the characters' speech, personalising the narrative, as well as prosodic and non-verbal components of a narrative. In the sample story provided by Jones et al. (2010) the storyteller provides a detailed description of the weather contributing to the alarming effect, the girl's appearance explaining the narrator's sudden urge to help her, and the girl's grave shown to the disbelieving driver by the girl's mother. The crucial detail is the fur coat which the narrator had given to the girl, later found folded on the grave. The dialogues with the girl and her mother are dramatised rather than recounted making the listener an involuntary witness. Syntactical structures and certain words are repeated, the tone and the pace of the narration are changed artfully with the listener falling into an enchanting rhythm. This indirect way of making the interlocutor understand and share the author's view, even if it is contrary to the listener's prior convictions, can be highly effective without imposing the speaker's authority: "The author abducts us … we are taken up in the story" (Snodgrass 2008: 1).

These traits of storytelling make the basis for the teacher's model. Mastering them constitutes the skills attained at the end of the zone of proximal development. This scheme includes the contextual aspect: storytelling should retain some traces of dialogicity, such as personalising the narration, asides to the listener, even without actual back channelling. As for the structural aspect, a story should include an introduction, background, problem, resolution, and comment, with pre- and post-narrative stretches optional. The strategies employed should be indirect, making use of stylistic, lexical, syntactical, prosodic, and non-verbal means. The model does not include the skill of sequencing these devices, which, according to Rühlemann, manifests itself in most original stories. This skill might be left outside the zone of proximal development in most classrooms as its lack does not interfere with identifying the frame of the performance as the frame of storytelling.

To scaffold the activities leading to attaining these skills, the teacher should also identify the starting point of the zone of proximal development, namely what the students already know about the genre and can do without the teacher's help. The first step in that direction with L2 students is to compare L1 and L2 native speaker's models, assuming that the learners are familiar with the conventions of the genre in their native culture. Generic traits missing from L1 genre model constitute the zone of proximal development, representing strategies of reaching goals uncharacteristic for the learners' native culture, new to them and enhancing their social experience if internalised. This part of the teacher's model designed for explicit instruction should be informed by comparative generic studies.

Unfortunately, these appear to be the less developed part of genre studies, so the educator frequently has to adopt the role of researcher, taking up contrastive research. This is exactly what I had to do while building the teacher's model of storytelling, drawing from Borissova's study of the Russian narrative (Borissova 2002: 246–256) for the description of the genre in the students' L1 culture.

The genre of Russian narrative appears to be similar in its crucial features to its English analogue in Rühlemann's description (2014). Its principal characteristic is dialogicity either implicating multiple narrators or requiring active involvement of listening participants. A recounting of events devoid of any traces of dialogicity constitutes a different, though related, genre of report, which lacks an evaluative component and carries out a merely informative function. Another major factor differentiating storytelling from other types of narrative is the choice of presentation strategies. To be recognised as such, a storyteller should make skillful use of detail, dramatisation and sequencing. Moreover, Borisova's list of structural components of a story corresponds to that of Rühlemann's, including pre- and post-narrative stretch, introduction, background, problem, resolution, and coda.

The contrastive analysis of storytelling in L1 and L2 cultures reveals a great deal of similarity in terms of context, structure, and strategies. However, there seem to exist culturally specific communicative norms to which storytellers should conform if they want their listeners to understand the point of the story. As Tannen maintains, "the point of the story is dramatized rather than lexicalized" (Tannen 2005: 41), therefore, divergence in national ways of dramatisation, including interaction of verbal and non-verbal elements of communication, appears to be crucial for the genre of storytelling.

Non-verbal elements of communication and their correlation with the verbal message have been shown to display clear cross-cultural differences since they were first investigated (Ekman and Frisien 1969). Mastering typical prosodic and non-verbal patterns of the new culture is apparently within the zone of proximate development for L2 learners.

Ekman and Frisien (1969) were the first to describe five possible relationships between verbal and non-verbal elements of communication. Repetition occurs when the information in the verbal and non-verbal messages is identical. If it is divided between verbal and non-verbal signs, this type of relationship is called complementation. When there is no verbal message in the communicative episode at all, substitution by non-verbal elements is likely to have taken place. In the case of contradiction, words and gestures send conflicting signals, and finally, the speaker can use non-verbal means to draw special attention to some part of their verbal message by emphasising or accentuating them.

Our analysis of interaction of verbal and non-verbal components in American and Russian stand-up comedy (Nikolaeva and Lobina 2018) revealed noticeable differences in how frequently these types occur in spoken English and Russian. American comedians seem to rely on emphasising their speech with gestures and mimicry to achieve a humorous effect, while Russian performers apparently resort to repeating verbal information in non-verbal elements more frequently than their American counterparts.

Researchers have suggested that predominance of a certain type of verbal/non-verbal interaction is linked with the speaker's perception of the context and the participants. Thus, the major function of repetition, according to Poyatos, is validating the sincerity of the speaker and creating the feeling of solidarity between the interlocutors (Poyatos 2002: 60). Accentuation, or emphasis, is associated with the speaker's intention to achieve maximal clarity. In its exaggerated form it may evoke the image of a drill instructor (Hickson and Stacks 1993: 265). Different roles of non-verbal elements in the message might reflect divergence in typical strategies of reaching out to the audience while projecting the image of a competent performer.

This is arguably attributable to the cultural identities of the performers. American culture is traditionally classified as a low-context discourse community. The term was suggested by Hall (1976) to describe the environment in which a communication process takes place. In low-context cultures communication is fairly independent of the environment, requiring the communicants to express their ideas directly, leaving as little as possible for the interlocutor to guess, or deduce from the context. Conversely, in high-context cultures, such as Russian, the context of interaction is rather informative, and the participants can draw freely from their shared knowledge. High-context cultures typically belong to the collectivistic type, where a sense of affinity with the audience is crucial for the speaker, while the risk of being misunderstood is almost negligible.

Thus, strategies of using non-verbal elements to reach out to the audience appear to be culturally specific and within the zone of proximal development for L2 learners mastering the genre of storytelling. Including them in the teacher's model and scaffolding classroom activities according to this model provide students with an opportunity to acquire the social skills of interacting with a new type of audience, together with an ability to adjust their communicative strategies to a changing context.

The crucial features included in the teacher's model of the genre of English storytelling for Russian learners were dialogicity, five-part structure, visualisation of events, and emphasising verbal messages by non-verbal means. As most of them are common for the genre in L1 and L2 cultures, it seemed at this stage that explicit instruction was necessary only in mastering the latter trait, while students could transfer the other storytelling skills from their experience within L1 culture.

The teacher's model of genre may serve as an assessment tool, providing both teachers and learners with a mould for estimating the effectiveness of the performance. However, to reveal the zone of proximal development of individual students, it should be contrasted with the students' prior genre knowledge.

10.4.3 Building the Student's Model

Although it is reasonable to suppose that students are familiar with generic features common for the two cultures and only need explicit instruction to internalise features specific for L2 culture (types of verbal/non-verbal interaction in the case of storytelling), actual prior genre knowledge may vary considerably between particular groups of students. On the one hand, learners' previous exposure to and experience of genres of L1 culture, as well as their genre competence, depend on a number of factors. No native speaker is equally proficient in every genre of their own culture. On the other hand, being foreign language students, learners enter the course with a certain level of L2 competence, including genre competence. Some generic features which are non-existent in L1 culture may be transferred from L2 genres acquired in the course of previous study.

The diversity of students' responses to the genre teaching assignments has been commented on by educators (see, for instance, Devitt 2006 and Soliday 2005). They concluded that to successfully internalise generic conventions, students have to "rework the voice of the other, the communal form, into their own individual words, intentions, and worldviews" (Soliday 2005: 82), which makes the process to a great degree individualised. Thus, the final working model of a genre cannot be created without estimating particular students' prior genre knowledge and consequently, without collaboration with the learners.

Therefore, at the third and final stage of building the student's model of storytelling the description of the genre was further modified in the classroom, with responsibility shared by the teacher and the students. In doing this I drew from interactive models of genre teaching aimed at synthesising implicit and explicit approaches suggested by the Brazilian school of genre teaching (Bawarshi and Reiff 2010: 187–189). They suggest that students produce an initial text in the genre being studied using their prior genre experience. Further steps include discussing genre samples, identifying their characteristics compared to similar genres, developing an outline of the text, producing the text, and getting feedback (Guimarães 2009). This sequence is supposed to ensure learners' involvement in the writing process, at the same time providing them with the necessary support.

I started my didactic sequence with a discussion of the genre context, in the course of which I made sure the learners were familiar with the social activity system the genre functions in, whether from their prior exposure to similar genres of their native culture, or from studying L2 genres. If the genre proves to be totally unfamiliar, there is little probability of learners' cognitive advance, as students would find themselves outside the zone of proximate development, unable to bridge the gap between their prior knowledge and new skills.

Interviews with education students in EFL communication classes proved that their previous exposure to the genre of storytelling was rather limited. The genres they admitted to being most familiar with were the literary short story, read for pleasure or as material for discussion in literature and stylistics classes, as well as various genres of everyday narratives such as reports and complaints. This, on the one hand, entailed difficulties in performing storytelling successfully, but, on the other hand, afforded opportunities for cognitive development. To reveal cognitive patterns of the students' prior genres closest to the target one both formally and contextually, students were guided through the step of initial 'early production' (following the didactic sequence suggested in Guimarães 2009).

The initial production was preceded by demonstrating the model sample of the story of a vanishing hitchhiker from the textbook *New Inside Out: Advanced Student's Book* (Jones et al. 2010) without any analysis of correlation between contextual and formal features. The textbook provides the audio of the story but no video material. Then the students were asked to produce a similar story in front of the class followed by an analysis at the next stage.

The analysis started with studying the teacher's model of storytelling. In a general discussion that followed, the students, aided by the instructor, contrasted the crucial generic features of the samples created in the stage of initial production with the model sample. The results were consistent with Devitt's finding that students rely on the genres from their prior experience when confronted with a new rhetorical situation (Devitt 2006). In rhetoric, the genre the speaker draws on to shape the suitable rhetorical response in an unprecedented situation is termed the antecedent genre (Jamieson 1975: 414).

Some of the students' narratives had a typical structure of everyday complaint. The parts of resolution and comment were missing. One of the students, Lusine, told a story of a boyfriend abandoning his partner. The introduction warned the listeners that they were in for a piece of personal experience. The background related the history of a relationship and the problem part included the boyfriend's unexpected disappearance and the desperate search for him. The following episode of finding him at last in the bosom of his other family did not serve as a resolution of the problem, merely deepening the main character/narrator's frustration. The listeners got the impression that Lusine's main purpose in telling the story was to get some moral support. A similar impression was produced by a story of another student,

Darya, about her parents' constantly favouring her brother at her expense. The story consisted of a series of episodes, each further aggravating the situation, but providing no solution.

A report was another antecedent genre structurally divergent from storytelling that the students drew on. Dasha presented an account of a singer's conflict with her fans, which was successfully resolved. The part which was supposed to be a comment expressed the narrator's delight in the happy outcome but carried no point across to the listeners, lacking the evaluative element.

Somewhat surprisingly, the choice of the wrong strategies by some students resulted in creating parables. The students' prior exposure to religious discourse seemed to be rather limited, nevertheless, they appeared to be familiar with the genre, I would presume through the educational discourse of L1 culture. Albina told a story of a girl's conflicts with her mother-in-law resulting in the young woman's decision to use poison. The situation was resolved by the fact that the substance she supposed to be lethal proved harmless, through a wise man's interference. While waiting for the results of her awful action the girl grew fond of her mother-in-law and repented.

The structure of the narrative coincided with that of a story, and the point was quite clear for the audience. Yet, the narrative was unlikely to secure the typical uptake of storytelling, which is further discussion of the topic or a story round supporting the point. Albina didn't use any visualisation devices, instead favouring an extremely direct strategy of presenting events. As a result, the listeners were not 'taken up' in the story, by just taking the narrator's position for granted.

As for the visualisation techniques the other students did use, the non-verbal elements in their communication mostly repeated the verbal message, which can be explained by interference of their L1 culture visualisation skills.

The only crucial generic feature that was present in most samples of initial production was dialogicity. The narrators felt the need for the listeners' support and included asides to the listeners in their stories, while the group provided remarks and questions, at times co-authoring the story.

Having noted and explained discrepancies between the formal features of the antecedent and target genres, the students, guided by the instructor, modified the teacher's model of the genre, outlining the zone of proximal development and building the student's model. At this last stage of modelling the genre, the zone of proximal development included the skills of expressing one's attitude to the problem through structuring the story properly, using indirect strategies of making a point, and establishing contact with the audience by emphasising the verbal message with non-verbal means of communication.

At the next step students did assignments based on the model, aimed at mastering the rhetorical strategies associated with the target genre. They practiced inventing plots including all the structural elements of the story, transformed indirect presentations of characters' interactions into stretches with direct speech, added details and repetition to succinct accounts of events, and identified the passages requiring pauses, and change of pace and tone to involve the listener, practicing those prosodic visualisation devices.

In a series of classes, the students learned to identify types of verbal/non-verbal interaction in authentic English language videos, and then took care to introduce emphasis into their utterances and reduced the amount of repeating the verbal message with mimetic means and gestures.

The following step involved producing the genre again, following the principle: do not act as you would in a similar context in your native culture, act as you would in a different context, employing a strategy characteristic of the genre under study. Such transfer of experience would appear to resemble Stanislavski's 'art of experiencing' (Stanislavski 2008), and in fact, called for some acting skills to be exercised by the students, especially as we targeted spoken genres. The task was facilitated using native speakers, real people, or fictitious characters presented by actors as role-models. I would suggest that the technique might be adaptable for written genres as well.

The final step of the didactic sequence required students' reflection of the genres produced based on the teacher's and groupmates' feedback and the teacher's model as an assessment tool. Comparing the texts created at the initial and final steps of production, the students realised that through mastering the genre of storytelling they acquired techniques of indirect persuasion, as well as skills of establishing rapport with the interlocutor through building a shared world rather than pleading for the listener's compassion.

10.5   Conclusion

In an attempt to overcome difficulties EFL students might face in striving to produce a genre of L2 culture and provide opportunities for their cognitive development, I built a model of the genre in three stages.

First, I drew on an existing description of storytelling to determine what a recipient of the genre expects of the storyteller. Then the description was abridged, leaving only the essential traits of the genre for students to master. In this way the outer boundary of the zone of proximal development was set, outlining the skills a foreign student should acquire to interact successfully in an L2 discourse community. The efficiency of the students' performance of the target genre can be assessed through interviewing the students themselves. Tannen suggests the aesthetic pleasure of the participants in friendly conversation as a criterion of communicative success (Tannen 2005: 191). Another way might be to ask native speakers to provide feedback on the texts produced by students. This could be done in the form of an interview or questionnaire, or by means of an experiment aimed at reconstructing the potential uptake of the genres, thus responding to Swales' recent call for genre researchers to undertake reception studies (Swales 2019: 81).

To establish the inner boundary of the zone of proximal development, its starting point, namely students' prior knowledge of the genre, I compared the relationships between formal and contextual features of the target genre to those existing in analogous genres of the learner's L1. Contrasting the strategies of achieving communicative purposes typical of local discourse communities, I determined a potential zone of proximal development for non-native learners of genres. Searching for ways to facilitate students' internalisation of new communicative and social skills, I involved them in confronting their prior generic experience with conventions of a new genre they are required to produce. In this way, we collaborated in mapping out their individual zones of proximal development.

The advance in cognitive development the students have made in a genre learning course might be estimated through observing the techniques they employ in further study. Confronted with new rhetorical situations, they may choose what Perkins and Solomon call 'low road' and 'high road' transfer (Perkins and Salomon 1988: 25). If learners demonstrate their aptitude to seek and reflect on connections between various generic contexts and forms, to adapt their skills and knowledge, and to use prior resources effectively they are likely to employ the 'high road' method of knowledge transfer. This might be indicative of an increase in the level of cognitive development. Choosing the 'low road' option, which involves "automatic triggering of well-practiced routines in circumstances where there is considerable perceptual similarity to the original learning context" (Perkins and Salomon 1988: 25) would suggest lack of ability to abstract skills from one context to be applied to another.

Interviewing students might also prove helpful for assessing the results of an L2 genre teaching course. Recent studies tend to consider genres to be bearers, articulators, and reproducers of culture (Beebee 1994), as well as "tools for accessing, critiquing, and bringing about change within cultures and publics" (Bawarshi and Reiff 2010: 151). In this light, teaching genres may be viewed as a possible factor of cultural dynamics, with the evolution of cultural models and patterns discernible not only at macro level of local cultures but also within specific, small-scale discourse communities.

References

Bawarshi, Anis S., and Mary Jo Reiff. 2010. *Genre: An Introduction to History, Theory, Research, and Pedagogy.* Indiana: Parlor Press and the WAC Clearinghouse.
Bazerman, Charles. 1994. *Constructing Experience.* Carbondale: Southern Illinois UP.
Bazerman, Charles. 2009. Genre and Cognitive Development: Beyond Writing to Learn. In *Genre in a Changing World*, ed. Ch. Bazerman, A. Bonini, and D. Figueiredo, 283–298. Fort Collins, CO: The WAC Clearinghouse and Parlor Press.
Beebee, Thomas O. 1994. *The Ideology of Genre: A Comparative Study of Generic Instability.* University Park: Pennsylvania State UP.
Borissova, Irene I. 2002. *Narrative as a Dialogical Genre* (In Russian), In *Speech Genres,* Issue 3, eds. V.E. Goldin, L.V. Balashova, V.V. Dementyev, K.F. Sedov, O.B. Sirotinina, M.Yu. Fedosyuk, 244–261. Saratov: College.
Cope, Bill, and Mary Kalantzis. 1993. *The Powers of Literacy: A Genre Approach to Teaching Writing.* Pittsburgh: U of Pittsburgh P.

Devitt, Amy J. 2006. First-Year Composition and Antecedent Genres. In *Conference on College Composition and Communication. Chicago, 24 March 2006*. Conference Presentation.

Devitt, Amy J. 2008. *Writing Genres*. Carbondale: Southern Illinois University Press.

Dolinin, Konstantin A. 1999. Speech Genres as a Means of Organizing Social Interaction (In Russian). In *Speech Genres*, eds. V.E. Goldin, L.V. Balashova, V.V. Dementyev, K.F. Sedov, O.B. Sirotinina, M.Yu. Fedosyuk, 8–14. Saratov: College.

Ekman, Paul, and Wallace V. Friesen. 1969. The Repertoire of Nonverbal Behavior. Categories, Origins, Usage, and Coding. *Semiotica* 1: 49–98.

Freadman, Anne. 1994. Anyone for Tennis? In *Genre and the New Rhetoric*, ed. A. Freedman and P. Medway, 43–66. Bristol: Taylor and Francis.

Freadman, Anne. 2002. Uptake. In *The Rhetoric and Ideology of Genre: Strategies for Stability and Change*, eds. R. Coe, L. Lingard, and T. Teslenko, 39–53. Cresskill, NJ: Hampton UP.

Freedman, Aviva. 1987. Learning to Write Again: Discipline-Specific Writing at University. *Carleton Papers in Applied Language Studies* 4: 95–116.

Guimarães, Ana Maria de Mattos. 2009. Genre Teaching in Different Social Environments: An Experiment with the Genre Detective Story. *L1—Educational Studies in Language and Literature* 9 (2): 27–47.

Gumovskaya, Galina. 2017. Secondary Language Personality of English Teacher. *Journal of Modern Education Review* 7 (7): 479–487.

Hall, Edward. 1976. *Beyond Culture*. New York: Doubleday.

Hickson, Mark, and Don W. Stacks. 1993. *NVC, Nonverbal Communication: Studies and Applications*. Madison (Wis): Brown & Benchmark.

Hyland, Ken. 2007. Genre Pedagogy: Language, Literacy and L2 Writing Instruction. *Journal of Second Language Writing* 16: 148–164.

Hyon, Sunny. 1996. Genre in Three Traditions: Implications for ESL. *TESOL Quarterly* 30: 693–722.

Hyon, Sunny. 2002. Genre and ESL Reading: A Classroom Study. In *Genre in the Classroom: Multiple Perspectives*, ed. A.M. Johns, 121–141. Mahwah, NJ: Lawrence Erlbaum.

Jamieson, Kathleen M. 1975. Antecedent Genre as Rhetorical Constraint. *Quarterly Journal of Speech* 61 (4): 406–415.

Jones, Ann M. 2008. Genre awareness for the novice academic student: An ongoing quest. *Language Teaching* 41 (2): 237–252.

Jones, Ceri, Tania Bastow, and Amanda Jeffries. 2010. *New Inside Out: Advanced Student's Book*, 2010. NY: Macmillan.

Kachru, Braj B. 1992. *The Other Tongue: English across Cultures*. Champaign: University of Illinois Press.

Koven, Michéle. 2007. *Selves in Two Languages: Bilinguals' Verbal Enactments of Identity in French and Portuguese*. Amsterdam: John Benjamins.

Laforest, Marty. 2002. Scenes of Family Life: Complaining in Everyday Conversation. *Journal of Pragmatics* 34: 1595–1620.

Luria, Alexandr R. 1970. The Functional Organization of the Brain. *Scientific American*. 222 (3): 66–78.

Martin, James R. 1997. Analysing Genre: Functional Parameters. In *Genre and Institutions: Social Processes in the Workplace and School*, ed. F. Christie and J.R. Martin, 3–39. London: Cassell.

Martin, James R., and David Rose. 2008. *Genre Relations: Mapping Culture*. London: Equinox.

Millar, Diane. 2011. Promoting Genre Awareness in the EFL Classroom. *English Teaching Forum* 2: 1–10.

Miller, Carolyn R. 1994. Genre as Social Action. In *Genre and the New Rhetoric*, ed. A. Freedman and P. Medway, 23–42. Bristol: Taylor and Francis.

Motta-Roth, Désirée. 2009. The Role of Context in Academic Text Production and Writing Pedagogy. In *Genres in a Changing World*, ed. C. Bazerman, A. Bonini, and D. Figueiredo, 317–336. West Lafayette: Parlor Press.

Nikolaeva, Olga A., and Yulia A. Lobina. 2018. Russian and American stand-up monologues: how verbal and non-verbal elements interact. In *Youth and Science: Word, Text, Personality: Proceedings of IV International Young Scholars' Conference*. Vol. 1, ed. Yu. Lobina, 11–16. Ulyanovsk: Ulyanovsk State University of Education.

Pavlenko, Aneta. 2006. Bilingual selves. In *Bilingual Minds: Emotional Experience, Expression and Representation*, ed. A. Pavlenko, 1–33. Clevedon, UK: Multilingual Matters.

Perkins, D.N., and Gavriel Salomon. 1988. Teaching for Transfer. *Educational Leadership* 46 (1): 22–32.

Poyatos, Fernando. 2002. *Nonverbal Communication across Disciplines*. Vol. I. Amsterdam/Philadephia: John Benjamins.

Rühlemann, Christoph. 2014. *Narrative in English Conversation: A Corpus Analysis of Storytelling*. Cambridge: Cambridge University Press.

Russell, David, and David Fisher. 2009. On-line Multimedia Case Studies for Professional Education: Revisioning Concepts of Genre Recognition. In *Theories of Genre and the Internet*, ed. J. Giltrow and D. Stein, 163–192. Amsterdam: John Benjamins.

Snodgrass, Klyne. 2008. *Stories with Intent: A Comprehensive Guide to the Parables of Jesus*. Cambridge: Wm. B. Eerdmans Publishing Co.

Soliday, Mary. 2005. Mapping Classroom Genres in a Science in Society Course. In: *Genre across the Curriculum*, eds. A. Herrington and Ch. Moran, 65–82. Logan: Utah State UP.

Stanislavski, Konstantin. 2008. *An Actor's Work: A Student's Diary*. Trans. and ed. J. Benedetti. London and New York: Routledge.

Swales, John M. 1990. *Genre Analysis: English in Academic and Research Settings*. Cambridge: Cambridge University Press.

Swales, John M. 2009. Worlds of Genre–Metaphors of Genre In *Genre in a Changing World*, eds. Ch. Bazerman, A. Bonini, and D. Figueiredo, 1–16. Fort Collins, CO: The WAC Clearinghouse and Parlor Press.

Swales, John M. 2019. The Futures of EAP Studies: A Personal Viewpoint. *Journal of English for Academic Purposes* 38: 75–82.

Tannen, Deborah. 2005. *Conversational Style*. Oxford: Oxford University Press.

Vygotsky, Lev S. 1986. *Thought and language*. Cambridge, Massachusetts: MIT Press.

Williams, Joseph, and Gregory Colomb. 1993. The Case for Explicit Teaching: Why What You Don't Know Won't Help You. *Research in the Teaching of English* 27 (3): 252–264.

Werzbicka, Anna. 1983. Genry Mowy. In *Tekst i zdanie*, eds. T. Dobrzyénska and E. Janus, 125–137. Wrocław: Ossolinium.

Chapter 11
Methods of Psycholinguistic Research as Possible Cognitive Approaches to Linguistic Data Processing

Irina V. Privalova

Abstract The efficiency of any study depends on consistency in the choice of material, methods and objectives. The effective examination of cognitive processes on the basis of verbal matter requires an integrated use of various methods, including psycholinguistic ones. Hence, the aim of this article is to discuss the advantages of psycholinguistic methods and the prospects of their employment in language and pedagogical design. In addition, the article provides an overview of the most popular psycholinguistic experimental approaches, such as the method of speech activity observation, semantic analysis, the method of semantic differential, and free and directed associative experiments. The advantage of each of these methods in the study of cognitive underpinning verbalized by language material is shown, and the examples of their practical use are demonstrated. The most popular mathematical and statistical procedures for processing obtained data as a result of psycholinguistic experiments are discussed. Specific examples demonstrate the effectiveness of the use of formulas, such as Student's t-distribution and the Cronbach's alpha coefficient. It is concluded that in order to establish the validity of the indicators obtained through psycholinguistic experiments, it is necessary to use mathematical and statistical data processing methods. Precise calculations guarantee the diagnostic value of the results.

Keywords Psycholinguistics · Associative experiment · Cognitive processes · Mental lexicon · Methods of verbal data processing

I. V. Privalova (✉)
Saratov State Medical University, Saratov, Russia
e-mail: ivprivalova@mail.ru

Leading Research Fellow of the Research Laboratory, "Intellectual Technologies of Text Management", Institute of Philology and Intercultural Communication, Kazan (Volga region) Federal University, Kazan, Russia

11.1　Introduction: On the Importance of Methodological Consistency

The value of all research is in its consistency. That is why there are two questions that come to the fore: what is the material and what methods are used for analysis? If the material and methodology are not consistent with the objectives of a research study, then the obtained results can hardly be qualified as valid ones. In an ideal research scenario, the topic of a study must be in agreement with all its components. As far as anthropocentric research of cognitive processes is concerned, controversies appear quite often in reconciling three major aspects—material, method and target of research. This reconciliation is increasingly difficult to accomplish in today's situation of transdisciplinarity. Dubrovskaya argues that modern linguistics

> … breaks the boundaries and refers to non-linguistic phenomena, also, modern linguistics involves the categories of analysis from psychology, political science, ecology and other areas of human life. As a result, the impression of scientific knowledge integrity is created. On the other hand, methodological inaccuracies, obscurity and blurriness are justified by anthropocentrism and the expansion of scientific borders. (Dubrovskaya 2019: 3)

"Methodological blurriness" may be observed, for instance, when it is proposed that the information impact on a recipient be investigated exclusively through text analysis; for example, political discourse is analysed and articles in newspapers and journals are considered with special emphasis on their lexical and grammar components. It is questionable that the analysis of the use of particular words and syntactic structures can provide enough information about recipients' reactions. Valid results are hardly achievable in this case since "impact" is a psychological category, and in order to get valuable information about impact, it is advisable to work with respondents. Another example of methodological inconsistency is the study of mental activity outcomes that are based solely on lexicographic sources, i.e., dictionaries. Sometimes the structures of concepts are discussed through references to lexical material. Meanwhile, the structure of a dictionary entry gives an idea of the semantic organization of a word. It also presents information about the links of a single verbal unit on the syntactic and paradigmatic levels. It is common knowledge that there is no absolute similarity between semantic field organization and lexical field organization. In addition, it is not a convincing option to draw conclusions about conceptual sphere composition based exclusively on analysis of the text matter of literary works—poems, novels, short stories, etc. Conceptual spheres, concepts, frames and propositions are cognitive phenomena; therefore, verbal material cannot give a true picture regarding their organization. On the other hand, questioning informants such as native speakers cannot provide enough information about the nature of cognitive phenomena. Thus, the results of an associative experiment would obviously not be enough to draw conclusions about the national-cultural specificity of mind of the representatives of a certain language community.

All the examples considered above demonstrate the attempts to understand the work of cognitive mechanisms using purely linguistic material, whereas cognitive processes provide the transformation of sensory information. The received information is converted from the moment when a stimulus hits a human being's receptors to the moment of a response. As a rule, this response is presented in a verbal form. The cognitive mechanism is liable for the accumulation of human knowledge about objects and phenomena of the real world. Indeed, a large body of knowledge is verbalized in the form of texts, various types of discourse and communicative practices.

In fact, all modern humanitarian studies are multidisciplinary. Psycholinguistics is a science that develops in line with the anthropocentric paradigm at the intersection of several scientific fields. Psycholinguistics exists in an interdisciplinary space, and therefore it is often difficult to "… disclose the limits beyond which other sciences start to unfold" (Klyukanov 2018: 18). At the present time, psycholinguistics is thought to be a unique field since it has its clearly defined scientific boundaries, but the pool of experimental methods is, however, an open set. It should be noted that the research object of modern psycholinguistics is also becoming more complicated. Some decades ago, the psychological features of speech generation and speech perception were the focus of psycholinguistics, whereas today, psycholinguists are more interested in linguistic consciousness and cognitive mechanisms of thought formation. Hence, they have to apply a whole range of different techniques in order to scrutinize mental processes. These are the reasons for problems in the choice of effective methods and methodological instruments. Another difficulty is the demarcation between the object and the subject of a study, its tasks and goals. These aspects should also be consistent with each other. When conducting interdisciplinary research (and contemporary psycholinguistic research is of such a nature), this aim becomes more complicated. The cases—in which methods from other scientific fields are involved—should be justified. As seen, in interdisciplinary research, the correspondence of tasks and methods is especially relevant.

As articulated earlier, the analysis of linguistic phenomena (literary works, electronic texts and dictionaries) in a particular language allows only the establishment of the possible ways of concept representation and their organization into a conceptual sphere. Contemplation of texts and vocabulary is clearly not enough to draw conclusions about mental categories and the process of image systematization. As we have already indicated, textual material may provide incomplete information about concepts and their structure. The totality of concepts is organized into a conceptual sphere, which is not identical to the mental category. Linguistic phenomena are quite informative when it comes to knowledge representation through the signs of a language system. As far as the distribution of knowledge into mental categories is concerned, it is necessary to arrange a set of practical experiments with informants. Research on cognitive issues is the domain of experimental psycholinguistics. Categorization is a complex, dynamic process, and it is good practice to conduct a number of psycholinguistic experiments, among which an associative experiment is of utmost importance.

Taking into consideration everything that has been said above, we suggest focusing on debating some relevant psycholinguist methods and their application. There is an attempt to show how the objectives relate to the tools used in the study of the material. Therefore, the target of this article is to discuss the most popular methods of modern psycholinguistics and the procedures of mathematical and statistical data processing. The article is an overview of the nature and aims at these methods and procedures in order to highlight possible approaches to the study of cognitive processes, which are represented by linguistic material. The review of psycholinguistic methods presented in the article may be of interest to a number of researchers working in the anthropocentric paradigm.

11.2   Psycholinguistics as a Science and Its Specificity in Studying Cognitive Mechanisms

Through the analysis of psycholinguistic discipline and its theoretical foundations, we aim to demonstrate that they have sufficient potential for cognitive process research and for a cognitive approach to language and pedagogical design. The theoretical foundations of psycholinguistics are based on the behavioural and non-behavioural structures of human activity. Psycholinguistics (as its name implies) is the combination of two independent sciences—linguistics and psychology. No wonder that many psychologists and linguists have contributed to its development. One should mention, among others, the intellectual contributions of the French sociologist Piaget (1969), American linguists Slobin and Green (1976) and Russian psychologist Vygotsky (2001). Extremely detailed historical insights on psycholinguistic discipline development, including the preparatory steps in its design, are presented in the monograph "A History of Psycholinguistics: The Pre-Chomskyan Era" by Willem Levelt (2012).

Psycholinguistics studies cognitive processes, and in this way, it has much in common with cognitive psychology and cognitive linguistics. The object of the study of cognitive psycholinguistics is the processes of perception and how a person obtains information from the outside world. The most popular issues are: how a person sorts out information and decrypts it, how information is transformed into knowledge, and the mechanisms that help organize and structure information and knowledge. Psycholinguists try to clarify how knowledge determines the mental activity of a person, i.e., behaviour, attention, memory, etc. Particular attention is paid to the study of conceptual sphere formation. At the end of the last and the beginning of this century, the term "concept" gained momentum. Studies of various concepts are still very popular. "Concept" is combined with the processes of information perception and the organization of knowledge since it is understood as a combination of knowledge about objects and phenomena of the world (Kubryakova 1997). In addition, specialists in cognitive issues are preoccupied with the studies of "frames", "prototypes", "categories" and "semantic fields" (Barsalou 1992; Lakoff and Jonson 1980; Lakoff 1982, 1987).

Psycholinguistic methods are believed to be efficient when they are applied to studying the work of the categorization mechanism and the construction of mental categories. Modern psycholinguists have managed to prove that categorization has a mental-verbal nature and is linked to the reflection of material reality and the formation of images and worldviews:

> Categorization is a process of ordering various phenomena (objects, events, actions, processes, qualities, relations, etc.) into different groups according to certain kinds of similarity. Although it can be a conscious act of determining what group a given item belongs to, primarily it is the most basic cognitive process with the function of providing cognitive building blocks for guiding our interaction with the environment. (Gyori 2013: 149)

With the development of the anthropocentric paradigm, the socio-cultural theory of Vygotsky (2001) is becoming increasingly called-for. It would not be much of an exaggeration to say that the socio-cultural theory of Vygotsky is still the most popular today. It deals with the thinking processes and speech activity of an individual. Socio-cultural theory confirms that a person, as a social being, is at the centre of speech activity since it is society that forms and regulates communicative behaviour. As seen, according to this theory, speech activity is an integral part of human activity. Thus, in traditional understanding, "psycholinguistics" is the science of the processes of speech perception and speech production. Within the framework of this discipline, language is studied in its connection with speakers and their activities. In the Russian scientific tradition, which is represented by the names of Leontyev (1975), Leontyev (2003), Tarasov (1987), Sorokin (1994), etc., psycholinguistics is interpreted as the theory of speech praxis. Leontyev argues:

> On the one hand, the subject of psycholinguistics is the correlation of a human's personality with the structure and functions of speech activity; and on the other hand, it examines language as the main "generative" image of the human world. (2003: 19)

In addition to cognitive linguistics, ethno-psycholinguistics can be called one of the new directions. Priorities in the development of cognitive linguistics belong to European and American scientists (Anderson 1983; Carston 1989; Chafe 1987; Langacker 1991), whereas Russian scientists have made great contributions to the development of ethno-psycholinguistics as well. Ethno-psycholinguistics is understood as a direction that considers the national-cultural component in speech activity. Any speech activity is nationally and culturally marked since the language, culture and consciousness of individuals are an inextricable trinity. Krasnykh defines the subject of psycholinguistics as a set of speech situations that take place in the context of national discourse. In addition, the subject of ethno-psycholinguistics is viewed as a national discourse in the totality of its manifestations and factors determining its cultural specificity (Krasnykh 2002: 10). Language helps an individual to identify himself or herself as a member of a certain ethno-linguistic and cultural community (Ufimtseva 1996; Krashykh 2002). Such an understanding of psycholinguistics is undoubtedly based on various areas of anthropocentric knowledge of the language.

Psycholinguists are of the opinion that the main focus of psycholinguistics should be on the thinking processes involved in language acquisition and its use. Back in 1934, in his work "Thinking and Speech", Vygotsky noted that thinking and speech duality is closely connected with the question of the relationship between various psychological functions and various types of consciousness activity. The central point of this whole problem is the connection of thought to word. Having analysed some aspects of the development of speech in phylogenesis and ontogenesis, Vygotsky comes to the conclusion that thought and words are not interconnected. The connection between them arises and grows in the course of the development of thought and word (Vygotsky 2001: 279).

The verbal product is considered by psycholinguists as an indicator of the work of thought processes. Language mediates the work of all cognitive mechanisms of a person, such as perception of reality, information processing and the construction of images. Scientists confirm that language has a close connection with mental activity. Inner thinking happens in verbal form, and distinctions between thought and its expression is a scientifically intriguing subject for exploration (Langland-Hassan and Vicente 2018). Linguistic cues influence mental representations that people form in order to understand language matter. The link between the general semantic knowledge about objects and the sentential context has been proven (Kang et al. 2020). The most vivid connection between mental processes and language is embodied in the concept of "mental lexicon":

> One question, which relates to the trade-off between computation and storage in language processing, is whether the mental lexicon is organized by morphemes or by words. (Treiman et al. 2003: 539)

The link between linguistic processes and cognitive structures has been noted in many studies in recent decades (see Bergen and Wheeler 2010; Glenberg et al. 1987; Zwaan 2016).

Psycholinguists confirm that language has a close connection with mental activity—they analyse the development of thought from design to utterance (Levelt 1989), or the model of word selection and the verbal design of thought (Levelt 1999). Psycholinguists operate with the terms that denote real phenomena, such as "internal speech" or "mental or internal vocabulary" of a person. They also confirm the existence of a connection between linguistic matter and the mental activity of an individual. Finally, when studying the characteristics of human intelligence, memory and brain pathologies, scientists turn to the analysis of speech reactions and language product (Luria 1979; Rhys et al. 2013). "Mental lexicon" seems to be the most curious phenomenon in terms of studying cognitive processes. Psycholinguists try to present the principles of human knowledge organization, referring to the mental lexicon of an individual (Zalevskaya 1990).

11.3 Theoretical Assumptions for Psycholinguistic Experimental Research

There are some theoretical grounds that can be applied to the experimental study of speech generation and information perception mechanisms, as well as the practical investigation of cognitive processes. Among many of them, there is a statement about the connection between language, mental activities and culture. This statement was first expressed as the idea of "an internal language form" by Humboldt (2000). Having analysed different languages, Humboldt, in his main linguistic work "On the difference in the structure of human languages and its influence on the spiritual development of the human race" (1836), drew the conclusion about the interrelationship between the nature of the language and the nature of the people (Humboldt 2000). Then, there were the ideas of Potebnya on the internal form of a word, which were expressed by him in his work "Thought and Language" in 1862. Most of those ideas appeared as a result of contemplations on Humboldt's works (Potebnya 1999). Moreover, it is difficult to imagine the development of psycholinguistics without the theory of linguistic relativity by Sapir (1949) and Whorf (1956), the psycho-sociological theory of Mead (1962) and the theory of historical ethnology of Boas (1984).

Of particular importance for the development of the experimental base of psycholinguistics are the ideas of Shcherba (2004), which he announced in his 1931 article "On the triple aspect of linguistic phenomena and experiment in linguistics". The scientist connected three aspects: language system, speech activity and speech material. Speech activity includes the processes of speaking and understanding, which are linked with the mechanisms of interpretation and sound matter production. Grammatical and lexicographical issues comprise the language system. Finally, the third aspect is linguistic material, in other words, all language matter that is produced by individuals of a particular socio-cultural group. This distinction was a real scientific breakthrough that is considerably indebted to the consistency of method, material and objectives.

The ideas of Shcherba are consistent with the ideas of Chomsky. This American linguist made a distinction between linguistic competence, which is considered as belonging to the field of linguistics, and linguistic performance, which is related to the field of psychology. Linguistic ability is believed to be something that constitutes the ability to speak a given language, and linguistic activity is represented by the utterances produced by a native speaker. Chomsky (1994) also put forward the thesis of the innate nature of linguistic structures, suggesting that a person's ability to learn a language is innate.

It is hard to debate the statement of Vygotsky that thinking and speech issues are some of the most difficult to investigate; therefore, their study should be carried out through a series of separate experiments. These experiments must be targeted towards "… concepts formation, the study of written speech in its relation to thinking, internal speech, etc." (Vygotsky 2001: 3). Accordingly, the identification of the role of language in mental processes, such as speech formation, speech generation and speech production, requires the involvement of subjects or informants.

The achievements in linguistics and psychology should be taken into account when compiling the pool of psycholinguistic experimental research. The effectiveness of the integral use of linguistic and psychological methods in conducting a particular psycholinguistic research study may have primacy. Indeed, language material can work as a guide to the area of cognitive mechanisms. Along with that, language, as an instrument of speech activity, is used by psychologists to determine the norm or pathology in the psychological state of subjects. For example, psychological questionnaires and psychological experimental tests are used to analyse various personality issues. For instance, a psychological technique for filling out sentences according to the Sacks and Levi Sentence Completion (SSCT) model (Sacks and Levy 1950) is suitable for the investigation of inner speech development. Undoubtedly, psycholinguistic experiments targeted to the evaluation of the syntactic correctness of sentences and statements can also be informative, specifically, as far as the peculiarities of constructing internal speech are concerned. In addition, surveys, interviews and observations are the sociological methods that are frequently used by psychologists, linguists and psycholinguists.

11.4   The Most Popular Psycholinguistic Methods and Examples of Their Use in the Research on Cognitive Mechanisms

In modern psycholinguistics, the widest array of methods and techniques is used to study cognitive processes, the most relevant review of which is presented in a multi-authored monograph "Research Methods in Psycholinguistics and the Neurobiology of Language: A Practical Guide" (De Groot and Hagoort 2017). In order to study the processes of language acquisition and information processing, the scientists have to apply achievements in areas such as neurology, programming, computational modelling, corpus linguistics, and the traditional methods of observation of language and behaviour.

In this part of the article, we will illustrate how different psycholinguistic experimental techniques can be used for analysing various aspects. These experimental techniques have been exploited by the author of this article on different stages of her scientific work. These ideas have been shaped in line with the Moscow psycholinguistic school, which is hallmarked by the works of Vygotsky (2001), Leontyev (1975) and Leontyev (2003), as well as by the works of the scientists of the Department of Psycholinguistics and the Theory of Communication at the Institute of Linguistics in the Russian Academy of Sciences: Tarasov (1987), Sorokin (1994), Ufimtseva (1996) and others. In addition, the possibility of personal cooperation with I. N. Gorelov, K. F. Sedov, A. A. Zalevskaya and V. V. Krasnykh could not but influence the theoretical underpinnings of our experimental investigations. In general, the empirical principles of the author's research are correlated with socio-cultural theory, the theory of speech praxis, the theory of linguistic consciousness of an individual and the national-cultural specificity of the linguistic consciousness of ethnic groups. We propose to consider the following review of methods as sharing experience and as contemplations concerning possibilities, limitations and constraints of each of these methods. In addition, the review presents the methods that are widely used in modern psycholinguistics and that have already proven their effectiveness.

11.4.1 In-Depth Interview Methodology

For example, in order to study the Internet-driven behaviour of young people, we used the in-depth interview methodology (Privalova and Kuptsova 2016). The method of in-depth interviewing came into psycholinguistics from sociology. Psychologists also use complex questionnaires in their practice. Survey material turns out to be very informative for solving certain psycholinguistic problems. The compilation of the questionnaire may cause a certain difficulty. The researcher must clearly understand what information he/she wants to receive and, based on this, compile the content and the sequence of questions. Thus, in our research (Privalova and Kuptsova 2016), the subjects were asked to fill in the questionnaire containing 14 questions. The answers to these questions were expected to provide us with both quantitative and qualitative characteristics of respondents. For example, a question containing evaluative information suggested a quantitative description of the object: "From what sources do you receive information? Determine its ratio in %." At the same time, the respondents gave detailed comments on questions such as: "How often do you watch TV? Which channels and programmes do you watch? If you don't watch TV at all, then, give your reasons for ignoring?" The questionnaire was presented in a written format, but we managed to talk with some informants as well. During an oral conversation with respondents, an interviewer has excellent opportunities to get detailed comments and to make some clarifications. An example of an in-depth interview is presented in our monograph on the study of youths' electronic communication (Privalova and Kuptsova 2016: 106–110).

11.4.2 The Methods of Speech Activity Observation

The method of *speech production observation,* along with the collection of language material that contains erroneous actions, was used by us for verbal attitude analysis in the speech of bilinguals. The ideas of Dmitri Uznadze about verbal attitudes served as the theoretical underpinnings. According to Uznadze, all mental processes are preceded by a special state of readiness for a certain activity. Such readiness means a peculiar adjustment which causes subjects to ensure mental or motor acts that provide an adequate reflection of the situation (Uznadze 1958: 88; Uznadze 1961:

66; Uznadze 1966). Verbal attitude is a special state that triggers speech mechanisms and mobilizes forces in individuals for speech (Privalova 1995: 14).

Uznadze noted that language attitudes give direction to speech mechanisms, i.e., perform the function of the "internal form of language" (in the terminology of Humboldt). The concept of language attitude explains such phenomena as the amalgamation of meaning and sound in a word and its correspondence to linguistic reality. Worth noting are the assumptions of psychologists about various types of attitudes as the mechanisms of foreign language text perception have proven to be rather efficient. The ideas about verbal attitudes can really explain a lot about the mechanism of erroneous actions in understanding a foreign text. However, the analysis of interpretations and translations may not be enough, and then the experimenter is expected to have a conversation with informants and ask them to offer explanations (post-experimental discussion technique).

In our research, all errors that occurred during foreign text perception were classified and interpreted from the point of view of verbal attitude influence. For example, the "relativity" of temporary forms in the Russian language, which is expressed in their counter-functioning with the syntactic structure, results in semantic distortions. Thus, the original sentence, "*In the forest, it becameas dark as the darkest night*" was translated by students as: "*The forest became as dark as it was the darkest night*"; whereas the correct variant is "*as it used to beon the darkest night*" (Privalova 1995: 85). It is of importance that the perception of the text is not always accompanied by understanding. Luria suggests differentiating perception and understanding, based on the two-sided nature of any language sign. This nature allows distinguishing between two stages in decoding: perception of the signified and perception of the signifier.

> The first phase is associated with the processes that decrypt the perceived language codes, and the second – with the decoding of the deep meaning that stands behind the perceived message. (Luria 1979: 291–292)

The examples given above illustrate that the potential of both linguistic and psychological methods is taken into account for developing the structure of a psycholinguistic experiment. Traditional linguistic methods aim at studying the language as a systemic-structural formation and texts as a set of semiotic signs. Among such purely linguistic methods, the following should be mentioned: structural–functional, definitional, component, stylistic, comparative, descriptive, and other types of analysis. And, at present, it is a commonly accepted fact that "… linguistic knowledge makes it possible to understand human consciousness" (Belyanin 2003: 128).

One more method of speech activity observation is the analytical assessment of semantic structures in the material of verbal activity of a person. The *semantic analysis* can provide rather valid data from the point of view of psycholinguistics. The connection between word and consciousness was noted by Luria:

> A word denotes things; a word identifies signs, actions, and relationships. A word unites objects into well-known systems, put it another way, it encodes our experience. (Luria 1979: 23)

There are various psycholinguistic experiments that are based on the study of the semantic structure of a word and its functions, for example, the methods of explication of words and definition of semantic meaning. Luria (1979) described the methodology for studying the comprehension of the verbal composition of a language in the process of speech development. For instance, the study of the categorization mechanism is based on decoding of the meaning of words in categorical procedures.

Linguistic and psychological approaches to the study of consciousness provide a different view of the nature of the mutually transitional relationship of super-sign and sign entities in reflective processes. However, it should first be recognized that due to objective reasons, all attempts to explain the mechanism of transformation of a super-semiotic reality into a semiotic one are empirical. Undoubtedly, the fact of the vital unity of language and consciousness remains widely acknowledged. The inter-subjective form of image existence is possible only in a semiotic form, the same form as that of the existence of meaning. The linguistic nature of mentality proven by Leontyev (1975) and Vygotsky (2001) is confirmed by the fact of its multi-level structure.

Some psycholinguistic techniques are based on the study of semantics. For example, the methodology for completing unfinished sentences is similar to the SSCT (Sacks and Levi Sentence Completion) method (Sacks and Levy 1950). Using this psycholinguistic method, subjects are invited to complete statements that may have varying degrees of initial design. Based on the produced options, one may judge the specifics of the syntactic organization and the deployment of syntactic structures. One more method is the "True–False" evaluation technique that allows drawing conclusions concerning the semantic similarities of some notions. Finally, the gradual scaling method should also be mentioned. Informants are offered a list of words from one semantic group that they rank depending on their significance. Then, using mathematical calculations, the highest and lowest ranked words are established and a grading scale is compiled. This scale gives an idea of the semantic affinity of verbal units that are close in meaning.

Among the psycholinguistic experimental studies, *the method of semantic differential* is in special demand. This method was proposed by one of the founders of the psycholinguistic discipline, Charles Osgood, and his colleagues (Osgood et al. 1957). The purpose of the experiment is to build the semantic space of a certain concept. For instance, informants are invited to characterize a specific or abstract concept via utilizing several (at least three) parameters. As a rule, a seven-point rating scale is offered to the informants. (It is noteworthy that there are questionnaires in which the number of specified parameters ranges from 5 to 9. However, filling out such questionnaires is time-consuming and tedious, and the results can be contradictory.) The choice of parameters and characteristics is predetermined by the objectives of the experiment. For example, the author of this article had a chance to participate in material collection for a scientific project carried out in the Department of Psycholinguistics and Communication Theory at the Institute of Linguistics, Russian Academy of Sciences, in the years 2013–2014. Within the framework of this project, several experiments were carried out in different countries in the world. The target of the experiments was to detect national and cultural characteristics of some abstract concept perceptions among the representatives of various ethno-linguistic cultures. Let us scrutinize the responses of the British informants that the author of this article managed to obtain. The concept of "power", for instance, is proposed to be evaluated on a seven-point scale (from -3 to $+3$), using criteria such as: *dark—light, passive—active, slow—fast, chaotic—regular, weak—strong, dangerous—safe, soft—solid,* etc. Some of the results of the experiment are presented in Table 11.1.

As seen, the conceptual classes are presented on the top line and their characteristics are given in the left column. If the number of informants is large enough (more than 500), a researcher will have an excellent opportunity to obtain socially fixed assessments of the key concepts. Alternatively, conducting an experiment among young people, one can make an assessment of a specific concept (for example, "power") to a certain age, social or national-cultural group. In order to get the results, the total number of points is determined and then divided by the total number of responses. (As one can see, mathematical calculations are indispensable in this case.) Undoubtedly, the method of semantic differential is effective in the study of axiological entities. One of the drawbacks of this method is that it requires the participation of a significant number of informants to obtain sufficient data for interpretation.

The most popular psycholinguistic technique is *an associative experiment*. This is a productive way to get to the information stored in a person's mind, which is often referred to as "a black box". Association (connection) is understood as a natural linking of mental processes (sensations, perceptions, thoughts, images, feelings, movements, etc.). The association is revealed in the manifestation of one of the processes that cause a manifestation of another or other mental processes (Spencer and Ziehen 1998: 5).

The association mechanism occupies a key position in speech-cognitive activity. The mechanism of speech understanding happens in the form of an association chain that arises in the mind under the influence of familiar images of words. The thinking process is finalized in words and utterances, and it also employs the work of an association mechanism. Any perception of reality is based on associative binding, the output of which represents the organization of information flows and its structuring. The use of associative techniques has a long tradition. The results of association research are so rich in information that they can be interpreted in a number of ways. The results can be considered, depending on the targets and objectives set by a researcher. Targets and objectives can be clearly seen if a hypothesis is stated and the research vocabulary is consistent.

There are two types of associative experiments—free and directed; in the first case, the subjects record any reactions that arise in response to a presented stimulus-word. In the case of a directed experiment, informants are limited in the choice of associates and in their total number. As seen, the purpose of the experiment may determine the interpretation of results, namely, semantic relationships and the choice of associates. The analysis of semantic links and of the semantic configuration of the sum total of reactions is performed, depending on the targets of the experiment. There have already been compiled some associative dictionaries that contain ready-made material for the study of semantic relations (Karaulov et al. 1996: 18).

Table. 11.1 Semantic differential scale

Criteria	Security	Homeland	Heartlessness	Family	Aggression	Poverty	Hard Work	Belief	Illegality	Irresponsibility	Power
Unpleasant—pretty	2	3	-3	3	-3	-3	2	3	-2	-3	-1
Dark—light	2	3	-3	3	-2	-1	3	2	-2	-2	-3
Ugly—beautiful	2	2	-3	2	-2	-2	3	3	-3	-2	-2
Passive—active	3	2	-1	3	-2	-1	3	2	0	-1	-1
Slow—fast	3	2	-3	2	-2	0	3	2	0	-3	2
Chaotic—orderly	3	2	-3	3	-3	1	3	2	3	-3	-3
Changeable—stable	3	3	-3	3	-3	0	3	2	-2	-2	-3
Unmoving—moving	3	1	-3	-1	2	3	-3	-3	2	2	-3
Simple—complicated	3	3	-3	3	2	3	3	3	3	1	3
Unusual—usual	3	3	-2	3	1	2	-1	2	1	3	3
Small—large	3	3	3	1	2	3	0	3	3	2	3
Weak—strong	3	3	3	3	3	3	3	3	3	-2	3
Light—heavy	3	2	3	3	3	3	2	3	2	2	3
Dangerous—safe	3	3	-3	3	-2	-2	3	3	-3	-2	-3
Soft—hard	3	2	3	3	3	3	3	3	3	3	3
Rough—tender	-3	-2	3	2	2	2	-3	3	-3	-3	-3

An associative directed experiment is the appropriate technique for studying the relationship between the external facet of a linguistic unit and its internal form. Associative experiments can be applied for different purposes, for example, in order to investigate the peculiarities of linguistic consciousness in representatives of various ages and professional, regional, social or ethnic groups. An associative experiment is also used to identify the features of specific concepts in the mentality of the representatives of a certain ethno-cultural group. The primary method for studying categorization is the associative experiment. For instance, a directed associative experiment in the format of attribute listing was used by Rosch and her colleagues to identify the characteristics of some basic concepts, such as "good" and "bad" (Rosch 1978: 387–389).

In our studies (Privalova 2005), we used a directed associative experiment to reconstruct the verbal images of the representatives of various ethno-linguistic cultures. The scientific hypothesis was based on the fact that the associates for a particular stimulus word, as well as their choice, are determined by the national-cultural specificity of the language consciousness of informants. The subjects were native speakers of Russian or American English and bilinguals. All stimulus words were grouped into six clusters: lexical universals, words with identical denotations and nationally, culturally labelled connotations, "internationalisms" with similar designata, hyperonyms and the words denoting Russian and American realities. As expected, the reactions to universal stimuli revealed the greatest number of coincidences, and the highest degree of national-cultural marking was noted in the associates of stimuli represented by culturally specific words (Privalova 2005: 340–348). The results of that directed associative experiment could be represented in the form of associative series. To put this in perspective, we presented the answers of two groups of respondents: American informants and bilingual informants (Russian people who were fluent in English and who had lived in the US for more than five years).

The associative reactions of the American informants to the word-stimulus "president" were as follows:

"President—_George Bush (39), leader (34), Clinton (11), power (10), powerful (7), Putin (7), politician (7), strong (6), authority (6), leadership (5), respect (5), no answer (4), America (4), important (4), controversy (4), White House (4), American flag (4), boss (3), CEO (3), control (3), George Washington (3), liar (3), dictator (3), head (3), ignorant (3), in charge (3), lies (3), of United States (3), puppet (3), Reagan (3), representative (2), responsibility (2), smart (2), suit (2), war (2), a generic president of something, but a male—more or less (1), a highly useful great potential danger (1), a picture of president Bush (1), absolute power corrupts (1), all knowing (1), American flag (1), American: not very smart, daddy's boy, wants too much (1), a mess (1), an elected public official who, only in rare cases, deserves the respect and admiration that his/her power and fame suggest"_ (Privalova 2005: 424).

The associative reactions of the bilingual informants to the word-stimulus "president" were as follows:

"President—_Путин (54), power (19), head (10), guarantor of the constitution (10), Буш (9), politics (8), Кремль (7), Россия (6), Bush (5), television (5), Constitution (5), leader (5), responsibility (5), strength (5), country (5), США (5), Putin (4),_ *state (4), government (4), respect (4), no answer (4), flag (3), power (3), Вашингтон (3), elections (3), head of the state (3), chief (3), Ельцин (3), Клинтон (3), puppet (3), Москва (2), White House (2), anthem (1), control (1), dissatisfaction (1), election (1), face (1), flowers (1), government (1), head (1), hymn (1), important (1), inaugural address (1), Iraq War (1), Lincoln (1), order (1), our honour (1), politics (1), president of US (1), respect and pride (1), ruler (1), Russia (1), state (1), Stop Bush! (1), trust (1), TV (1), USA president (1), well-known (1)"* (Privalova 2005: 403).

All reactions that are received as responses to one stimulus word can be grouped into an associative field. (Sometimes the associative field is called an "associative-verbal network", implying that all components of this unity are somehow connected.) Next, an analysis is made of the components included in this field. For example, in the associative field of the stimulus word "president", one can notice such elements as: concrete and abstract nouns, proper names, phrases, phraseological units, extracts of sentences, whole sentences, paragraphs of reflection, pop-references, etc. The content of an associative field does give an idea of the structure of internal speech—the construct that is located between unfolding thoughts and produced speech messages. Hence, the verbal component of an associative field is informative in studying cognitive mechanisms.

It is worth noting that an associative field is not congruent to a semantic field. It is inappropriate to put an equal sign between an associative field and a semantic field. A semantic field is organized around a word-hyperonym, and its components are words-hyponyms. A semantic field includes the words of various parts of speech united by common features. However, sentences, text segments and mini-texts cannot comprise a semantic field. All verbal units in a semantic field are interconnected in meaning. The main method for semantic field research is discourse study of various types, in other words, linguistic products of speech activity.

Let us proceed to some close analysis of the associative field of the word-stimulus "president" in the group of American informants. As seen, there are proper names: George Bush (39), Clinton (11) and George Washington (4). There are the associates linked with national-cultural symbolism as well and the associates representing various attributes of a stimulus word. Cultural symbols that pop up as images of the word incentive "president" confirm that they contain information with an emotive property—America (4), White House (4) and American flag (4)—that is significant in only one ethno-linguistic culture. The evaluative nature of associative reactions is observed in the appearance of such associates as elections, laws, constitution and government. The national marking of an object such as "constitution" is revealed in associative reactions in American subjects. For instance, the associative reaction "freedom" (13) has not been observed in Russians. It indicates the absence of connections between the images verbalized by such language units as "constitution" and "freedom": fairness (4), guidelines (4), important (4), sacred (4), amendment(s) (5), foundation (3) and history (3). All answers for one stimulus word have been statistically processed (Privalova 2005: 332). An example of calculations of the quantitative characteristics of an associative experiment is presented in Table 11.2. ˙

Table. 11.2 The numerical characteristics of an associative experiment in a group of subjects – representatives of the American ethno-linguistic culture on the word-stimulus "president"

The total number of associative reactions	Total number of associates	Number of recurring reactions	The number of repeating associates	Single reactions (associates)	Number of failures (cases when the subjects failed to provide any response)
387	212	210	35	177	5

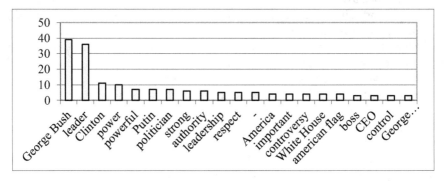

Fig. 11.1 Top 20 associates for the word-stimulus "president"

Another possible type of the material presentation is the top 20 frequency associates, as in the example given below in Fig. 11.1 (Privalova 2005: 450).

The results of large-scale psycholinguistic associative experiments, in other words, the aggregation of associative norms, are recorded in dictionaries. Among these dictionaries, the most well-known are: the dictionary by Deese (1965), the English Associative Thesaurus (Kiss et al. 1972), Leontyev's "Dictionary of Associative Norms of the Russian Language" (Leontyev 1977) and the most complete of the Russian-language associative dictionaries, "Russian Associative Dictionary", in four volumes (1994–1996) (Karaulov et al. 1996).

The *validity of the results* of psycholinguistic experiments is of utmost importance. While studying mental activity and linguistic consciousness, scientists receive not direct but indirect data in the form of verbalized (materialized) images. The answers from a large number of informants (at least 100 people, although the required number is 500) need to be obtained in order to acquire sufficient validity. The material with which psycholinguists work is abundant, complex and subjective. Therefore, the utilization of a software product, as well as mathematical and statistical methods helps establish the validity of existing indicators. For example, the methods of mathematical processing of Microsoft Excel data can be used when calculating the data and analysing the results of an associative experiment. Among other mathematical methods, the following should be mentioned: the formation of the tables of experiment associates for each stimulus word and automatic summation of the number of reactions received per experiment for each stimulus word and the number of failures.

The statistical verification method, known as *Student's distribution or t-test*, is utilized in order to find the validity of the obtained indicators. As a rule, Student's distribution is used to prove the validity of sociological indicators. Based on the example of our study, we will consider how the Student's formula was used to calculate the ratio of linguistic parameters obtained as a result of an associative experiment. As far as we know, such an approach has not been applied previously when describing the correlations between groups of stimuli and sets of associates. There are six types of data in our associative experiment (see the lines in Table 11.3), namely: the total number of associative reactions, the total number of associates, the number of repeating reactions, the number of repeating associates and the number of individual reactions (associates). Thus, the following approach to representing data validity is proposed. First, it is worth providing the indicator of the relative magnitude of the difference between the groups, or a measure of difference between the groups – t with the use of Student's statistics, which makes it possible to compare heterogeneous values. If $t < 1.84$, the difference between the groups is insignificant, which allows us to talk about their comparability. Secondly, the calculation of the error probability index is *alpha*. The generally accepted error indicator is considered

Table. 11.3 Comparison of the indices in six experimental groups

Data	Average deviation 1	Standard deviation 1 (standard error of the mean)	Average deviation 2	Standard deviation 2 (standard error of the mean)	t	df	alpha
The total number of associative reactions	526.40	23.33	411.20	7.79	10.47	5	0.0001
The total number of associates	227.20	25.92	227.80	15.71	0.04	8	0.9658
The number of repetitive reactions	358.00	40.22	230.80	19.54	6.36	7	0.0004
Number of repetitive associates	58.80	9.73	47.40	4.04	2.42	6	0.0519
Single reactions (associates)	168.40	22.17	180.40	16.23	0.98	9	0.3542
Number of rejections	15.60	3.65	2.40	1.34	7.60	6	0.0003

an alpha value of less than 0.5, and then with most values passing at a significance level of 0.01, the indicators are considered valid. The results of a comparative study between groups are represented in Table 11.3 (Privalova 2005: 335).

> Finding the indicator of the relative value of the difference between the groups, or measures of difference between the groups – *t* using Student's statistics makes it possible to bring heterogeneous values to the same values (Privalova 2005: 334).

In other words, the Student's distribution method is used to show the validity of the results and to equalize heterogeneous indexes. As seen, the internal consistency of characteristics describing a single object can be calculated using such statistical measurements as reliability analyses, better known as *the Cronbach's alpha coefficient* (Ermolaev 2003). Due to the complexity of manual calculation of the Cronbach's alpha coefficient in the process of data processing, one can use the computer program SPSS. It is also possible to create special (or individual) software products. There were 763 informants in our associative experiment and they produced 38,317 reactions. Hence, a special software application was designed in order to process the data (Privalova 2005: 329–333).

A quantitative analysis of the language material and the application of statistical and mathematical methods are two different things, and they should be carefully distinguished. Quantitative methods are limited to counting certain linguistic units, for example, the total number of words in a text or the number of proper names in a text segment. By using mathematical or statistical techniques, it is possible to establish various types of correlations between the specific groups of linguistic phenomena and show their general representativeness (see the example above). In addition, in mathematical and statistical methods, correlative relationships are established between two (or more) indicators, with the help of formulas and coefficients. Regretfully, in some contemporary surveys, quantitative analysis is treated as a mathematical method.

11.5   Conclusion

To conclude, modern psycholinguistics is a scientific branch of knowledge that has an interdisciplinary nature. It is a complex science and it combines the achievements of psychology and linguistics. An experiment with the aim of collecting material should be at the centre of any psycholinguistic research. But each study is unique since the object of a survey and the targets are unique. Therefore, along with generally accepted methods (associative experiment, semantic differential method, etc.), it is possible to develop unique experimental methods. Thus, for each new scientific task, the famous Russian psycholinguist Gorelov proposed a new experimental technique. For example, it has been done in the experiments defining the link between visual images and concepts or for the experiments focusing on specific features of the synesthesia mechanism (Gorelov 2003). As has already been noted, the pool of psycholinguistic experimental methods is an open set that offers exciting opportunities for psycholinguists to demonstrate their creativity in carrying out scientific tasks.

All in all, the thoughts presented above are individual contemplations on the possibilities of experimental study of cognitive processes. The description of the experiments is presented as an overview, rather than a guide for conducting research on cognitive mechanisms' effects. The readers are expected to be interested in the prospects and advantages of such experiments. Hopefully, the review of experimental techniques contributes (to some extent) to the cognitive approach to language and pedagogical design.

References

Anderson, John R. 1983. *The Architecture of Cognition*. Cambridge: Harvard University Press.

Barsalou, Lawrence W. 1992. Frames, concepts, and conceptual fields. In *Frames, Fields, and Contrasts*, ed. A. Lehrer and E.F. Kittay, 21–28. Hillsdale, NJ: Lawrence Erlbaum Associates.

Belyanin, Valery. 2003. *Psycholinguistics*. [Psiholingvistika.] Moscow: Flinta.

Bergen, Benjamin, and Kathryn Wheeler. 2010. Grammatical aspect and mental simulation. *Brain and Language* 112 (3): 150–158.

Boas, Franz. 1984. *Anthropology of Modern Life*. Wesport, CT: Greenwood Press.

Carston, Robyn. 1989. *Linguistics: The Cambridge Survey. Vol.3. Language: Psychological and biological aspects*. Cambridge: Cambridge University Press.

Chafe, Wallace L. 1987. *Cognitive Constraints on Information Flow: Coherence and Grounding in Discourse*. Amsterdam: John Benjamins Publishing Company.

Chomsky, Noam. 1994. *Bare Phrase Structure*. Cambridge, MA: MIT Press.

Deese, James. 1965. *The Structure of Associations in Language and Thought*. Baltimore, MD: John's Hopkins Press.

Dubrovskaya, Tatiana. 2019. Introduction. The problem of method in modern linguistics and language teaching. [Predislovie. O probleme metoda v sovremennoj lingvistike i lingvodidaktike.] In *Modern Developments in Linguistics and Language Teaching: The Problem of Method* [Soveremennyje Napravlenija v Lingvistike i Prepodavanii Jazykov: Problema Metoda], *III International Conference Proceedings, Penza, 24–27 April 2019, Vol. I Methods in Linguistics*, ed. T.V. Dubrovskaya, 3–4. Penza: Penza State University Publishing House.

Ermolaev, Oleg. 2003. *Mathematical Statistics for Psychologists*. [Matematicheskaya statistika dlya psihologov.] Moscow: Moscow Psychological and Social Institute: Flinta.

Glenberg, Arthur, Marion Meyer, and Karen Lindem. 1987. Mental models contribute to foregrounding during text comprehension. *Journal of Memory and Language* 26: 69–83.

Gorelov, Ilya N. 2003. *Selected Works on Psycholinguistics*. [Izbrannye trudy po psiholingvistike.] Moscow: Labyrinth.

de Groot, Annette, and Peter Hagoort, eds. 2017. *Research Methods in Psycholinguistics and the Neurobiology of Language: A Practical Guide*. New York: Wiley-Blackwell.

Gyori, Gabor. 2013. Basic level categories and meaning in language. *Argumentum* 9: 149–161.

Humboldt, Wilhelm. 2000. In *Selected Works on Linguistics*. [Izbrannye trudy po yazykoznaniyu.] Moscow: OJSC IG Progress.

Kang, Xin, Anita Eerland, Gitte H. Joergensen, Rolf A. Zwaan, and Gerry T. M. Altmann. 2020. The influence of state change on object representations in language comprehension. *Memory and Cognition* 48: 390–399.

Karaulov, Yuriy N., Yurij A. Sorokin, Evgenij F. Tarasov, Natalia. V. Ufimtseva, and Galina A. Cherkasova. 1996. *Associative Thesaurus of the Russian Language. Russian Associative Dictionary.* [Associativnyj tezaurus russkogo yazyka. Russkij associativnyj slovar'.] Vol. 1–4. Moscow: Institute of the Russian Language

Kiss, George, Clark Armstrong, and Roy Milroy. 1972. *The Associative Thesaurus of English.* Edinburgh: University of Edinburgh, MGC Speech and Communication Unit.

Klyukanov, Igor. 2018. *Message and Oblivion.* [Soobshchenie i zabytie.] Moscow: St. Petersburg: Center for Humanitarian Initiatives.

Krasnykh, Victoria. 2002. *Ethnopsycholinguistics and Linguoculturology.* [Etnopsiholingvistika i lingvokul'turologiya.] Moscow: ITDGK "Gnosis".

Kubryakova, Elena S., ed. 1997. *A Brief Dictionary of Cognitive Terms.* [Kratkij slovar' kognitivnyh terminov.] Moscow: Moscow State University.

Lakoff, George. 1982. *Categories and Cognitive Models.* Berkeley, CA: University of California.

Lakoff, George. 1987. *Women, Fire and Dangerous Things: What Categories Reveal about the Mind.* Chicago: The University of Chicago press.

Lakoff, George, and Mark Jonson. 1980. *Metaphors We Live By.* Chicago: The University of Chicago press.

Langacker, Ronald W. 1991. *Foundations of Cognitive Grammar: Volume II: Descriptive Application.* Stanford, CA: Stanford University Press.

Langland-Hassan, Peter, and Agustín Vicente, eds. 2018. *Inner Speech: New Voices.* Oxford: Oxford University Press.

Leontyev, Alexei N. 1975. *Activity. Consciousness. Personality.* [Deyatel'nost'. Soznanie. Lichnost'.] Moscow: Politizdat.

Leontyev, Alexei A, ed. 1977. *Dictionary of Associative Norms of the Russian Language.* [Slovar' associativnyh norm russkogo yazyka.] Moscow: Moscow State University Publishing House.

Leontyev, Alexei A. 2003. *Fundamentals of Psycholinguistics. [Osnovy psiholingvistiki.]*, 3rd ed. Moscow: Meaning.

Levelt, Willem. 1989. *Speaking: From Intention to Articulation.* Cambridge, MA: MIT Press.

Levelt, Willem. 1999. Models of word production. *Trends in Cognitive Sciences* 3 (6): 223–232.

Levelt, Willem. 2012. *A History of Psycholinguistics: The Pre-Chomskyan Era.* New York: Oxford University Press.

Luria, Alexander. 1979. *Language and Consciousness.* [Yazyk i soznanie.], ed. E.D. Chomsky. M: Moscow State University Publishing House.

Mead, George H. 1962. *Mind, Self and Society.* 2nd ed., ed. C.W. Morris. Chicago: University of Chicago Press.

Osgood, Charles, George Suci, and Paul Tannenbaum. 1957. *The Measurement of Meaning.* Urbana, Chicago and London: University of Illinois Press.

Piaget, Jean. 1969. *The Mechanisms of Perception.* New York: Basic Books.

Potebnya, Alexander. 1999. *Complete Collection of Works.* [Polnoe sobranie trudov.] Moscow: Labyrinth.

Privalova, Irina. 1995. *Psychological Attitude in the Understanding of Foreign Text (Based on Russian and English Languages).* [Psihologicheskaya ustanovka v processe ponimaniya inoyazychnogo teksta (na materiale russkogo i anglijskogo yazykov).] The PhD dissertation. Saratov.

Privalova, Irina. 2005. *Interculture and Verbal Sign (Linguo-Cognitive Basis of Intercultural Communication).* [Interkul'utra i verbal'nyj znak (lingvokognitivnye osnovy mezhkul'turnoj kommunikacii).] Moscow: Gnosis.

Privalova, Irina, and Natalia Kuptsova. 2016. *Digital communication of the youth.* [Elektronnaya kommunikaciya molodezhi.] Saratov: Saratov State University Publishing House.

Rhys, Catrin, Christiane Ulbrich, and Mikhail Ordin. 2013. Adaptation to Aphasia: Grammar. *Prosody and Interaction. Clinical Linguist Phonetics* 27 (1): 46–71.

Rosch, Eleanor. 1978. Cognition and Categorization. In *Cognition and categorization*, ed. E. Rosch and B.B. Lloyd, 27–48. Hillsdale, NJ: Lawrence Erlbaum Associates.

Sacks, Joseph M., and Sydney T. Levy. 1950. The Sentence Completion Test. In *Projective Psychology*, ed. L.E. Abt and L. Bellak, 357–402. New York: Knopf.

Sapir, Edward. 1949. The Grammarian and his Language. In *Selected writings of Edward Sapir in language, culture and personality*, ed. D.G. Mandelbaum. Berkeley: University of California Press.

Shcherba, Lev. 2004. *Language System and Speech Activity.* [Yazykovaya sistema i rechevaya deyatel'nost'.] Moscow: URSS l.

Slobin, Dan, and Judith Green. 1976. *Psycholinguistics.* [Psiholingvistika.] Trans. E.I. Egnevitskaya. Moscow: Progress.

Sorokin, Yurij. 1994. *Ethnic Conflictology (Theoretical and Experimental Fragments)* [Etnicheskaya konfliktologiya (teoreticheskie i eksperimental'nye fragmenty).] Samara: Russkij Licej.

Spencer, Grant, and Theodor Ziehen. 1998. *Foundations of Psychology. Physiological Psychology in 14 Lectures.* [Osnovaniya psihologii. Fiziologicheskaya psihologiya v 14 lekciyah.] Moscow: AST-LTD.

Tarasov, Evgenij. 1987. *Trends in the Development of Psycholinguistics.* [Tendencii razvitiya psiholingvistiki.] Moscow: IYA RAN, Nauka.

Treiman, Rebecca, Charles Clifton, Jr., Antje S. Meyer, and Lee H. Wurm. 2003. Language comprehension and production. In *Comprehensive Handbook of Psychology, vol. 4: Experimental psychology,* 527–548. New York: Wiley.

Vygotsky, Lev. 2001. *Thinking and Speech. Mind, Consciousness, Unconscious.* [Myshlenie i rech'. Psihika, soznanie, bessoznatel'noe.] Moscow: Labyrinth.

Ufimtseva, Natalia. 1996. Russians: The Experience of yet Another Self-Knowledge. [Russkie: opyt eshche odnogo samopoznaniya.] In *Ethnocultural Specificity of Linguistic Consciousness,* 139–161. Moscow: IYA RAN.

Uznadze, Dimitri. 1958. The Experimental Basis of the Psychology of Set. [Eksperimental'nye osnovy psihologii ustanovki.] *Experimental Studies on the Psychology of Set* 1: 3–126.

Uznadze, Dimitri. 1961. The Main Provisions of the Set Theory. [Osnovnye polozheniya teorii ustanovki.] *Experimental Foundations of a Psychological Set.* Tbilisi: Publishing house of the Georgian Academy of Sciences.

Uznadze, Dimitri. 1966. *Psychological Research.* [Psihologicheskie issledovaniya.] Moscow: Nauka.

Whorf, Benjamin Lee. 1956. *Language, Thought and Reality: Selected Writings of Benjamin Lee Whorf*, ed. J.B. Carroll. Cambridge: Technology Press of Massachusetts Institute of Technology.

Zalevskaya, Aleksandra. 1990. *Word in the Lexicon of Man.* [Slovo v leksikone cheloveka.] Voronezh: Voronezh State University.

Zwaan, Rolf. 2016. Situation Models, Mental Simulations, and Abstract Concepts in Discourse Comprehension. *Psychonomic Bulletin & Review* 23 (4): 1028–1034.

Chapter 12
Teacher Personality as a Factor of Pedagogical Design

Ekaterina N. Shchaveleva, Andrei N. Kuznetsov, and Yulia V. Pushkina

Abstract This chapter explores in-depth studies of teacher personality and its effect on pedagogical design in the framework of course design and course delivery. The research is based on quantitative and qualitative methods, including surveys, interviews, comparative analysis, and computational method. Three categories of stakeholders were embraced, students, teachers, and program administrators, with a total of 382 respondents. The research was mapped out in four phases: two synchronous and two asynchronous. The research questions were: (1) What teacher qualities account for successful pedagogical design? and (2) What correlation exists between each of the revealed teacher qualities and pedagogical design? The findings included a set of eleven key teacher qualities nominated by stakeholders: responsibility, sociability, industriousness, goal-orientation, creativity, punctuality, attentiveness, proactiveness, fairness, empathy, and exactingness. The authors demonstrate and illustrate that these qualities are reflected in both course design and course delivery, and could thus be a subject of formation during both a teacher's pre-service and in-service periods. Further research perspectives are highlighted, such as approaches to the evaluation of teacher performance, including 360-degree feedback; designing a course that is closely connected to a teacher's qualities; and shaping a teacher's personality as a factor of pedagogical design.

Keywords Pedagogical design · Course design · Course delivery · Teacher personality · Structured interview · Student satisfaction · Teacher qualities · Russian culture

E. N. Shchaveleva (✉) · Y. V. Pushkina
National University of Science and Technology 'MISiS', Moscow, Russia

A. N. Kuznetsov
Center of Education Systems Management, Institute of Education Management of Russian Academy of Education, Moscow, Russia
e-mail: andremos@inbox.ru

12.1 Introduction

The problem of pedagogical design has recently become an issue of interest, specifically in the context of the increase in MOOCs and SPOCs. Researchers have been investigating the factors that affect a course and make it successful from an array of perspectives. This chapter considers the factors as applied to the phenomenon of pedagogical design holistically, and irrespective of the way a particular course is delivered: whether it is face-to-face, blended, or online. The chapter thus focuses on pedagogical design rather than on course design, the former being a broader framework of metadidactic studies. Taking into account that pedagogical design absorbs course design, however, both course design and course delivery factors will be considered.

As early as the 2000s,

technological characteristics, the pedagogical structure of courses, and their relationship to student learning and satisfaction with the course delivery medium (Arbaugh 2005: 135)

were treated as factors of a good course. Kosyrev et al. (2017) would identify the key issues and approaches to the teacher-training curricula development and course design with account of the characteristics of the national education system. Qin and Tan (2018) note that problems of course design

could be traced to inherent deficiencies in its design, creation, and implementation, which are rooted in contextual factors at levels of system, institution, faculty, and course.

Asoodar et al. (2016: 704) categorised the course design factors into six dimensions, "learner dimension, instructor's dimension, course dimension, technology dimension, design dimension, and the environment dimension". Earlier, Gamage et al. (2015) proposed ten dimensions affecting MOOC development: interactivity, collaboration, pedagogy, motivation, a network of opportunities/future directions, assessment, learner support, technology, usability, and content. Later, Al-Fraihat et al. (2017) suggested an alternative ten-dimensional model in view of e-learning in general, and grouped it into planning, readiness, management, support, pedagogical, technological, faculty, institution, evaluation and ethics clusters. This set of course design categories was extended by Gokdas and Torun (2017) who addressed design, proficiency, and exertion.

Li et al. (2017) analysed the role of the evaluation system. Hammarlund et al. (2015) and Linder (2017) postulated that a transparent alignment of assignments and assessment, clarity of purpose, goals, and guidelines comprise the cornerstone of a solid course. In addition, "continuous opportunities for communication and collaboration" have been considered, together with the problem of overcoming the

primarily internal factors, e.g., low self-efficacy, difficulties to plan the work effectively and adapting to a new environment. (Hammarlund et al. 2015: 12)

In this connection, Lencastre et al. (2010: 4288) highlighted

design of the educational environment; development and implementation of the online curricular units and evaluation.

Moore emphasised "content organization and presentation along with minimizing non-essential cognitive load" (Moore et al. 2014: 143).

According to the reviewed publications, researchers would scrutinise the issue of a tutor's guidance as a factor in pedagogical design. Panchoo (2015: 7463) stipulates "a properly designed virtual environment with appropriate tools, relevant learning strategies, and the guidance of a tutor". Guiding students throughout a course "helps them to refine their project and ideas and to articulate their creative minds" through "experiencing, thinking as well as redoing and rethinking" (Vaziri 2010: 250), which requires increased responsibility from the teacher as their mentor. This added teacher value is associated with "an expectation of more explanatory and supportive tutor intervention" (Stepanyan et al. 2009: 367).

From the student perspective, scholars propose student epistemic beliefs (Conn et al. 2011), management of student expectations (Jesurasa et al. 2017), student cognitive styles (Oh and Lim 2005) and learning styles (Moallem 2007; Nielsen and Kreiner 2017) as essential factors in pedagogical design.

The literature review revealed that teacher personality is rarely considered as a factor in efficient pedagogical design, although many researchers note the importance of a teacher's character for the learning process.

Zinchenko et al. (2020: 11) emphasise "human readiness and participation in the development and realization of new types of socio-professional activities". Yasan Ak and Yendi (2018) showed the identifiable relationship between the personality traits of pre-service teachers and their attitudes towards the perspective profession. Rezaei et al. (2019: 1342) mentioned

> the importance of uncovering the relationship between five big personality traits and teachers' personality factors,

which are openness to experience, conscientiousness, extraversion, agreeableness, and neuroticism (Ak and Yendi 2018). According to Senchyna (2017: 123)

> the prerequisite of humanities teacher's professional development is his/her ability for reflection which involves self-cognition, self-analysis and activity self-assessment, as well as understanding the way he/she is perceived by others as a personality.

Thielmann et al. (2019) note a teacher's sensitivity, engagement, equilibrium, stability, and optimism; whilst Doo et al. (2020) indicate the importance of openness to experience for a tutor's self-efficacy and work engagement, and state that altruism does not have a direct bearing.

The two research questions raised in this chapter are:

- What teacher qualities affect successful pedagogical design (both course design and course delivery)?
- What is the correlation between each of the revealed teacher qualities and pedagogical design?

The study was conducted from the perspectives of three stakeholders: students, teachers, and program administrators.

12.2   Data and Methodology

The research was conducted in the Department of Modern Languages and Communication, National University of Science and Technologies (NUST) 'MISiS' (Moscow, Russia), which delivers two Bachelor programs under the degree of linguistics: *Translation Studies* and *Teaching Modern Languages and Cultures*. The format of the program is that students apply for Linguistics and split into two programs when they become third year students. Although there are two hypothetical streams of preferences in terms of teacher qualities that might be characteristics of the two groups of students (translators-to-be and teachers-to-be), there is strong belief that those differences may be considered negligible in the context of the current research: all these students come from more or less homogeneous linguistic-educational and socio-cultural backgrounds.

The research was both qualitative and quantitative. The analysis was based on data collected through surveys with the use of questionnaires for both teachers and students, together with structured interviews. The analysis of the surveys required the use of computational methods.

The research comprised four phases. The Phase I research question was 'What qualities of a teacher's personality affects the various behaviours of students?' The survey was used as a research method. The respondents had to identify which of the teacher qualities was most influential in their behaviour. The survey included 315 students majoring in linguistics: 149 first year students, 90 s year students, 57 third year students (26 of whom were taught *Translation Studies* and 31 were taught *Teaching Modern Languages and Cultures*), and 19 fourth year students (eight from *Translation Studies* and eleven from *Teaching Modern Languages and Cultures*).

Phase II was the most extended stage, and lasted four months (March–June 2020). It aimed to reveal whether the teachers working on the programs possessed the qualities identified in Phase I. These qualities became the basis of the questions included in structured interviews with 65 teachers working on both programs. The list of qualities was added by program administrators as the authors believe that not only students can determine the success of the program, although their opinions matter. The prior expert evaluation by program administrators provided background for those interviews.

Phase III involved the survey conducted with students who were to identify whether the teachers possessed qualities from the list compiled in Phase II. The research methods thus included the survey with further comparative analysis. This phase required massive calculations, so computational methods were used.

The series of interviews in Phase II proceeded with the feedback survey carried out in Phase IV, which was synchronous with Phase III. The teachers were given a platform on which to share their post-interview comments.

Google Forms was used as the media for all surveys conducted during the research.

12.3 Results

Phase I

Both literature review and the longitudinal research have shown that the personal qualities of a teacher affect the level of satisfaction a student gets from the course. The authors assumed that the qualities could affect a student through different ways, i.e. personality development, academic development, and professional development. A list of 40 features has currently been made, which could be involved in the academic atmosphere and displayed by a teacher:

• spiritual generosity	• singularity
• flexibility	• wittiness
• humanity	• responsible
• diplomacy	• compassion
• dynamism	• tactfulness
• benevolence	• decency
• cordiality	• acumen
• pro-activeness	• punctuality
• culturality	• self-reflection
• sincerity	• self-confidence
• sociability	• self-discipline
• creativity	• modesty
• leadership	• fairness
• softness	• tolerance
• attentiveness	• exactingness
• assertiveness	• industriousness
• probity	• goal-orientation
• innovativeness	• good humour
• impartiality	• sensitivity
• optimism	• empathy

The analysis revealed the qualities recognized by the majority of students when their answering the question. The qualities were ranked in each category, which is shown in Table 12.1.

The analysis also showed that students responded to qualities affecting personality development (21 qualities noted by more than 200 students) more gladly than those of professional development (10) or academic development (1). Students do not acknowledge that a teacher's personality affects their academic behaviour. Students believe these are qualities that an 'ideal' teacher should possess, regardless of the circumstances.

All the qualities were compared and ranked according to the responsiveness of the respondents, irrespective of their attributing them to a particular group. The list was thus shortened to the ten most popular characteristics among the students (according to the number of mentions), which comprised the basis of our study:

1. Responsibility
2. Sociability

Table 12.1 Top ten qualities affecting various student outcomes

Personality development	Academic development	Professional development
Spiritual generosity	Responsibility	Responsibility
Sincerity	Creativity	Sociability
Good humour	Industriousness	Industriousness
Cordiality	Punctuality	Pro-activeness
Benevolence	Attentiveness	Leadership
Optimism	Pro-activeness	Exactingness
Modesty	Goal-orientation	Goal-orientation
Empathy	Sociability	Innovativeness
Sensitivity	Exactingness	Punctuality
Humanity	Impartiality	Flexibility

3. Industriousness
4. Goal-orientation
5. Creativity
6. Punctuality
7. Singularity
8. Attentiveness
9. Pro-activeness
10. Fairness

Phase II

The authors conjectured that teacher qualities could be evaluated from two viewpoints: students and administrators (expert evaluation). The expert evaluation is the most important, because it is not only student opinions that matter, but equally the judgment of the administrators who run the program and are responsible for both achieving the program outcomes and an efficient course design that complies with the requirements of the government and the educational institution.

For this reason, the authors worked out a list of questions that could help to reveal whether an educator possesses certain qualities. The list of qualities was slightly changed as a development of the list that had been used within the previous phase. Singularity and creativity were not distinguished, and the administrators added exactingness and empathy to the list. The administrators consider the former to be an essential quality for program effectiveness; whilst the latter was hypothesised as a quality that could affect the level of a student's satisfaction. The questions were included in the structured interview with the teachers ($N = 65$), and conducted from March through June 2020, both face-to-face and via distance. The qualities themselves were not named during the interview but used to help the interviewees reflect upon the teaching habits associated with those qualities. The questions were from the

Table 12.2 The qualities and questions

Quality	Questions
Attentiveness	Do you note changes in student behaviour?
Sociability	How do you tackle problems in your communication with students?
Punctuality	Do you have a backlog when checking student papers?
Empathy	Do you ask students the reasons for their underperformance?
Fairness	Are you lenient with students who attribute their backlogs to extenuating circumstances?
Exactingness	What do you understand to be the quality work of a student?
Responsibility	Do you normally schedule your teaching activities?
Industriousness	How much time do you normally spend when preparing for a lesson?
Creativity/singularity	Do you vary your teaching materials and practices?
Pro-activeness	Do you voice your professional and personal concerns associated with your department activity?
Goal-orientation	What are your professional objectives?

teaching paradigm, as it has more bearing on pedagogical design and is thus more administrator-centred. Examples of such questions are listed in Table 12.2.

The interviews with the teachers lasted from 30 to 60 min, depending on the interviewees' answers and their sociability. The results of the interviews enabled an expert evaluation of the teacher qualities to be obtained. This was measured on a five-band scale, where 3 is the standard level; 2 and 4 are low and high levels respectively; and 1 and 5 are extremes, as shown in Fig. 12.1. These extremes could hinder the teaching process. For instance, if a teacher was awarded 1 for punctuality, or being late to check papers, that could lower the level of student satisfaction. Conversely, a teacher might be awarded 5 for creativity because they spent too much time on that, so that the other aspects of the teaching process suffered. The results were analysed and the weakest qualities were identified. These turned out to be attentiveness (average 2.87) and creativity (average 2.9). The latter could be ascribed to the fact that teachers are overloaded with work, and lack the time to create new materials or activities for their learners. Attentiveness, on the other hand, is worth an in-depth investigation. Both, however, were approximate to the standard level.

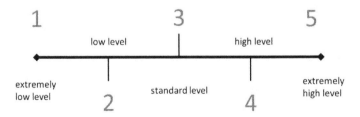

Fig. 12.1 The levels of qualities possessed

Table 12.3 The percentage of deflection

Points of deflection	Percentage
0	34.8
1	44.2
2	17.3
3	2.7
4	1.0

Phase III

The next step of the study was to ask students their opinions about whether the teachers of the two programs possessed the qualities mentioned above. The results might be somewhat subjective, but the authors of the research acknowledge that this piece of information could be beneficial for the program because that the program is seen from the consumers' perception. It may affect the program's attractiveness to university applicants. The authors also inquired whether the students were satisfied to work with one teacher or another.

The results of this survey were compared to the Phase II findings to reveal any differences in perception.

The analysis showed that in most cases (nearly 80%) the expert evaluation either coincided with the student evaluations, or featured a one-point deflection, although there was also some serious deflection (shown in Table 12.3).

In the students' perceptions the weakest qualities of their teachers are pro-activeness (2.7), goal-orientation (2.6), creativity (2.51), and empathy (2.48). On average, student evaluations were 0.5 points lower than the expert evaluations. It is noteworthy that creativity appeared to be the weakest quality in both evaluations.

The authors also attempted to investigate the correlation between the level of satisfaction with the teachers and the qualities these teachers possess. The review of the results indicates that no particular qualities affect the level of student satisfaction, although some tendencies can be seen. Creativity, pro-activeness, goal-orientation, empathy, sociability, and punctuality somewhat raised the level of satisfaction. Conversely, exactingness had a negative effect here. At the same time, all the qualities together had a strong impact on students' positive perceptions of a teacher.

Phase IV

Once the series of interviews was complete, the survey was launched to obtain feedback about the interviews. The feedback survey showed that not only did the interviews help the qualities to be revealed, but it also offered an opportunity for reflection on teaching habits. Nearly 70% of the teachers reported that they were ready to revisit their teaching habits (Fig. 12.2).

The interview also enabled teachers (57.8%) to focus on some of their teaching habits. The respondents noted that they had not paid attention to their habits before (shown in Fig. 12.3). At the same time, over 40% appeared to be insensitive to the

Fig. 12.2 Readiness to revisit teaching habits

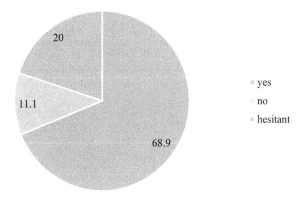

Fig. 12.3 New foci of teaching competencies

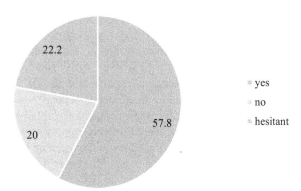

interview. This could be explained by either their holistically shaped personality or inflexibility.

Despite this, the majority of the interviewees reported the positive effect of the interview on their professional well-being. The respondents acknowledged that the interview provided them with the opportunity of voicing their concerns and sharing their opinions about the program, their interaction with students, and self-reflection (Fig. 12.4). Moreover, the teachers who were interviewed during the COVID-19 lock-down confessed that the interviews supported them and helped them in their spiritual well-being, helping their forced professional isolation and personal 'solitude'.

12.4   Discussion

The qualities established in this research could be required for successful pedagogical design, and both the students and the administrators should expect them from the teachers employed by the program.

Fig. 12.4 Positive effect of the interviews

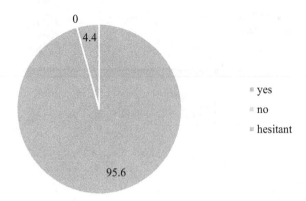

The authors presume that there is a correlation between the personal qualities of teachers and their ability to design a course. Effectively designed courses could increase the level of student satisfaction, and hypothetically would contribute to their mastery of the program. In light of this, this chapter provides the authors' views about reflection on the teacher qualities in course design.

Sociability is a quality that extends beyond personal interaction and might be reflected in a teacher's inclination and ability to choose interactive forms of teaching. In this case, the teacher would actively employ forms such as discussions, debates, brainstorming, and Q&A sessions in the teaching process. This is particularly vital for teaching foreign languages and affects language acquisition.

Industriousness is reflected in the process of course design. An industrious teacher would demonstrate precision and thoroughness in the development of the course syllabus. From the administrators' point of view, it also leads to meeting deadlines for submitting the ready-made syllabi, even under a heavy workload.

Pro-activeness manifests itself through teaching strategies in the active search for novel teaching resources, for example, socio-human, technical, financial, and so on. A pro-active teacher does not react to student behaviour but foresees the challenges that may be encountered and that are projected in the course design.

Creativity is closely correlated with pro-activeness. A teacher may implement self-tailored materials in concordance with the needs of students and institution, and demonstrate the flexibility of the curriculum through context-centeredness, which would be grounded in student-centeredness, the availability of resources, and so on.

Responsibility and punctuality are qualities that help teachers meet the rigid deadlines prescribed for both themselves and their students. This may also affect their attitude towards various aspects of the course design, such as thorough the development of rubrics. The latter also corresponds to fairness, empathy, and exactingness, although these qualities are more important in course delivery than course design. These three play a major role in assessment: while designing assessment and rubrics a teacher may consider student proclivities, and thus foresee their ability to complete the assignments. In this context, the rubrics might be student-centred or content-centred, challenging and rigid, or student-friendly, and so on.

Goal-orientation is associated with a teacher's ability to attain outcomes. In course design it manifests itself in thoroughly planned course outcomes, aligned with the respective content, assessment, and rubrics. For such teachers, the course content is grounded on the foresight of the development (including fluctuations) of the professional field for which the students are being prepared.

Course design is also dependent on the teacher's qualities as manifested through their teaching behaviour. All of these impact the course delivery and therefore the level of student satisfaction with the particular courses, and the program overall.

A teacher's qualities are believed to impact course design through course delivery. For example, the course itself could be designed by a professional with all mentioned qualities be on a high level, but a teacher delivering the course may hypothetically suffer from a lack of fairness and punctuality. In the context of Russian culture, this could lead to a negative student perceptions of the course in contrast to the perception of the same course delivered by a more fair and punctual teacher.

The research demonstrated that it is essential for students to see a number of personal qualities in their teacher to guarantee a high level of satisfaction with a teacher and the relevant course. There are qualities that affect course perception, and these should be further developed. The study showed that a lack of creativity could have a slightly negative affect on course perception. Considering teaching practice, creativity like some other qualities, is not an inborn entity but is a gainable skill.

The authors postulate that personality qualities are may be shaped further in the in-service period of a teacher's development. This may be implemented in two ways: (1) structured interviews, where a teacher is given a chance to reflect upon their teaching habits and revisit them (e.g. exactingness or empathy), or (2) seminars conducted by program administrators, where teacher trainers offer specifically elaborated assignments with which to practice skills (e.g. creativity or pro-activeness).

The authors believe that these qualities could alternatively be shaped during a teacher's pre-service period within teacher training programs at university. Research (Pushkina and Schaveleva 2018) was carried out in 2018 and demonstrated the effectiveness of pedagogical cases offered to senior students majoring in *Teaching Modern Languages and Cultures* at NUST 'MISiS'.

Further studies could be carried out as a follow-up to the present research, to address the in-service development of personal qualities so that the dynamics of a student's course satisfaction can be observed.

The current research demonstrated that the evaluation of a teacher's performance should not be subjected to student perceptions as a single factor. As has been illustrated, the evaluations of students and experts differ in some instances. There are qualities that students underestimate, which are determining factors of course success in terms of student outcomes (e.g. exactingness). This brings the authors to the concept of a holistic evaluation of teacher performance: 360-degree feedback (Schaveleva et al. 2019).

It is also the authors' contention that the ultimate objective of the pedagogical design is its adaption to the teacher's personality. The global idea that underpins further research is that a teacher's personality may be a precursor to pedagogical design. It becomes specifically important if a teacher boasts considerable and program-valuable practical experience but their teaching skills are not sufficient. The course design should also be centred around a teacher's personality: the course should accentuate the teacher's best qualities. Hypothetically, that will improve the quality of teaching and thus increase student satisfaction.

The study demonstrated that structured interviews improve a teacher's well-being (both personal and social), so they could greatly contribute to the effectiveness of their teaching performance. The teachers also noted that the interviews gave them an opportunity to provide their feedback about the program directly to the administration. This encourages the authors to proceed with the elaboration of interview scenarios to support teachers during the academic year.

This all paves the way for the follow-up research that is planned in NUST 'MISiS'.

12.5 Conclusion

In this research the authors identified a set of teacher qualities that affect successful pedagogical design: course design and course delivery. Students clearly distinguish between the qualities affecting their various behaviours in the context of their course mastering. The students thus agree that the majority of these behaviours affect their personality development, which is necessary because most students are still undergoing the process of personality formation. The qualities valued by students were responsibility, sociability, industriousness, goal-orientation, creativity, punctuality, singularity, attentiveness, pro-activeness, and fairness. As an outcome of expert evaluation, the authors altered the list of qualities by adding empathy and exactingness. The surveys and interviews used proved to be relevant research methods in this context.

The second research question regarding the correlation between each of the revealed teacher qualities and pedagogical design was addressed in the Sect. 12.4. The chapter gives an insight into the ways the qualities can and indeed do affect pedagogical design, which provides soundly for student satisfaction with an individual course and the program overall.

The authors admit that the outcomes of the research might have been affected considerably by two objective parameters. The first of those is the linguistic bias of the students participating in the survey, which could influence their humanistic nomination of teacher qualities. The second parameter appeared to be the cultural background of both the students and the teachers, the Russian culture, which is predominantly feminine (Kuznetsov and Obuobi-Donkor 2019), and might dictate personality preferences in terms of the qualities that are expected of the partner in communication.

The current research is far from exhaustive and could be the basis of follow-up studies of the personality development of teachers and students, as well as the strategic development of pedagogical design, factors affecting the level of student and teacher satisfaction, and approaches to the evaluation of teaching performance.

Acknowledgements The research was carried out through the courtesy of administrators at the Department of Modern Languages and Communication, NUST 'MISiS' (Moscow, Russia). The authors would like to express their appreciation for the efforts of students and teachers on the Bachelor's program in Linguistics, NUST 'MISiS' for their participation in this research.

References

Al-Fraihat, Dimah, Mike Joy, and Jane Sinclair. 2017. Identifying success factors for E-learning in higher education. In *Proceedings of the International Conference on e-Learning*, eds. L. Campbell, R. Hartshorne, 247–255. Curran Associates, Inc., New York.

Ak, Nehir Yasan, and Bahar Yılmaz Yendi. 2018. The relationship between personality and attitudes towards teaching profession of pre-service teachers. In *EDULEARN Proceedings*, eds. L. Gómez Chova, A. López Martínez, I. Candel Torres, P. 3887.

Arbaugh, J. Ben. 2005. Is there an optimal design for on-line MBA courses? *Academy of Management Learning & Education* 4 (2): 135–149.

Asoodar, Maryam, Shahin Vaezi, and Balal Izanloo. 2016. Framework to improve E-learner satisfaction and further strengthen E-learning implementation. *Computers in Human Behavior* 63: 704–716.

Conn, Samuel S., Simon Hall, and Michael K. Herndon. 2011. Student epistemic beliefs as a catalyst for online course design: a case study for research-based elearning. *Cases on Building Quality Distance Delivery Programs: Strategies and Experiences,* 177–199.

Doo Min, Young, Meina Zhu, Curtis J. Bonk, and Ying Tang. 2020. The effects of openness, altruism and instructional self-efficacy on work engagement of MOOC instructors. 2020. *British Journal of Educational Technology,* 51(3) (May): 743–760.

Gamage, Dilrukshi, Shantha Fernando, and Indika Perera. 2015. Factors Leading to an Effective MOOC from Participants Perspective. In *8th International Conference on Ubi-Media Computing (Umedia) Conference Proceedings*, 230-235. Curran Associates, Inc., New York.

Gokdas, Ibrahim, and Fulya Torun. 2017. Examining the impact of instructional technology and material design courses on technopedagogical education competency acquisition according to different variables. *Educational Sciences-Theory and Practice* 17 (5): 1733–1758.

Hammarlund, Catharina Sjodahl, Maria H. Nilsson, and Christina Gummesson. 2015. External and internal factors influencing self-directed online learning of physiotherapy undergraduate students in Sweden: a qualitative study. *Journal of Educational Evaluation for Health Professions,* 22 (June): 12-33

Jesurasa, Amrita, Kelly Mackenzie, Hannah Jordan, and Elizabeth C. Goyder. 2017. What factors facilitate the engagement with flipped classrooms used in the preparation for postgraduate medical membership examinations? *Advances in Medical Education and Practice* 8: 419–426.

Kosyrev, Vasitiy P., Petr F. Kubrushko, and Andrei N. Kouznetsov. 2009. TVET and Teacher-training curricula: a developed national perspective. In *International Handbook of Education for the Changing World of Work: Bridging Academic and Vocational Learning*, eds. R. Mclean, D. Wilson, 1285–1292. Springer Science+Business Media B.V.

Kuznetsov, Andrei, and Dorcas Obuobi-Donkor. 2019. International marketing of educational services: literature review and intercultural case-study aimed at establishing dependence of school attractiveness on education as an ethnic value. In *INTED2019 Proceedings*, eds. L. Gómez Chova, A. López Martínez, I. Candel Torres, 7856–7864. Valencia: IATED Academy.

Lencastre, José A., Angélica Monteiro, António Moreira, and Délio Carquejo. 2010. Organization and management of online learning environments. In *3rd International Conference of Education, Research and Innovation* (ICERI2010), ed. IATED, 4288–4294. Madrid: IATED–International Association of Technology, Education and Development.

Li, Dahui, Qi. Fan, and Xuefeng Dai. 2017. Personal training evaluation system design for high education. *Eurasia Journal of Mathematics Science and Technology Education* 13 (7): 4333–4342.

Linder, Kathryn E. 2017. *The Blended Course Design Workbook: A Practical Guide.* Sterling, Virginia: Stylus Publishing LLC.

Moallem, Mahnaz. 2007. Accommodating individual differences in the design of online learning environments: a comparative study. *Journal of Research on Technology in Education* 40 (2): 217–245.

Moore, Joi L., Camille Dickson-Deane, and Min Z. Liu. 2014. Designing CMS courses from a pedagogical usability perspective. In *Perspectives in Instructional Technology and Distance Education: Research on Course Management Systems in Higher Education*, ed. A. Benson and D. Whitworth, 143–169. Charlotte, NC: Information Age Publishing.

Nielsen, Tine, and Svend Kreiner. 2017. Course evaluation for the purpose of development: what can learning styles contribute? *Studies in Educational Evaluation* 54 (September): 58–70.

Oh, Eunjoo, and Doohun Lim. 2005. Cross relationships between cognitive styles and learner variables in online learning environment. *Journal of Interactive Online Learning* 4 (1): 53.

Panchoo, Shireen. 2015. Online learning environment information system: architectural design based on online learners' activities. In *INTED Proceedings,* eds. L. Gómez Chova, A. López Martínez, I. Candel Torres, 7463–7468.

Pushkina Yulia V., and Ekaterina N. Schaveleva. 2018. Development of personal competencies within pre-service teacher training: a case study of a Russian University. In *10th International Conference on Education and New Learning Technologies (EDULEARN),* 2983–2987.

Qin, Melissa Xiaohui, and Xiongkai Tan. 2020. Examining a SPOC experiment in a foundational course: design, creation and implementation. *Interactive Learning Environments.* DOI: https://doi.org/10.1080/10494820.2020.1722710.

Rezaei, Omid, Mehrdad Vasheghani Farahani, and Fatemeh Musaei Sejzehei. 2019. Relationship between novice versus experienced efl teacher's big five personality traits and their ambiguity tolerance and risk taking. *Journal of Applied Research in Higher Education* 11(3): 1342-1351.

Senchyna, Natalia. 2017. Peculiarities of the development of humanities teachers' pedagogical reflection. *Science and Education* 5: 123–127.

Schaveleva, Ekaterina N., Anastasia I. Iatcenko, and Andrei N. Kuznetsov. 2018. 360-degree Feedback for teacher's portfolio development: research in quality assurance at the university level. In *10th International Conference on Education and New Learning Technologies (EDULEARN),* 2995–3000.

Stepanyan, Karen, Richard Mather, Hamilton Jones, and Carlo Lusuardi. 2009. Student engagement with peer assessment: a review of pedagogical design and technologies. *Advances in Web Based Learning–ICWL 2009, Lecture Notes in Computer Science* 5686 (August), eds. G. Goos, J. Hartmanis, and J. van Leeuwen, 367–375.

Thielmann B., T. Yurkul, I. Zavgorodnij and W. Kapustnik. 2019. Relationships of personality traits and workplace-related patterns of behavior and experience by female teachers. *Zentralblatt Fur Arbeitsmedizin Arbeitsschutz Und Ergonomie* 69(3): 133–143.

Vaziri, Tala. 2010. Reinventing teaching methods to foster creative and innovative minds the role of teachers' guidance in the future success of students. In *4th International Technology, Education and Development Conference* (INTED 2010), eds. L. Gómez Chova, A. López Martínez, I. Candel Torres, 250–255.

Zinchenko, Yuriy P., Evgeny M. Dorozhkin, and Ewald F. Zeer. 2020. Psychological and pedagogical bases for determining the future of vocational education: vectors of development. *Education and Science* [Obrazovanie i Nauka], 22(3): 11–35.

Chapter 13
Phonetics as an Art: Real or Surreal Assessment Criteria?

Natalya V. Sukhova

> What upsets people is not things themselves but their judgements about things
> Epictetus (Cited from Geary 2005: 73)

Abstract The chapter addresses one of the controversial issues in second language pronunciation assessment: why raters give different ratings even if the scoring procedure is valid and the criteria are consistent. The research aimed at tackling the question with the help of neuroaesthetic methodology. The Vienna Integrated Model of top-down and bottom-up processes in Art Perception allows the experimental ratings to be analysed from the rater's perspective and the speech sample to be compared with an art object as far as its evaluation is concerned. The experimental material consisted of a student's speech sample, which was a part of a vast annotated data set (collected over a four-year teaching period), the student's pronunciation ratings and a pilot survey of various raters with their assessment strategies. The results of the academic assessment of the student's phonetic performance and the analysis of the survey answers correlated well with the neuroaesthetic model. The correlation covered the main processing elements: (1) pre-classification; (2) perceptual analysis; (3) implicit memory integration; (4) explicit classification; (5) cognitive mastery; (6) secondary control and (7) self-awareness, metacognitive assessment.

Keywords Phonetics · Phonological and phonetic competence · L2 pronunciation · Assessment · Neuroaesthetics

13.1 Introduction

It is well known that phonetics is a study of acoustic and articulatory characteristics of speech (Akhmanova 2010: 496). However, it is not only a study, but it is also the whole scope of acoustic and articulatory (physiological) features of a given language

N. V. Sukhova (✉)
National University of Science and Technology 'MISiS', Moscow, Russia

and consequently of a given speaker of a given language. In other words, the fact that any speaker has his/her phonetics also holds true.

This presupposition evokes a number of implications which underlie this paper. Firstly, the phonetic inventory in a broad sense, as an ideal phonetic set–phonemes, intonemes, etc.–belongs to a language (e.g. Kodzasov and Krivnova 2001). Secondly, an individual speaker possesses a phonetic inventory as s/he has acquired it, namely, having allophonic and prosodic realisations of a certain ideal phonetic inventory, in a broad sense. Thirdly, these realisations are varied to a degree that is not comparable to variations at any other linguistic levels (cf. grammar or semantics). The extent to which phonetic features differ across speakers is the maximum possible (Pierrehumbert 2003).

Some questions which arise in regard to phonetics are both *philosophical,* and hence thought-provoking but not necessarily having any answers linking the language to the world (e.g. Blackburn 2017) in general, and *practical*, i.e. those which should supply the addresser with concrete solutions (e.g. Kirshner 2003).

The *philosophical* field encompasses such queries as the following: Why do I like the sound of someone's speech and dislike someone else's? What makes me say that French speech sounds pleasant to me even though I have no mastery of the French language? Why would a student strive to sound like a native speaker of English without being able either to say who this native speaker is or what exactly s/he likes about this hypothetical native-like speech?

Broader consideration of *philosophical* issues may lead us to the Saussurian dichotomy of *langue* which is an abstract system of internalized, shared rules governing a certain national language; and *parole* designating actual oral and written communication by a member or members of a particular speech community (Saussure 1983).

Thus, the questions raised above would present a battle field of some idealized foreign language (cf.: *langue*) and what the person has as his own speech (cf.: *parole*).

The *practical* domain is more well-formed and seemingly obvious and is thus traditionally present in applied linguistics. The agenda is as follows: how to teach phonetic disciplines; how to teach a person to speak a language, the phonetics of a language, second language (L2)[1] pronunciation, etc.; and how to assess all inter- and intrapersonal articulatory differences that we hear at an acoustic level.

This chapter attempts to address the principles of assessment in phonetics and of phonetics in teaching English, looking for the answers in both philosophical and practical domains.

The main premises for this search are the following:

- One of the components of linguistic competence, i.e. the ability to speak a language, is *phonological and phonetic competence*, i.e. the ability to perceive and produce speech based on the knowledge of articulatory and acoustic features of speech as well as of rhythmic and intonation patterns (CEFR 2018).

---

[1] In this chapter, I take a broad view of second language, i.e. encompassing the language of natural and artificial bilingualism.

- Teachers of English and also other educators (e.g. examiners of international examinations) regularly attend to the phonological and phonetic competence by either *developing* or *assessing* it.
- There are debates on how to *develop* phonological and phonetic competence, e.g. what its components are, how to teach intonation, what methods to use nowadays, etc. (Eliseeva 2019).
- There are controversies concerning how to *assess* phonological and phonetic competence—whether to apply the criteria which would fit the multicultural world of nowadays (CEFR 2018) or to employ a traditional Russian approach of imitation and full copying of the original material (Eliseeva 2019), etc. (Ashby and Ashby 2017).

These tasks of developing and assessing phonological and phonetic competence are usually tackled within a pedagogical realm and are frequently left unsolved (Derwing 2019). Teachers are struggling with competence assessment, as they are unable to have objective criteria. English as the *lingua franca* complicates the matter, causing, on the one hand, phonological and phonetic competence to be somewhat redundant as far as intelligible and comprehensible speech goes (see some chapters in Kang and Ginther 2018); hence, the whole idea of the necessity of teaching phonetics traditionally or developing competence, on the other hand, is jeopardised.

Thus, more precisely, the paper *aims* at seeking an answer to a philosophical question: Why does it all happen to phonetics?

I would immediately suggest an unexpected solution: phonetics is an art, and I will try to show how it can be dealt with as an art object.

Advances in neuroscience have prompted an exploration of the possible links between human linguistic competence, speech production and speech perception, and the way we "assess" or perceive speech in real communication. The findings further on may help to objectivise the phonetic criteria to be assessed in teaching.

The chapter is organised into 6 sections. Section 13.1 is an introduction where the research question and the background premises are stated. Section 13.2 focuses on the phonetic and phonological performance and its assessment. The key notions of intelligibility and comprehensibility are explored as we find them in the relevant literature. The figure of the rater is also introduced with all his/her sociolinguistic peculiarities which influence a rater's assessment of the speech. Section 13.3 is about our data and methodology used in the research. The data were collected at the National University of Science and Technology "MISiS" for a large-scale phonetic project. However, the recurrent problem, or rather a difficulty in assessing phonological and phonetic competence, has led the author to abandon the pedagogical methodology and answer a philosophical question of why the assessment depends so much on the rater even though there are assessment criteria imposed, e.g. by the programme designer. The survey in which experts and non-phoneticians took part supports the author's predictions coming from the findings in neuroscience. Section 13.4 presents the results of the analysis based on the neuroaesthetic methodology, students' data and the survey responses. Section 13.5 critically turns to several key limitations of the applied methodology and the possibility to review the conclusions. Section 13.6 gives an overview of the research and the conclusions drawn from the findings.

13.2   Assessment: General Considerations

Assessment is "the act of judging or deciding the amount, value, quality, or importance of something, or the judgment or decision that is made" (Cambridge Dictionary).

The last two decades have seen a burgeoning of empirical studies on second language (L2) pronunciation in general (see the latest issues of *Journal of Second Language Pronunciation, Studies in Second Language Acquisition, TESOL Quarterly*, among others) and a renewed focus on pronunciation assessment, in particular.

As noted above, teaching and assessment go hand in hand with phonetics as we tend to teach key phonological and phonetic phenomena and then assess them as well.

Within language assessment, the field of phonological and phonetic competence evaluation, or more broadly how the students do speaking and listening tests, is usually the most controversial one (see chapters in Kang and Ginther 2018) and in "many types of language programmes teachers tend to avoid assessing pronunciation" (Derwing 2019: 29).

The key variables of the phonological and phonetic competence assessment are intelligibility, comprehensibility, and the figure of the rater, as Kang and Ginther observe (2018). However, Thomson (2018) suggests that there are still three leading constructs in L2 pronunciation: "intelligibility, comprehensibility and accentedness" (ibid.: 23).[2] These constructs should be measured and eventually assessed.

Intelligibility is defined as "the extent to which a speaker's message is actually understood by a listener" (Munro and Derwing 1995: 76). Comprehensibility refers to listeners' "judgement on a rating scale of how difficult or easy an utterance is to understand" (Derwing and Munro 1997: 2). These findings as Kennedy and Trofimovich (2017) argued, "stimulated a debate about the appropriate targets and effective methods for pronunciation instruction" (Ibid.: 262).

The rater's figure brings us to the relationships between (1) the social role of the speaker and the listener and (2) the language background of the speaker and the listener. The paths of these relations are intertwined as we can have such combinations as:

- a social role:

  - teachers—students
  - teachers—teachers
  - students—students

---

[2] We do not touch on the notion of *accentedness* in this paper.

- a language proficiency:

    – native speakers—L2 speakers
    – L2 speakers—L2 speakers (the same L1 + L2 proficiency level)
    – L2 speakers—L2 speakers (a different L1 + L2 proficiency level)

Some other variations of all those are also possible.

Yan and Ginther (2018) dwell upon a dichotomy of a listener and a rater. Further research into this field shows that the listener can evaluate the speech and usually does it in a very biased way. Thus, we can suggest that the rater's opinion will be more objective than a plain listener's one.

Reid et al. found that "social context and generational differences" are important in rating L2 speaking performance (2019: 419). The raters were native speakers of English.

Saito et al. (2019: 1133) have examined

> how L2 users assess comprehensibility of foreign-accented speech according to a range of background variables, including first language (L1) profiles, L2 proficiency, age, experience, familiarity, and metacognition.

There were lenient and strict groups of listeners. So, comprehensibility was valued more by the lenient group of listeners, whereas the strict listeners were "strongly attuned to phonological accuracy" (Saito et al. 2019: 1133).

Nagle et al. (2019) took a dynamic approach to L2 comprehensibility. The raters and the speakers were L2 Spanish users. The results highlighted that

> certain problematic features and individual episodes caused listeners' impressions to converge, though substantial individual variation among listeners was evident. (Nagle et al. 2019: 647)

Summing up the findings and opinions on a speaker with his/her intelligibility and on a rater with his/her comprehension of the former, we can infer a number of key issues in assessment that are relevant to our paper.

Firstly, there are numerous sociolinguistic and extralinguistic components that impact the assessment that can also be assigned to a high influence of individual differences across speakers and listeners (or raters, in our case).

Secondly, as a result, the assessment rarely proceeds according to the assessment criteria even though they are developed and provided to the rater.

Hence, one important challenge of this work is to try to find the explanation to "the vicious circle" of the assessment.

In this chapter we seek firstly to trace how university teachers of phonetics assess phonetic and phonological competence: whether there are any criteria, what those criteria are and how we can explain those criteria, and whether they are methodologically grounded or are "impressionistic".

Thus, these goals comprise the following questions:

- What are the assessment criteria established at the department level to assess the students' performance during *A Practical Course in Phonetics*[3]?
- What are the assessment criteria established at the department level to assess the students' performance during the *Cambridge English: Advanced* (CAE) mock exam?
- What are the assessment criteria which teachers of phonetics report that they refer to (the survey results)?

The idea of this project emerged when the teaching staff of the department and its administration perceived a discrepancy between the pedagogical efforts of the teachers of phonetics and dissatisfaction with students' phonetics, which other teachers claimed. We have decided to find out what exactly teachers (both phoneticians and non-phoneticians) mean when they say that "his/her phonetics is bad" and to compare it to the objective reality of the students' performance. Broadly speaking, the aim here is to pinpoint the criteria of assessment in the mock exam (non-phoneticians) and in the course (phoneticians), which could reveal the discrepancy.

The second goal of this chapter is to seek an explanation to the extensively contradictory results of the first part of the queries (see Sect. 13.4.1). Here I will attempt to correlate the perception of students' phonetics to the perception of art objects.

13.3   Data and Methodology

13.3.1   A Broader Context of the Material for This Study

Participants

We recorded bachelor's students at the Department of Modern Languages and Communication at the National University of Science and Technology 'MISiS' (Moscow, Russia). All of them were students of the bachelor's programme in linguistics. The recordings were made from 2018 to 2019.

There were 81 students, from 18 to 20 years old: 19 males and 62 females. All of them gave a written consent for the audio recordings to be investigated and publicly demonstrated for the scientific purposes.

Recordings

There are 4 subsets of audio recordings in *.wav* format:

(1)   the recordings done after the 1st semester of their studies (winter 2018)
(2)   the recordings done after the 2nd semester of their studies (spring 2018)
(3)   the recordings done after the 3rd semester of their studies (winter 2019)
(4)   the recordings done after the 4th semester of their studies (spring 2019)

---

[3] Hereafter we will use 'course' for "A Practical Course in Phonetics".

The recordings are the oral part of the exam (mock CAE): speaking. In our department, this is a traditional exam for the discipline called "A Practical Course of English".

The computer and the microphone used to record were set on the table in front of the participants. So, the participants felt at ease with the equipment.

The first two subsets were recorded when there were two students talking, answering the questions of the examiners. The last two subsets were recorded when there were three students present.

There were always two examiners present during the speaking part.

The mean duration of the recordings was 14 min 10 s.

The information was stored on a Google sheet where we registered the following data:

- the student's name
- his/her date of birth
- his/her credits for speaking part (1–4 semesters)
- his/her credits for the course (1–4 semesters)
- his/her examiners' names for the speaking part
- his/her teachers for the course
- the duration of the recording

The recordings are stored on different Google disks and on the department's server.

Assessment Scales

We keep the assessment history of the students. More concretely, we have their credits for each semester for the speaking part (see the above 4 subsets of recordings) and we have their credits for the course that also covered the same 4 semesters. The credit systems for the course and for the exam were different and that is why the information is in percent to equal the calculations.

Assessment criteria for the course written in the programme documents[4] are as follows (Table 13.1):

Table 13.1 shows that phonetic and phonological competence is assessed very thoroughly in the course; at least the assessment scale allows for doing it and presupposes it. "To articulate correctly" actually means a lot: you pronounce, for instance, the diphthong [eɪ] as in *main*, keeping its nucleus as a front, mid-open (narrow variation), unrounded vowel and then proceed to its glide; when the tongue rises a bit up towards the articulation of vowel [ɪ], the space between the jaws is reduced (Tsybulya 2013: 68). "To maintain all the processes" means that the student is aware of the fact that the diphthong [eɪ] (1) should sound longer in the position before the voiced consonant (as it is in *main*) and (2) it can be monophongised in the word's final position before the pause or in the monosyllabic words before the voiced consonants. It can be pronounced as [e:] or [e], e.g. Let's stay [ste:], shall we, Jane [dʒe:]

---

[4] "A Practical Course in Phonetics" has a syllabus that has been approved by the programme's administration.

Table. 13.1 Criteria to assess the spoken tasks of the course

Criteria	Credits			
	5	4	3	0
Phonetics	All sounds are articulated correctly; all the phonetic processes are maintained	All sounds are articulated correctly, but not all the phonetic processes are maintained	Some sounds are articulated incorrectly; not all the phonetic processes are maintained	All sounds are articulated incorrectly; none of the phonetic processes are maintained
Prosody	Prosodic contours are correct	Prosodic contours are correct, but there are some minor inconsistencies	Prosodic contours are mainly correct, but there are some gross mistakes	Prosodic contours are totally incorrect

Assessment criteria for the CAE exam are explicitly written in the Handbook for the CAE exam (C2 Proficiency Handbook 2020: 58), and the department staff report that they have observed them.

Figure 13.1 demonstrates the assessment scales designed in terms of phonology, which seem to resemble other approaches to phonological competence (cf. Guide for teachers, IELTS 2020). This proves the idea that phonology is a grey area when it comes to teaching and especially assessing, in contrast to linguistics where phonology can hardly be defined as "under-researched" (e.g. see Zsiga 2013).

Piccardo conducted an extensive research and highlighted the major pitfalls of, for example, CEFR phonological assessment (2016: 9) which was similar to the CAE assessment scale:

- The existing scale Phonological Control does not capture this conceptual apparatus and appears fully unrealistic when it comes to issues such as accent, or progression (particularly in moving from B1 to B2).
- Furthermore, it is not consistent as it mixes such diverse factors as stress/intonation, pronunciation, accent and intelligibility without providing clear indication of progression in any of these factors specifically.
- It is not complete, which results in jeopardizing its applicability and usefulness.

Piccardo's thorough report eventually resulted in a newer version of CEFR in 2018 in which all suggested changes to the phonological scales were accepted (see this version of the scale in CEFR 2018: 136), and the author states that:

> this analytic grid can provide the basis for teachers to include appropriate objectives for phonology in their teaching and to develop assessment criteria appropriate to the level(s) concerned. [...] The provision of this more realistic, analytic scale will foster attention to phonological aspects in language teaching, encourage a more analytical and comparative approach and thus contribute to the awareness and effective communication of our learners. (Piccardo 2016: 23)

Berger attempted to create "a differentiation for academic speaking at C1 and C2 in the form of common reference points" (Berger 2020: 85). C1 and C2 descriptors

C2	Grammatical Resource	Lexical Resource	Discourse Management	Pronunciation	Interactive Communication
5	Maintains control of a wide range of grammatical forms and uses them with flexibility.	Uses a wide range of appropriate vocabulary with flexibility to give and exchange views on unfamiliar and abstract topics.	Produces extended stretches of language with flexibility and ease and very little hesitation. Contributions are relevant, coherent, varied and detailed. Makes full and effective use of a wide range of cohesive devices and discourse markers.	Is intelligible. Phonological features are used effectively to convey and enhance meaning.	Interacts with ease by skilfully interweaving his/her contributions into the conversation. Widens the scope of the interaction and develops it fully and effectively towards a negotiated outcome.
4	Performance shares features of Bands 3 and 5.				
3	Maintains control of a wide range of grammatical forms.	Uses a range of appropriate vocabulary with flexibility to give and exchange views on unfamiliar and abstract topics.	Produces extended stretches of language with ease and very little hesitation. Contributions are relevant, coherent and varied. Uses a wide range of cohesive devices and discourse markers.	Is intelligible. Intonation is appropriate. Sentence and word stress is accurately placed. Individual sounds are articulated clearly.	Interacts with ease, linking contributions to those of other speakers. Widens the scope of the interaction and negotiates towards an outcome.
2	Performance shares features of Bands 1 and 3.				
1	Shows a good degree of control of a range of simple and some complex grammatical forms.	Uses a limited range of appropriate vocabulary to give and exchange views on familiar and unfamiliar topics.	Produces extended stretches of language with very little hesitation. Contributions are relevant and there is a clear organisation of ideas. Uses a range of cohesive devices and discourse markers.	Is intelligible. Intonation is generally appropriate. Sentence and word stress is generally accurately placed. Individual sounds are generally articulated clearly.	Initiates and responds appropriately, linking contributions to those of other speakers. Maintains and develops the interaction and negotiates towards an outcome.
0	Performance below Band 1.				

Fig. 13.1 Assessment scales extracted from C2 Proficiency Handbook for Teachers (C2 Proficiency Handbook 2020: 58)

were taken, and they underwent keyword analysis. As a result, there was a list of keywords unique to a particular level or shared by both (Berger 2020: 93). This list was then correlated to bands, such as full academic, advanced academic, general academic, full operational, effective operational (based on Berger 2015: 289; Berger 2020: 95). The author stated that the calibrated scales should be more "context-neutral and constructor-oriented".

Summing up all we know about the assessment in a broad sense (see Sect. 13.2), we can assume that the assessment criteria of phonological and phonetic competence in the CAE mock exam and the phonetics course are various; however, they try to objectivise the speech the assessor hears, each in their specific way.

13.3.2   A Narrow Context for the Present Study

Participants

The pilot study consisted of the recordings of one student and a survey in which seven teachers took part.

The student (EP[5]) is a female, aged 18 to 19 years old throughout our longitudinal recordings. There are four recordings of her from semesters 1-4 at the mock exam CAE (speaking part). She had two different teachers during her phonetics course.

The teachers who participated in the survey were four phoneticians and three non-phoneticians at the tertiary level from different institutions in Russia. All were female (see more details about the respondents below in the subsection).

Pilot data set

We have chosen 4 recordings of EP to study in the pilot project. The first criterion was connected with the teachers of phonetics; EP had different teachers during semesters 1-2 and semesters 3-4. That would "objectivise" the results of EP's phonetics course for our purposes. The second criterion was her marks—good and excellent (in %) for all 4 semesters in phonetics and satisfactory marks for the CAE exam. Even though it is hard to extract the mark specifically for the phonology there, it is a good benchmark of language competence in general (Domahs et al. 2015: 5).

EP's case is one of many which shows the keystone contradiction and general dissatisfaction in our department among teachers and the administration. The general claim is that the teachers of phonetics do not teach phonetics, and students do not improve their phonological and phonetic competence during the two-year course.

Survey

Initially the idea of the survey was to go beyond the teachers of our department to have a "third" opinion, so there were 3 teachers who were not faculty members.

There were 7 teachers; they were all Russian-speaking females. The pedagogical experience in teaching English ranged from 3.5 years to more than 40 years, and of teaching phonetic disciplines, it ranged from 0 to more than 40 years. Thus, there were 5 people who considered themselves phoneticians, and 2 people who thought they were non-phoneticians. For more detail on this, see Table 13.2.

The survey was conducted via a Google form and consisted of 10 questions. The audio recordings of EP were incorporated into the form. The survey participants could listen to them as many times as they wished.

---

[5] EP stands for the student's first name and a surname in our data storage.

Table. 13.2 The metadata of the survey participants

Name	How many years have you been teaching English?[b]	How many years have you been teaching phonetic disciplines?	Would you call yourself a phonetician (i.e. a person who specialises in phonetics or any of its aspects)?
AS[a]	3.5	0.5	Yes
IM	11	0	No
UE	28	19	Yes
AT	26	7	Yes
GV	Over 40	0ver 40	Yes
EI	42	20	No
NT	Over 40	0ver 40	Yes

[a]The letters in the first column stand for the initials of the teachers.
[b]These are questions from the survey.

13.3.3 Methodological Premises. Neuroaesthetics: How We Perceive Objects and Life Experiences

What happens when we listen to speech? Do we just listen to the acoustic waves, do we perceive the content, or do we encounter the environment? Obviously, these questions have some answers which are congruent with a specific situation. Namely, we can only listen to waves (in case you do not know the language), we can comprehend an interesting lecture, but practically all the time we encounter and get engaged with the whole communicative environment.

Having said that, I have attempted to seek some solutions to those questions, and more precisely to the questions related to how we perceive our students' speech and how we assess it in cognitive science and specifically in neuroaesthetics.

Neuroaesthetics has established itself as "a serious discipline with an aim to scientifically examine aesthetics from a neurobiological perspective" as we find in the review article on neurobiology of embodied aesthetics by Kirsch et al. (2016: 57).

This review shows that some scholars suggest that:

> esthetic experiences emerge from the interaction between neural systems involved with sensory-motor processes (sensation; perception and motor system), emotion-valuation processes (reward; emotion; wanting and liking), meaning-knowledge processes (expertise; context and culture). (Kirsch et al. 2016: 57)

The aesthetic experience in this definition resembles very much the assessing experience in which I am interested: there is a motor activity of articulation, we use our expertise in evaluating speech, we experience the emotions towards what we hear and eventually give a grade to a student.

This train of thought has prompted me to delve into neuroaesthetics and look at the explanatory opportunities of its models.

Pelowski et al. (2017: 81) described a model

how people may encounter/react to the environment, using a number of general processing
sequences that are not confined to any specific stimulus.

Interestingly, they introduced the model "for theoretically and empirically
addressing the psychological experience of art" (Pelowski et al. 2017: 82), visual
art, to be precise.

The article discusses in a very detailed way *The Vienna Integrated Model of
top-down and bottom-up processes in Art Perception* (VIMAP). The model is multi-
staged and contains a lot of elements, which

explicitly connect early bottom-up, artwork-derived processing sequence and outputs to
top-down, viewer-derived contribution to the processing sequence. (Pelowski et al. 2017:
82)

Finally, the authors give

one more direction for a holistic consideration, and concomitant interpersonal and processing
differences. [...] This model also took the step of considering personality, prior experience
and classifications held by a viewer, which were shown to feed into the processing experience,
leading to focus on certain elements (style vs. content) or emotional input. (Pelowski et al.
2017: 82, 85)

They have summarised aspects that should be included in a theory of processing
art in Table 13.3.

Even though it is a viewing experience, the elements of the model may fit quite
well to perceiving one's speech.[6] Personality plays a crucial role in speech production
and speech perception variability.

Below, in Sect. 13.4.2, I would like to show the possible links between the model
for processing arts and the steps to assess someone's phonological performance. I
would not go deep into VIMAP, comparing only the key aspects of a model as they
are listed in Table 13.3.

13.4 Results

13.4.1 Assessment Results: Course in Phonetics and Mock CAE Exam

The student EP had different teachers during two years of the phonetics course.
The curriculum itself for the discipline "A Course in Phonetics" was designed as a
continuous programme starting from the segmental level (semesters 1–2) up to the
suprasegmental level. The teaching material was based on discourses of different
genres (phonostylistics) in semesters 3–4. There were two academic hours per discipline in all 4 semesters (i.e. 1 h and 30 min per week of in-class studies). The

---

[6] Unlike the visual system, where visual objects and scenes are frequently stationary, the hallmark
of the auditory system is time (Gage and Baars 1978: 144).

Table. 13.3 Key aspects and questions for a model of processing art (taken from Pelowski et al. 2017: 83)

Art processing aspect	Type of processing	Model questions
Low-level artwork derived features: • symmetry, lines, colours, balance • gist impression • patterns, identifiable objects	Bottom-up, early/intermediate vision	• How do individuals generally process and respond to specific artwork features? • How do features guide attention, arousal, judgement?
Viewer personality, knowledge, training, context: • general background, memories, associations, culture • art-related expertise • mood of viewer • artwork labels, extra information • social/personal settings	Largely automatic, but also top-down processing; intermediate and late vision	• How do these aspects interact with or influence perception or attention? • How do context/viewer characteristics influence the prevalence of certain judgements or preferences? • Why and how does art produce differing outcomes for different individuals?
General outputs: • emotion/affect • physiology, action • evaluation • meaning, understanding	Automatic/bottom-up processes and "secondary" top-down response	• Can these [general outputs] be connected to both low-level artwork processing stages and/or to top-down viewer response?
"Second-order" responses and "secondary top-down processing": • deeper meaning • new implications/perceptions • learning • adjustments in emotion/judgements	Top-down viewer response	• How do responses/output change or evolve within experience—i.e. how do we move between emotions? • How do we come to novel interpretations and new perceptions? • How can we be changed/transformed by our experience with art?
Art-specific anecdotes, special experiences: • profound harmony, flow • intense emotion/loss of self • disruptive interactions • detached "aesthetics" vs felt pragmatic emotion	Automatic/bottom-up processes and "secondary" top-down response	• How do we explain these and connect them to mundane processing experience? • How do we explain the relationships between recently targeted aesthetic states like chills, awe, crying and feeling moved?
Longitudinal impacts: • changes in personality, worldview • relation with art • social judgement • impact on health and well-being	Automatic/bottom-up processes and "secondary" top-down response	• Does one interaction with art impact subsequent behaviour or interaction? • Is viewing art objectively good for you?

(continued)

Table. 13.3 (continued)

Art processing aspect	Type of processing	Model questions
• The brain: functional connection to correlates and network	Automatic/bottom-up processes and "secondary" top-down response	• How do theoretical cognitive/behavioural components connect to our neurological function and past imaging findings? • What are the broader systems and networks that underlie the appreciation of art? • What is the organisation of systems leading to top-down responses and higher meaning and to aesthetic emotions—e.g. awe, horror, disgust?

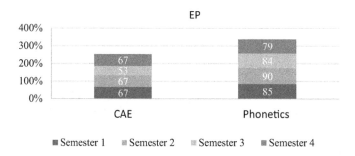

Fig. 13.2 EP's assessment results (%) for "A Course in Phonetics" and for a mock CAE exam

discipline ends up (4th semester) with an exam. The exam covers phonostylistics mainly, though the overall phonetic and phonological competence is also assessed.

Figure 13.2 shows the overall performance of EP in the course in phonetics (the right column) and her performance on the CAE mock exam (the left column). We also can trace EP's performance during the semesters.

As Fig. 13.2 demonstrates, during the 1st semester (year 1 of her studies) EP had an excellent mark for the phonetics course (85%[7]) and a satisfactory mark for CAE (67%). We can assume that EP's phonological competence was very high, though her overall linguistic one is poor.

The 2nd semester's marks were approximately the same with an increase in "phonetics" score—90%. The results for the CAE were the same—67%. Interestingly, this was the end of the 1st year of studying, and there was no improvement in language mastery in general, but an improvement in phonetics as the assessment results show.

---

[7] There is a table of convergence of percent into marks in our department. It runs like this: 51–69% is a satisfactory mark, 70–84% is good, and 85–100% is excellent.

The 3rd semester showed the same tendency even though the teacher of phonetics was different: 84% for phonetics and 53% for the CAE exam. As the phonological competence was decreasing, the overall linguistic score was even worse.

The 4th semester—the end of the 2nd year—was the end of the phonetics course and the last CAE mock exam for our bachelor's students. EP performed well (79%) in phonetics and satisfactorily on the CAE exam (67%).

Thus, we can trace the tendency of EP's satisfactory performance on the exam and a rather good performance in the phonetics course. The contradiction in the assessment results has prompted seeking a solution elsewhere rather than in the course's criteria and the programmes' curricula.

13.4.2   Assessment Results: Survey

The survey has shown those perceptual aspects where processing of phonological information and the processing of art objects converge. Table 13.4 depicts connections between the survey questions and the key aspects of the processing art model as I see them.

Table 13.4 allows for a broad interpretation as far as the processing of phonological information and the assessment process go. The interpretation I will undertake will account for both and will correlate with the neuroaesthetic model.

13.4.2.1   How Do Individuals Generally Process and Respond to Specific [Artwork] Features? How Do Features Guide Attention, Arousal, Judgement?

The *first question* in the questionnaire was about general liking and disliking of EP's speech. The respondents had to choose the respective figure on the scale from 1–5, where **1** is *I dislike* and **5** is *I like*. The majority of phoneticians chose 3, whereas 1 and 2 were chosen an equal number of times by both phoneticians and non-phoneticians.

The answers can correlate with the individual *cognitive processing styles.*

> Cognitive processing style refers to psychological dimensions representing preferences and consistencies in an individual's particular manner of cognitive functioning, with respect to acquiring and processing information. (Yu and Zellou 2019: 138)

The same ideas are found in Ausburn and Ausburn (1978), Messick (1976) and Witkin et al. (1977). The individual differences in executive functions can manifest themselves here. These manifestations are translated into switching between tasks and mental sets, constant monitoring of working-memory content, and deliberate overriding of dominant or prepotent responses (Yu and Zellou 2019, p. 138). As Yu and Zellou (2019: 138) state "these components […] have all been implicated in variation in phonological processing".

13.4.2.2 How Do These Aspects Interact With or Influence Perception or Attention? How Do Context/Viewer Characteristics Influence the Prevalence of Certain Judgements or Preferences? Why and How Does Art Produce Differing Outcomes for Different Individuals?

These stage questions (see Table 13.4) do not correlate with any of the survey items, as it is about the respondents. However, those questions are directly connected to the individual differences in processing phonological information and the speaker's background and experience, i.e. in other words, the way that respondents assess EP's samples correlate with their own L2 pronunciation (or language proficiency if we go further).

Table. 13.4 The convergent features of the survey questions and the key aspects of the processing art model

Art processing aspect	Model questions	The questions from the survey[a]
Low-level artwork derived features: • symmetry, lines, colours, balance • gist impression • patterns, identifiable objects	• How do individuals generally process and respond to specific artwork features? • How do features guide attention, arousal, judgement?	(1)[b] Listen to a student's speech and assess her phonetics: • you do not like her phonetics 1 • you like her phonetics 5
Viewer personality, knowledge, training, context: • general background, memories, associations, culture • art-related expertise • mood of viewer • artwork labels, extra information social/personal settings	• How do these aspects interact with or influence perception or attention? • How do context/viewer characteristics influence prevalence of certain judgements or preferences? • Why and how does art produce differing outcomes for different individuals?	_[c]
General outputs: • emotion/affect • physiology, action • evaluation • meaning, understanding	• Can these be connected to both low-level artwork processing stages and/or top-down viewer response?	(2) Listen to a student's speech. Mark in the table below the phenomena in which you think the student's speech is poor. This is according to your overall impression of vowels, consonants and prosody. • Poor • Good • Excellent • Difficult to say

(continued)

Table. 13.4 (continued)

Art processing aspect	Model questions	The questions from the survey[a]
"Second-order" responses and "secondary top-down processing": • deeper meaning • new implications/perceptions • learning • adjustments in emotion/judgements	• How do responses/output change or evolve within experience—i.e. how do we move between emotions? • How do we come to novel interpretations/new perceptions? • How can we be changed/transformed by our experience with art?	(3) Could you specify your decisions in the previous question? Write what exactly is poor and what exactly is excellent (if at all in any cases).
Art-specific anecdotes, special experiences: • profound harmony, flow • intense emotion/loss of self • isruptive interactions • detached "aesthetics" vs felt pragmatic emotion	• How do we explain these and connect them to mundane processing experience? • How do we explain the relationships between recently targeted aesthetic states like chills, awe, crying and feeling moved?	(5) How have you assessed this audio excerpt? Can you specify your train of thought on this and comment on two variants of assessment (mine and yours)?
Longitudinal impacts: • changes in personality, worldview • relation with art • social judgement • impact on health and well-being	• Does one interaction with art impact subsequent behaviour or interaction? • Is viewing art objectively good for you?	
• The brain: functional connection to correlates and network	• How do theoretical cognitive/behavioural components connect to our neurological function and past imaging findings? • What are the broader systems and networks that underlie the appreciation of art? • What is the organisation of systems leading to top-down responses and higher meaning and to aesthetic emotions—e.g. awe, horror, disgust?	(4) Listen to the student's speech again and assess her phonetics academically: you still have a 5-grade system (i.e. from 1 (min.) to 5 (max.)). Write your own scale of assessment and give the student a mark.

[a]The questions are given here as they went in the survey.
[b]This figure shows the order of the question in the survey. The order in which respondents answered proved to be critical.
[c]This row stays empty as there were no survey questions where respondents could reveal their personality explicitly. For more on that, see below Sect. 13.4.2.2

Phonological processing is understood to mean any sort of language processing that involves linguistically relevant sounds, which broadly encompasses not only the parsing of the speech signal into phonological categories and the processing of phonological categories in context, but also the parsing of words into higher-order prosodic units. (Yu and Zellou 2019: 132)

What varies?

- realisation of a phonetic category;
- perceptual orientation to acoustic details during phoneme perception;
- the production and perception of coarticulated speech;
- usage of lexical information.

For example, there is a strong correlation between L2 perception and production of vowel phonemes (Komar 22: 161). There is a positive correlation between vowel perception and vowel production, and vowel perception might precede vowel production (Ibid.).

The same findings are reported for the consonants, the coarticulated speech and so on (for more details, see Yu and Zellou 2019: 134). I dare suggest that these facts might prove that individual differences in the perception of phonological information influences the way a person not only perceives someone's speech but also assesses it even though the perception-assessment process is professionally bound.

This variability across speakers has a number of reasons, one of which is the speaker's background and experience. Here it correlates very well with the key aspect from the model "viewer personality, knowledge, training and context".

A primary source of individual variability is speakers' prior experience (linguistic or otherwise) as evidenced in how foreign-language learners acquire nonnative sounds and sound sequences, and how language borrowers incorporate them into their native language. (Yu and Zellou 2019: 135)

Learners differ

in their ability to perceive L2 contrastive vowels and consonants on the basis of L1 and L2 language experience and the degree of perceived phonetic similarity between L1 and L2 speech sounds. (Mora 2007: 1)

These differences do not come solely from the linguistic experiences per se but also from behavioural experience (e.g. musicians process lexical tones better than non-musicians), social experience (e.g. those people who have bigger networking circles are better at vowel perception in noise) and from their knowledge of what sound sequences are possible and impossible in their native language (Yu and Zellou 2019: 136).

However, having said all that, it cannot be stated in a straightforward fashion that there is a direct perception-production link.

The conditions under which a perception—production link emerges remain vague and require further investigation. Under certain circumstances and with certain goals, a production—perception link for individuals has been observed. In other circumstances, perceptual behavior appears to be influenced by community-wide patterns. These arch for understanding the conditions and contexts under which a direct production—perception link emerges as an active force in phonological processing remains an important avenue for future studies and can provide more evidence for the nature of the representations and mechanisms active in phonological processing. (Yu and Zellou 2019: 138)

13.4.2.3   Can These Be Connected to Both Low-Level [Artwork] Processing Stages and/or to Top-Down Viewer Response?

The *second question* in the questionnaire was about liking particular elements of EP's speech. More precisely, the respondents had to evaluate the vowels, consonants and prosody of EP's speech as poor, good or excellent and mark if it was difficult to say.

The data was distributed across and among the respondents (phoneticians and non-phoneticians) unequally, see Figs. 13.3 and 13.4.

As the figures indicate, opinions were divided, and evidently the responses were compliant with the model, whereby the "viewer's" responses depend on the experience and progress with experience. Moreover, this stage included the perception of the combination of separate elements of the perceived object (for a comparison, see Pelowski et al. 2017: 88). In the second question, the combination of elements was comprised of segments (vowels and consonants) and suprasegmentals (as prosody). Regardless of specific constituents, speech was perceived holistically, not as a complex of elements.

If, for example, we consider the responses for *vowels,* then we see that they were in the majority of cases twofold; vowels were estimated (perceived) as either *poor* or *good*, regardless of the respondent being phonetician or not. That can be explained by experience; more experienced teachers gave a *poor* grade to vowels, whereas less experienced teacher gave a *good* one.

The responses for *consonants* were more uniform; all the respondents considered them *poor*. Here the explanation may lie in the nature of consonants; there are many

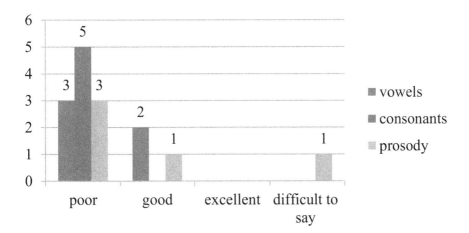

Fig. 13.3 The answers to the second question by *phoneticians*

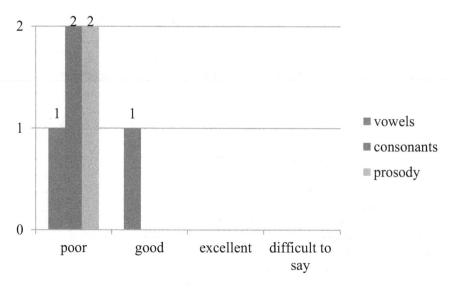

Fig. 13.4 The answers to the second question by *non-phoneticians*

English consonants which differ from Russian ones. Thus, the mismatching effect can elicit the *"poor"* mark.

The *prosodic contour* was very difficult to evaluate in detail; it is simpler to speak about overall communicative intelligibility if the parameters are not specified (as here in the survey). Hence, we see this difficulty reflected in the responses from *poor* to *good* to *difficult to say*.

13.4.2.4 How Do Responses/Output Change or Evolve within Experience? How Do We Move Between Emotions? How Do We Come to Novel Interpretations, New Perceptions? How Can We Be Changed/Transformed by Our Experience with Art?

The *third question* in the survey was to specify the decisions made previously (an open question). The respondents listened to EP's sample a maximum of 4 times and a minimum of 2 times.[8]

The whole idea was to trace the change in perception once the respondents were exposed to EP's speech more often.

The experienced teachers elaborated on segments and suprasegments (see example #1 below).

---

[8] The respondents listened to EP's speech for the second question and the third question, where they could refer to the audio 3 times to evaluate vowels, consonants and prosody.

(1)　Vowels and consonants are not of good quality: no reduction of vowel length in the unstressed position; some consonants betray non-native quality of enunciation (/h/, /θ/, etc.; prosody is non-native (the final melodical contour sounds strange. There's too much lilt in intonation). (GV)[9]

Young teachers mainly used an "impressionistic" description, employing such terms as "incorrect" and "do not sound right" (see example #2 below).

(2)　Intonation (fall rise doesn't correspond to the message and meaning, but at least she tried to use some of the tones). No aspiration, /θ/ doesn't sound correct, /r/ at the end of the word is also incorrectly pronounced. (AS)

The rest of the responses also addressed vowels, consonants and prosody evaluation, except one response which was as follows: "The intonation is poor".
The model suggests that this is the 3rd stage of perception in which

> features are segregated or grouped to form larger units corresponding to intermediate stages of vision. This stage also involves focus on details, which were detected in the initial visual perception, with the viewer giving these aspects further scrutiny [...]. (Pelowski et al. 2017: 88)

This all corresponds very well with the responses described above: more detailed analysis along the three aforementioned lines and further scrutiny of these elements are needed.

13.4.2.5　How Do We Explain These and Connect Them to Mundane Processing Experience? How Do We Explain the Relationships Between Recently Targeted Aesthetic States like Chills, Awe, Crying and Feeling Moved? Does One Interaction With Art Impact Subsequent Behaviour or Interaction? Is Viewing Art Objectively Good for You?

The *fifth question*[10] was to specify the train of thought when respondents were evaluating EP's speech and to comment on the variants of assessment.
　　Here we encountered a variety of opinions. Some respondents said they evaluated it academically with no explanation of what it was (AT) or "just sounds bad" (EI).
　　Some were quite explicit with respect to trying to find out how they actually evaluated (see examples # 3, 4 and 5 below).

(3)　Intonation first, then other criteria. (Because it stood out). I gave 4 in the first place, then checked each criterion individually and changed my mind. (AS)
(4)　First I thought that everything was included in the 1st scale, but then after listening to the recording for a few times, I realised that even though there are issues with prosody and pronunciation of consonants, I still can understand

---

[9] The respondent is GV. Hereafter the respondent's text is fully preserved.

[10] With respect to the corresponding question number, see Table 13.4.

everything that the person is saying. I decided to combine vowels and consonants into the category "pronunciation" and add a new category "clarity". I
think the "clarity" category is important here because sometimes people may
have the same issues in phonetics—in pronunciation and prosody; however,
their speech might be incomprehensible. In this excerpt, even though there are
some significant problems with phonetics, it is possible to understand what the
person is saying. (IM)

(5)   The overall effect of speech is satisfying. However, non-native quality of speech
       is obvious. (GV)

The model shows that at this stage the individuals

have general pleasant or unpleasant reactions to prototypicality[11] ([…]), novelty, etc. […]
In addition to classification and identification of formal or conceptual elements, […] this
stage includes an initial check/classification of the specific emotion—beyond basic positive
or negative valence—elicited by a work, which would also inform attention (i.e. pragmatic,
emotion-evoking focus on content or detached motion-minimising focus on style/form) and
processing mode (pragmatic vs aesthetic). (Pelowski et al. 2017: 89)

13.4.2.6   How Do Theoretical Cognitive/Behavioural Components Connect to Our Neurological Function and Past Imaging Findings? What Are the Broader Systems and Networks That Underlie Appreciation of Art? What is the Organisation of Systems Leading to Top-Down Responses and Higher Meaning, and to Aesthetic Emotions? E. G. Awe, Horror, Disgust?

The *fourth question*[12] was to proceed with the assessment in an academic way.
The respondents had to be explicit about their grades on a 5–1 scale (where 5 is
excellent and 1 is poor) when providing the criteria. Then they evaluated EP's overall
performance and gave her a mark according to the scale.

The marks were 2, 2.5 and 3 (see Fig. 13.5).

If we analyse the explanations the respondents gave for their criteria descriptions,
we can single out the following parameters:

- the descriptors *poor, good and excellent* were attributed to vowels, consonants
  and prosody on a joint basis. For example, "1—vowels, consonants and prosody
  are poor" (AS)
- the descriptors were missing for 2 reasons: 1) they were not stated at all; and 2)
  the descriptors, suggested by the author, were acknowledged.

This finding is also concomitant with the model which runs that

Here, the perceptual and contextual elements uncovered in the bottom-up processing above
are met with a more top-down executive consideration in which viewers attempt to locate

---

[11] In our case in phonetics that would be the English speech of a native speaker.

[12] About the corresponding question number, see Table 13.4.

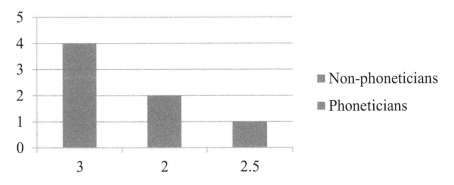

Fig. 13.5 The mark for EP's overall performance

and combine all information collected in the prior processing stages in order to form one coherent meaning, matching this to initial schema and expectations, and then attempt to formulate an appropriate evaluative or physical response, culminating in the creation of meaning, associations, evaluations [...]. (Pelowski et al. 2017: 89)

13.5 Limitations

The methodology has some limitations in my opinion.

The study by Pelowski et al. (2017) described a model "how people may encounter/react to the environment, using a number of general processing sequences that are not confined to any specific stimulus" (Ibid.: 81), thus prompting me to compare their model and the assessment of phonetics. However, I assume that there should be other studies included and analysed, like those that consider the processing of music, for example, and work on neurolinguistics.

Besides, visual perception is definitely different from auditory perception (especially in processing time), and that should be taken into account. But the idea of comparing them on the basis of phonetics seemed very promising, exactly because of the linguistic formulations as when we describe our experience of viewing the painting, we use a narrative similar to that used when reporting about someone's speech.

The other drawback, as I see it, is the limited number of teachers (assessors) who participated in the survey, 7 seems sufficient for a pilot study.

Future research may take a wider perspective of perception, more participants and more samples of speech to assess and delve more deeply into the neuroaesthetic model of processing.

13.6   Conclusions

The present paper aimed at tackling a set of philosophical and practical questions with an overall query of why it all happens to phonetics. The pilot research undertaken has shown what the possible answers could be.

Firstly, the comparative analysis of the stages of the neuroaesthetic model of processing art objects and those of the assessment of phonological and phonetic competence can align. More concretely, teachers assess a student's phonetics as a viewer "assesses" art objects. Thus, an unorthodox hypothesis is that phonetics is an art.

Secondly, this observation can have broader implications for L2 phonetic and phonological assessment in general. The results of the survey disclose the idea that the criteria of assessment stem from the following: (1) the object itself (the phonological and phonetic properties of speech); but what is more, (2) the rater's personality, knowledge, training and context; (3) general outputs; (4) other responses in similar or different situations; (5) special experiences; and this can cause (6) longitudinal impacts on speech perception.

Thirdly, an attempt to explain why phonological and phonetic competence is so difficult to assess has been made. The answer here can be that this competence intertwines the rater's and speaker's phonological awareness and peculiarities of their phonological processing together with the assessment criteria, thus making it a very complex blend.

Acknowledgements I express a sincere gratitude to my colleagues Dr. Galina Vishnevskaya, Dr. Tatiana Dubrovskaya and Prof. Maria Lukanina for their thoughtful comments on the initial version of the chapter. I stay responsible for any remaining drawbacks.

References

Akhmanova, Olga S. 2010. *Dictionary of Linguistic Terms.* [Slovar' linguisticheskikh termiov.] Moscow: Librokom.

Ashby, Michael, and Patricia Ashby. 2017. Unruly Intonation. In Sounds and Melodies Unheard: Essays in Memory of Rastislav Šuštaršic. *Linguistica LVII* 1: 29–45.

Assessment. Cambridge Dictionary. https://dictionary.cambridge.org/ru/словарь/английский/ assessment. Accessed 8 June 2020.

Ausburn, Lynna J., and Floyd B. Ausburn. 1978. Cognitive Styles: Some Information and Implications for Instructional Design. *Educational Communication and Technology* 26: 337–354.

Berger, Armin. 2015. *Validating Analytic Rating Scales: A Multi-Method Approach to Scaling Descriptors for Assessing Academic Speaking.* Frankfurt am main, Germany: Peter Lang.

Berger, Armin. 2020. Specifying Progression in Academic Speaking: A Keyword Analysis of CEFR-Based Proficiency Descriptors. *Language Assessment Quarterly* 1 (1): 85–99.

Blackburn, Simon W. 2017. Philosophy of Language. *Encyclopedia Britannica.* https://www.britan nica.com/topic/philosophy-of-language. Accessed 8 June 2020.

CEFR Common European Framework of Reference for Languages. 2018. Learning, teaching, assessment: Companion volume with new descriptors. Strasburg: Council of Europe.

C2 Proficiency Handbook for Teachers (v. 168194). https://www.cambridgeenglish.org/Images/168 194-c2-proficiency-teachers-handbook.pdf. Accessed 4 March 2020.

Derwing, Tracey M. 2019. Utopian Goals for Pronunciation Research Revisited. In *Proceedings of the 10th Pronunciation in Second Language Learning and Teaching conference, Iowa State University, September 2018*, eds. J. Levis, C. Nagle, and E. Todey, 27–35. Ames, IA: Iowa State University.

Derwing, Tracey M., and Murray J. Munro. 1997. Accent, Intelligibility, and Comprehensibility: Evidence from Four L1s. *Studies in Second Language Acquisition* 20: 1–16.

Domahs, Ulrike, Hubert Truckenbrodt, and Richard Wiese. 2015. Editorial' Phonological and Phonetic Competence: Between Grammar, Signal Processing, and Neural Activity. *Frontiers in Psychology*, 6.

Eliseeva, Ulyana V. 2019. *The Methodological Potential of Multimodal Corpora in Teaching English Phonetics (A Suprasegmental Level)*. [Metodicheskij potencial mul'timodal'nyh korpusov pri obuchenii fonetike anglijskogo jazyka(suprasegmentnyj uroven').] Bachelor's thesis, Moscow, NUST "MISiS".

Gage Nicole M., and Bernard J. Baars. 2018. Music and Sound Perception. In *Fundamentals of Cognitive Neuroscience*, 143–184. Academic Press.

Geary, James. 2005. *The World in a Phrase. A Brief History of the Aphorism*. NY, London: Bloomsbury.

IELTS: Guide for teachers. Test Format, Scoring and Preparing Students for the Test. 2017. https://ielts.com.au/wp-content/uploads/2019/04/IELTS_Guide_for_teachers_2017.pdf. Accessed 13 June 2020.

Kang, Okim, and April Ginther, eds. 2018. *Assessment in Second Language Acquisition*. NY: Routledge.

Kennedy, Sara, and Pavel Trofimovich. 2017. Pronunciation Acquisition. In *The Routledge Handbook of Instructed Second Language Acquisition*, ed. L. Shawn and S. Masatoshi, 260–280. NY and London: Routledge.

Kirsch, Louise P., Cosimo Urgesi, and Emily S. Cross. 2016. Shaping and Reshaping the Aesthetic Brain: Emerging Perspectives of the Neurobiology of Embodied Aesthetics. *Neuroscience and Biobehavioral Reviews* 62: 56–68.

Kirshner, Howard S. 2003. Speech and Language Disorders. *Office Practice Neurology* 2nd edition. Elsevier: Churchill Livingston, 890–895.

Kodzasov, Sandro V., and Olga F. Krivnova. 2001. *Fundamental Phonetics*. [Obschaya fontetika.] Moscow: RSUH.

Komar, Smiljana. 2017. The Relationship between the Perception and Production of Four General British Vowels by Slovene University Students of English. In Sounds and Melodies Unheard: Essays in Memory of Rastislav Šuštaršic. *Linguistica LVII* 1: 161–171.

Messick, Samuel. 1976. *Individuality in Learning*. San Francisco: Jossey-Bass.

Mora, Joan C. 2007. Methodological Issues in Assessing L2 Perceptual Phonological Competence. *Proceedings of the PTLC 2007 Phonetics Teaching and Learning Conference*, 1–5. London: Department of Phonetics and Linguistics, University College London.

Munro, Murray J., and Tracey M. Derwing. 1995. Foreign Accent, Comprehensibility, and Intelligibility in the Speech of Second Language Learners. *Language Learning* 45 (1): 73–97.

Nagle, Charles, Pavel Trofimovich, and Annie Bergeron. 2019. Toward a Dynamic View of Second Language Comprehensibility. *Studies in Second Language Acquisition* 41 (4): 647–672.

Pelowski, Matthew, Patrick S. Markey, Michael Forster, Gernot Gerger, and Helmut Leder. 2017. Move Me, Astonish Me'Delight My Eyes and Brain: The Vienna Integrated Model of Top-down and Bottom-up Processes in Art Perception (VIMAP) and Corresponding Affective, Evaluative, and Neuropsychological Correlates. *Physics of Life Reviews* 21: 80–125.

Piccardo, Enrica. 2016. *Common European Framework of Reference for Languages: Learning, Teaching, Assessment. Phonological Scale Revision*. Process Report. Strasburg: Council of Europe.

Pierrehumbert, Janet B. 2003. Probabilistic Phonology: Discrimination and Robustness. In *Probabilistic Linguistics*, ed. R. Bod, J. Hay, and S. Jennedy, 177–229. Cambridge, MA: MIT Press.

Reid, Kym T., Pavel Trofimovich, and Mary G. O'Brien. 2019. Social Attitudes and Speech Ratings: Effects of Positive and Negative Bias on Multiage Listeners? Judgments of Second Language Speech. *Studies in Second Language Acquisition* 41 (2): 419–442.

Saito, Kazuya, Mai Tran, Yui Suzukida, Hui Sun, Viktoria Magne, and Meltem Ilkan. 2019. How Do Second Language Listeners Perceive the Comprehensibility of Foreign-accented Speech? Roles of First Language Profiles, Second Language Proficiency, Age, Experience, Familiarity, and Metacognition. *Studies in Second Language Acquisition* 41 (5): 1133–1149.

Saussure, Ferdinand, de. 1983. *Cours de Linguistique Generale*. Translated by R. Harris, London: Duckworth.

Thomson, Ron. 2018. Measurement of Accentedness, Intelligibility, and Comprehensibility. In *Assessment in Second Language Acquisition*, ed. O. Kang and A. Ginther, 11–29. NY: Routledge.

Tsybulya, Nadezhda B. 2013. *A Practical Course of English Phonetics: the British and the American Variants.* [Kurs prakticheskoj fonetiki anglijskogo jazyka. Britanskij i amerikanskij variant.] Moscow: Gnozis.

Witkin, Herman A., Carolann Moore, Donald R. Goodenough, and Patricia W. Cox. 1977. Field-dependent and Field-independent Cognitive Styles and Their Educational Implications. *Review of Educational Research* 47: 1–64.

Yan, Xun, and April Ginther. 2018. Listeners and Raters: Similarities and Differences in Evaluation of Accented Speech. In *Assessment in Second Language Acquisition*, ed. O. Kang and A. Ginther, 67–89. NY: Routledge.

Yu, Alan C.L., and Georgia Zellou. 2019. Individual Differences in Language Processing: Phonology. *The Annual Review of Linguistics* 5: 131–150.

Zsiga, Elizabeth C. 2013. *The Sounds of Language: An Introduction to Phonetics and Phonology.* Malden MA, Oxford: Wiley-Blackwell.

Index